Critical Voices
in Criminology

Critical Perspectives on Crime and Inequality

Series Editor
Walter S. DeKeseredy, University of Ontario Institute of Technology

Advisory Board
Shahid Alvi, University of Ontario Institute of Technology
Meda Chesney-Lind, University of Hawaii at Manoa
Mark Israel, Flinders University of South Australia
Barbara Perry, University of Ontario Institute of Technology
Claire Renzetti, Saint Joseph's University
Martin Schwartz, Ohio University

Critical Perspectives on Crime and Inequality presents cutting edge work informed by these schools of thought: feminism, peacemaking criminology, left realism, Marxism, cultural criminology, and postmodernism. In an age of instrumental reason and increasing state control, the need for critical and independent analysis of power and social arrangements has never been more acute. Books published in this series will be monographs for scholars and researchers, as well as texts for course use.

Titles in Series:

The Politics of Organized Crime and the Organized Crime of Politics,
by Alfredo Schulte-Bockholt

Advancing Critical Criminology: Theory and Application,
edited by Walter S. DeKeseredy and Barbara Perry

Symbolic Gestures and the Generation of Global Social Control,
by Dawn Rothe and Christopher W. Mullins

Charting Women's Journeys, by Judith Grant

Criminal to Critic, by James E. Palombo with Randall G. Shelden

Policing Race and Place in Indian Country: Over- and Underenforcement,
by Barbara Perry

Critical Voices in Criminology, edited by Chris Powell

Critical Voices in Criminology

edited by
CHRIS POWELL

LEXINGTON BOOKS
A division of
ROWMAN & LITTLEFIELD PUBLISHERS, INC.
Lanham • Boulder • New York • Toronto • Plymouth, UK

Published by Lexington Books
A division of Rowman & Littlefield Publishers, Inc.
A wholly owned subsidiary of The Rowman & Littlefield Publishing Group, Inc.
4501 Forbes Boulevard, Suite 200, Lanham, Maryland 20706
www.lexingtonbooks.com

Estover Road, Plymouth PL6 7PY, United Kingdom

British Library Cataloguing in Publication Information Available

Library of Congress Cataloging-in-Publication Data

Critical voices in criminology / edited by Chris Powell.
    p. cm. — (Critical perspectives on crime and inequality)
  Includes bibliographical references and index.
  ISBN 978-0-7391-2032-3 (cloth : alk. paper) — ISBN 978-0-7391-2033-0 (pbk. : alk.
paper) — ISBN 978-0-7391-3977-6 (electronic)
  1. Critical criminology. 2. Criminology. I. Powell, Chris, 1951–
HV6019.C753 2009
364—dc22   2009013861

The paper used in this publication meets the minimum requirements of American
National Standard for Information Sciences—Permanence of Paper for Printed Library
Materials, ANSI/NISO Z39.48-1992.

∞™ The paper used in this publication meets the minimum requirements of American
National Standard for Information Sciences—Permanence of Paper for Printed Library
Materials, ANSI/NISO Z39.48-1992.

Printed in the United States of America

Dedicated to my late mother,
DORIS MAY POWELL 1924–2009

Contents

Preface

To my knowledge there have been just two collections of criminological articles dedicated to exploring the life stories of criminologists. (Holdaway and Rock 1998; Geis and Dodge 2002)

This is the first to focus on critical criminologists. The idea emerged from my teaching two courses on a fairly regular basis. One was called "the sociology of criminology" and taught whilst I was a lecturer in Social Theory and Criminology at the University of Wales, Bangor from the mid 1990s to 2000, and the other "reflexive criminology" which is currently taught at the University of Southern Maine where I am a member of the criminology department. The courses are essentially the same, the name changed due to the sociologists unwillingness to permit academics from outside their department (even those with PhD's in sociology) to use the "S" word. We learn a little about how the pragmatic compartmentalization of what passes for knowledge can be structured to accord with perceived group interests.

Moving away from that somewhat sour note I would like to be far more positive and offer my sincere thanks to those people who have helped in the production of this work. The basic position underpinning it is that "criminological" work is a construction, and that if we seek to understand criminology more fully it assists us if we acquire better insights into the conditions of that construction. Without the "constructors" then, no book. I thank them all for their willingness to join in an enterprise perhaps quite foreign to them, maybe even somewhat threatening. Some people lay themselves quite bare here. I thank too, all those students at Bangor and USM who were willing to engage with something a little different and offered supportive comments.

I thank all the people at Lexington. They have all shown considerable patience, patience probably developed from having to deal routinely with academics! To Walter Dekeseredy, the series editor of *Critical Perspectives in Crime and Inequality*, and the editorial board, I also owe a great debt. Here at USM I'm grateful to Dean Devinder Malhotra, who released a little money which made life easier, and especially to Rosemary Miller, the administrative assistant in the criminology department who helped me in every way she could—and with considerable humor and tolerance. Ann Brushwein, of USM's Information and Technology Users services was both efficient and tolerant. I thank my good friend and colleague Piers Beirne. He is a continuingly supportive presence.

Finally, three notes of regret. This book would not have been produced without the initial contribution of Kimberly Cook, who was to have been co-editor. I am sure, that had she felt able to continue her involvement, the whole process would have been conducted more quickly and with greater efficiency. Personal differences and her own departmental circumstances combined to lead her to the conclusion that she had to withdraw from the project, and indeed to pull the article she'd written for it. That article is both intellectually rigorous and immensely moving, and I very much hope she feels able to publish it one day.

The famous Dutch abolitionist, Louk Hulsman, was to have added his "critical voice" to this collection. Due to his sad passing he was unable to fulfill his promise. His work inspired many of us and hopefully will continue to do so.

Finally I wish to acknowledge my dear mother Doris, who also died whilst this work was in preparation. She never understood fully what I was doing, and worried constantly about me, but she loved and supported me unconditionally. She was a wonderful person, and so much more than a mere "Sister of Christ," which was the only status granted her in the humanity-denying Catholic funeral service.

REFERENCES

Holdaway, S., and Rock, P. (1998). *Thinking about Criminology*. Toronto: University of Toronto Press.

Geis, G., and Dodge, M. (2002). *Lessons of Criminology. Cincinnati:* Anderson.

Introduction

Traditionally readers confronted with criminological literature are presented with little more than thumbnail sketches as to the social characteristics of the authors, or indeed of their motivations. Typically one learns of their status, their institutional location, their supposed credentials for writing what they have, and their presumed entitlement to be taken seriously. If we bother to concern ourselves with prefaces, forewords, and so forth (and I suspect few people do), we may gain a sense of their broader connections with other scholars, with academia, and other institutions. Rarely are we presented with a more detailed impression of the authors. Butch Cassidy's famous question; "who are those guys?" isn't one we're expected to be interested in. Whilst the "humanities" launched their assaults on it, authorship wasn't considered to be relevant in "scientific" circles, as "professional competence" seemingly rendered such matters unimportant. Indeed, positivistic assumptions surrounding such issues as "reproducibility of results" for example, explicitly denied the validity of pursuing further detail. In more recent years increasing numbers of critically minded scholars have become more aware of authorship as an issue; that it matters who is in a position to do the addressing. As a result, it is now not uncommon for authors to attempt to "locate" themselves quite typically *en passant* during a discussion of methodological issues. Perhaps significantly the "self identifiers" overwhelmingly appear to be those on the critical side of scholarship. Such partial identification may be helpful in assisting our reading/ understanding of the final product, but it is by necessity, rather limited.

The writers in this collection have been invited to break one of academia's more potent taboos—the denial of the relevance of authorship promoted by the "grammatically based" veto on using the subjective I. Here the authors were not required to hide behind the collective securities of "one" and "we." From time to time perhaps, "bad" grammar can constitute "better" politics? It seems to me that we should not deny our own unique place in the cosmos, with our own histories, our own geographical, economic, and gender loca- tions—in sum our own "baggage." The objectivist myth of pretending such factors may be disregarded (whilst professionally expedient) has always been an exercise in mystification. Thus writing in the first person invites the en- tirely reasonable response on behalf of the reader to ask—"So, who are you anyway?" Even though we can't realistically provide potted personal histories of ourselves every time we put pen to paper (and who's to say which the "rel- evant" bits might be for any given reader?) we can at least draw attention to work having been produced by a living human being, with her or his own axes to grind. This may be an ethical requirement really. Admittedly I have not always been or felt able to adopt my ideal strategy—breaking with convention has its costs in terms of credibility. The "personal" is not easily equated with the "professional," and in practice one ends up making compromises. Com- puter software which routinely "corrects" the "personal" as "ungrammatical" also helps or hinders in this process! The broader "subjective" "objective" question is of course central to this book, and many of the contributors clearly struggled for various reasons with concerns over "objectivity." Overgeneral- izing a little this was more of an issue with younger scholars, probably closer to, and more mindful of, traditional doctoral training. Nevertheless many people expressed anxieties at different stages. E-mails referred specifically to "trying to avoid being too self-indulgent," "getting too personal," "avoiding war stories," and such. One of the authors stated, "I didn't find it in me to get too personal—not sure why." Indeed reading these chapters provides a clear indication of just how difficult it can be to address such reservations.

So there are genuine academic concerns about appearing to lack "objectiv- ity," and they stem from a variety of sources. "I ing" clearly foregrounds the self. Traditionally many have conceived of the scholar as a background figure, operating behind the scenes from a sheltered academic environment, telling others "how things are" before slipping back into peaceful (and relatively unaccountable) obscurity. It's a romanticization clearly, but nevertheless it's an image that has appealed to many academics. It's a mode of operation which critical scholars should probably regard with a degree of ambivalence. Some of those privileged people in their ivory towers may not have manifestly linked their academic work to activist involved citizenship in the ways which critical scholars may have preferred. However their skeptics reticence about endorsing, for instance, populist authoritarianism, often earned them the displeasure of the political elites, who from time to time deemed them potentially, even actually, subversive. That same reluctance to too publicly endorse has been connected to traditional academic (at least posture of) humility.

The sophisticated version of "knowledge" is that it is conditional, constantly open to contestation and, probably, eventual refutation. A degree of distancing qualification from one's conclusions was therefore prudent. However, things have changed, and continue to change at some pace. Today a far more bullish ethos prevails, one in which in the name of public "accountability" and "relevance" scholars are not only encouraged to boast of their "accomplishments" but are effectively sanctioned if they do not. This new game, clearly a function of the increasingly intensified marketization of the university sector, is played by most (even "critical") scholars, though for some I hope with a degree of embarrassment.

This has an impact upon how academics can function institutionally. Scholars are cognizant of what it takes to establish, sustain and develop their careers within institutional contexts. Work is read and evaluated by colleagues, departmental heads and administrators. There is a balance to be struck between demonstrating one's value and productivity and appearing arrogant and superior. "Stars" can be celebrated by administrators and distrusted or even resented by colleagues. Getting "too personal" can provide potential rivals with dangerous ammunition. Indeed, with specific reference to this collection I can openly state that one, in my opinion, rather wonderful and incredibly moving paper was pulled for precisely this reason. *So—Who are* these *guys?*

Criminology is a multidimensional discipline. Whilst all of the authors of this collection are or have at some time been considered criminologists or have contributed to criminology programs, only some (obviously mostly the younger ones) hold formal qualifications in criminology or, more commonly in the US, criminal justice. Most of us are qualified sociologists, and we probably still regard ourselves as such. We come to consider "crime" with sociology's skeptical lens—and perhaps our reluctance to suspend that skepticism is what enables us to embrace self-definition as "critical" criminologists. That said "critical criminology" is a rather broad church. It has its fundamentalists, its moderates, even its agnostics. All are represented here. One of the contributors is reluctant to see himself as a critical criminologist, though his influence upon those who do see themselves as such has been significant. Intellectually we take differing perspectives on just how useful and valid the category of "crime" is. Some of us would wish to expand the use of the label, others to reconfigure it, and others to abolish it in favor of a less highly charged alternative. Again this collection represents all tendencies. Politically the authors clearly place stress on differing dimensions of what most critical criminologists would identify as "social domination." We hear Marxist, socialist, feminist, civil libertarian, and anarchist voices. Critical criminology is rightly associated with social activism and the vast majority here are indeed such. The chapters indicate the links between experience, academic work, and activism, demonstrating the connections between them.

This group is also socially diverse. Some come from more, others less privileged backgrounds. One or two were privately "educated," most were not. There is diversity of gender and sexual orientation; there is diversity of ethnicity, of nationality, and of religious upbringing. There are at least (depending on one's definition) three immigrants. A serious attempt has been made to obtain contributions from people of different ages and at different stages of their careers. Thus our authors include those relatively new to academic criminology, others in the middle and later stages of their careers, and two who are officially or semi-retired. Some are well known "names" in critical criminology, some probably will be, and maybe one or two are not and would prefer it that way. Hence author selection has been conducted with the intention not only of registering the meaningfulness and implications of authorship, but to infer sites of conflict, debate, resistance, and change, for sure within the context of critical criminology, but also within criminology as a social accomplishment. An aim has been to render the intellectual tradition of criminology more visible, as situated within the broader sociostructural contexts of changing societies and institutions.

In order to try to obtain a limited degree of consistency I sent all the potential contributors a list of themes which they might have wished to reflect upon. Emerging as some sort of officially acknowledged criminologist usually requires at least some level of engagement with crime-related ideas at under-graduate and/or graduate level. What were people expected to learn about? Who seemed to be the primary definers of the discipline? Who were the key influences, both positive and negative? What were the factors involved in de-termining a doctoral or other major topic? Were there obstacles/inhibitors as well as supportive people around?

I invited people to explore the conjunctures of time and space. Was being a student in the 1960s and 1970s a vastly different experience from that of the 1980s and 1990s? What about the places in which one studied? I sug-gested people might explore the mundane realities of finding employment, negotiating a niche for themselves, and dealing with any "turf wars" which may have occurred. I asked about the availability of funding and the practical realities of conducting critical research. Finally I requested that the authors might consider speculating as to the meaning of their experiences in terms of understanding better the social purposes of/for criminology.

As I anticipated people emphasize different things. That was after all an essential part of the exercise. However it is striking that relatively few seek to dwell on the negative, perhaps a little surprising given that we are critical criminologists. In the main, difficulties encountered are engaged with in a highly generalized and vague manner. This is, perhaps, as it should be. Critical criminologists understand the complexities involved in "playing the victim." They should, theoretically at least, be able to avoid personalizing issues, rather understanding them in broader structural senses. The difficulty might be, reversing Mills (2000) for a moment, that in order to make inroads into the political arena, it's necessary to identify the issues—and in order to do that there have to be cases.

There is an understandable reluctance to hang dirty linen out in public. It's not often very pragmatic to too openly critique "obstructive" tutors, col-leagues, and/or administrators. Reading these chapters suggests what should be obvious, that newer scholars are somewhat more reticent than the older ones. If Dylan's observation that when you have nothing, there's nothing to lose has some value, and the control theorists advise us that when you've got something you've got something to lose, then perhaps when you've got all you need and you're rather old, then the chances are that you won't lose it. I'd call it the "Jimmy Carter" effect, whereby it seems easier to describe the "dark side of how it is/was" when you've left or are about to leave. There's no real virtue in this; if a risk, it's a relatively low one.

I'm expressing, of course, the perspective from a negative Frankfurtian-influenced element of critical criminology, and am offering the observation as just that. Of course the world of critical criminology is full of generous mentors and colleagues who have been willing to go that extra mile. It is right to identify them and to speak of the value of the various supportive networks now in place, often due to the energy and commitment of those people. Paying homage to the pioneers of critical criminology is an honest and honorable thing to do.

REFLECTION AND CRITICAL SCHOLARSHIP

Brown (2002) in the course of an argument supporting it warns us that "reflection can of course be a dangerous enterprise, its results sometimes inconsequential, self indulgent, sanitized, and prey to the vagaries of memory." I concur. Some of us may feel that such can be nothing other than narratives. Yet narratives give meaning to our lives and listening to those of others may help us to understand how they see the world and act in it a little more clearly. Critical criminology is concerned with unpacking conventional crime stories and how they get told. It's valuable to describe the enduring legacy of criminology as essentially reflecting versions of "order" held to by "privileged white guys." No critical criminologist has been immune to its influence and the authors here are both laying out their responses to it and articulating their own narratives. As I've indicated they can be very different. Criminology, even its critical variety, is not an equal opportunities profession. Some of our authors have had to struggle more than others to be heard and here we obtain some sense of that. I think they have engaged with a process of some value. Lowenthal (1983) suggests that media analysts should concern themselves with asking who says what to whom, why, how, where, and with what consequences. The converse questions—who does NOT, and so forth are of equal importance. The authors reflect on their own "channeling" processes and in so doing allow us to a deeper awareness of the more subterranean dynamics at play.

I'd suggest this is important because it's a key step toward recognizing that what passes for criminology is, as with everything else, the result of a series of constructions, constructions performed by social actresses and actors in a variety of contexts. Cast light on the authorship question and one is better equipped to open up broader issues deriving from a closer assessment of those contexts. In turn such a reflexive exercise allows us to develop a more critical evaluation of the discipline of Criminology, and the social functions (for good and/or ill) which it may perform.

Whilst most criminologists are of course for criminology, an increasing number now feel themselves to be marginal to it or "accidentals," and a few indeed would describe themselves, a la Stan Cohen (1988) as against it. Therefore the deconstruction of criminology, even perhaps especially, one's own version of it, is no mere exercise in "self indulgence." Gouldner (1971) identifies the need for a sociology of sociology. This volume is an attempt to contribute to a "sociology of criminology" or a reflexive criminology.

REFERENCES

Brown, D. (2002). Losing my religion. In Carrington, K. and Hogg, R., (eds.), *Critical Criminology*. Wilton, UK.

Cohen, S. (1988). *Against Criminology*. New Brunswick: Transaction.

Gouldner, A. (1971). *The Coming Crisis of Western Sociology*. New York: Equinox.

Lowenthal, L. (1983). *Literature and Mass Culture*. New Brunswick: Transaction.

Mills, C. W. (2000). *The Sociological Imagination*. New York: Oxford University Press.

1

Butterfly or Dinosaur? Criminological "Journeyman" and Romantic Pessimist

CHRIS POWELL

There are other things in my life apart from professional work. Last Christmas an ex-partner and dear friend sent me a card indicating "All he really wants to do is watch the football" (soccer) which, if extended to reading about it and many other sports, playing idiosyncratic squash, walking a dachshund, and listening to rock music, accounts for what I do with the rest (most) of my life. As with squash I'm a "B+" sort of academic, capable from time to time (I like to think) of producing "A" grade cameos. Whilst I'm not a "name" in the sense that most of my fellow contributors to this collection are or in some cases will surely be, I suppose I've achieved a modest level of "success," having worked in one or two good universities where I've pulled my weight in terms of publications and teaching.

My journey into criminology was in one sense the result of a series of coincidences, though as usual if one seeks roots one can find them easily enough. My paternal grandfather, who I never met, was a village constable in a rural part of the English Midlands. A family (apocryphal?) story relates how he turned down the offer of promotion to sergeant in a nearby city because he thought there were "real" criminals there. He was given two stripes for his jacket and allowed to remain in the countryside, the only "corporal" in the history of the British police. He clearly lacked ambition—or perhaps he just preferred drinking after hours with his friends and playing soccer and billiards? A well-known breakfast cereal box provided information on various occupations and one on "The Police" semi-seduced me with its references to vital social service/protection, combined with an active and varied outdoor life and a lack of perpetual supervision. On reflection this was probably my first encounter with the "glossy brochure" versions of what passes for "reality" which I've been so eager to demolish in the various courses I've taught over the years on "Crime and Social Control" or "Theorizing Social Control/Institutions."

Then there's my Catholic background. Obsessed as it is with inspiring guilt, which can easily be assuaged by subordinating oneself to a "greater" power, it saturated me with discourse on deviance and punishment. There's probably a paper to be written someday about the number of lapsed Catholics who have drifted into criminology—and particularly, I suspect, its more critical versions. Actually at a conference in the middle of the night en route to a bathroom I came across one of the contributors to this volume looking ashen faced. When I asked him what the matter was he told me he thought he'd seen a nun! My parents were loving, gentle, and essentially conservative people. Those familiar with Merton's fatalists or McKenzie and Silvers's "angels in marble" (1968) would recognize them. They were upper working class people who did what they were told because they'd been convinced that they should, rather than because they believed that so doing would lead to fortune. I was led to believe that the police were my friends; that the system was just, and if I worked just a little harder at school I could get a job as a teller in a bank and come home from work clean. Unfortunately when I left the house (where things indeed seemed courteous and reasonable) I found myself betrayed. At school I found myself "piggy in the middle" between school bullies and what at the time I felt to be "psychopathically" violent teachers. Both groups seemed equally volatile, unpredictable, and requiring of avoidance. (This was good training for walking in large American cities seemingly only populated by drug dealers or cops. It also prepared me for the dark side of academia, I suppose?!) This wasn't how it should be. Later I saw real police in action, brutally attacking people peacefully protesting against the Vietnam War. I wanted to understand what was going on.

I had some conception by my mid-teens that the "system" represented injustice rather than justice. I started to read anarchist literature, which made mention of "crime-free" societies. "Crime" obviously meant violence and aggression, and these places sounded good to me. Of course they were "crime-free" because there was no codified law. I learned that a little later! It seemed to me that if I was going to get a handle on "truth" I was going to have to study sociology. After all, the people whom I observed being most actively engaged in protesting the panoply of injustices of which I was rapidly becoming aware were sociology students such as Rudi Dutschke and Daniel Cohn-Bendit. Initially I made an abortive attempt to become an English teacher. However the faculty at the College of Education thought my interest in the theatre of the absurd too bohemian. During that time I also got an important insight into the use of power. The failure of obviously bright but leftist students to get job offers after teacher certification led to the belief amongst many of us that they had been blacklisted. When the college "authorities" categorically denied that such a list existed, students broke into the administrative offices and found it.

Eventually I scrambled onto a degree course in sociology. I exchanged my literature books for sociology ones with a student moving in the opposite direction. When I asked why she was changing she said—"Sociology has no soul." After a few weeks I realized why it was she'd come to that conclusion. At that time sociology was still dominated by a complacent brand of Parsonian functionalism. Whilst my tutors seemed to prove on a daily basis that methodology, theory, and, incredibly, even anthropology were boring subjects, and all apparently led to the inevitable conclusion that our existing version of "social order" was the best which could be achieved (come back Hegel, all was forgiven). I only had to leave the lecture hall, look around or even just listen to a Dylan, Jefferson Airplane or Crosby, Stills and Nash album, to realize this was not so. I concluded that the students were reacting *against* received sociology, rather than being inspired *by* it. I remember my first day taking a "social structure" course. The lecturer looked at us, smiled sardonically and announced—"So here we have another group of young women wanting to help people and of young men wanting to bring about revolution." It pains me to say it, but he wasn't far wrong either.

I attended lectures and seminars conscientiously and liked most of the faculty, but was disappointed and frustrated. My grades reflected this, being decidedly average. In my second year though, everything changed. A new member of staff was appointed and I signed up for his optional course on the sociology of deviance. He was a graduate student of one of the "new criminologists," it was his first job and he was simultaneously laconic and dynamic.

His course accomplished far more than merely familiarizing and exciting me
with new criminology; it also made me acutely aware of the importance and
fascination of theory. Marx became more than a lecture placed somewhere
between Durkheim and Weber en route to the dustbin of history. For the first
time I was introduced to the various micro theories (hardly mentioned in the
official "theory"course) and I was captivated by them. As with so many others
I struggled to reconcile micro and macro perspectives and in honesty I still
do. I continue to think it's worth the effort though. I revisited those boring
reactionary old theorists and began to realize that they were so much more
interesting than I'd thought.

It's conventional and far too easy to romanticize the early and mid-1970s.
Then again it's far too easy to dismiss them as well. Overall I'm quite willing to assert that this was the time when sociology and criminology became
intellectually mature. Any process of maturation inevitably involves the odd
experimental blip—but even failed experiments can be pedagogically valuable
and exciting. George Harrison observed that we must surely be learning from
our mistakes. As did George a lot of people had their pretentious side, but
at least they had pretensions to *something*. Many of the men, no doubt, had
their "revolting" side, as feminist voices were struggling to be heard even in
"radical" circles. It wasn't yet automatically assumed that feminists' concerns
be taken seriously or even that lip service needed to be paid to taking them
seriously. What was happening though, was that sociology, led I'd suggest by
the sociology of deviance, began to perform what I think is its rightful task
of suspending belief in prevalent institutional arrangements and definitions
of reality. If one had been encouraged to do so, and had been led to look in
the right places, one could have found this skepticism amidst the writings of
the "founding fathers" of course, but the new breed generally gave us rather
more than a nod here and a wink there. Suspension of belief logically and
inexorably led to the challenging of it. I managed to persuade the sociology
department at the University of Leeds to accept me on a master's course in
"the Sociology of Organizations." I thought myself a con man throughout this
period. I knew I didn't belong amongst these smart people. Driving toward
the university always involved anxiety as to whether I'd reach a "restroom"
in time. Perhaps, though, I could scramble through somehow and get a job
teaching liberal studies in a college of further education? By now the thought
of paid employment was concerning me for the first time. Hitherto I'd held

to the mid-1960s notion that "in the future" society would be organized on the basis of human need. In Britain it's conventional to regard the election of the conservative government under Margaret Thatcher as a watershed, when progressive hopes were dashed, but for me it was several years earlier with the defeat of the Upper Clyde shipbuilders in 1974. If the "hippy dream" seemed less of an option it would become necessary to support myself. I thought lecturing would allow me to do the things I wanted to do—comfortably, independently, and morally. I still think such is the human ideal and that being in academia, certainly through the earlier part of my "career" gets as close to it as I was ever going to be. After some early hiccups I got my MA. I thought at the time that mid-level analysis was a little unsatisfactory, lacking the overview of macro and the detail of micro perspectives. I focused on police organizations and persuaded the department to let me write a dissertation on "phenomenological and conflict approaches within the sociology of deviance." I suggested (and still do) that these approaches shared the bedrock standpoint of any sociological enterprise in that they assume a skeptical stance with regards to "common sense" understandings as to the purpose of cultural patterns and social institutions. Both invite that suspension of belief with regards to the conventions of normal everyday existence, subjecting such things to a thoroughgoing reflective gaze. It has been widely argued that the phenomenological perspective (of which postmodernism is perhaps the most recent manifestation) encourages a placing for the sociologist as an ironist. This is all well and good, and there is a case to be made for the sociologist as a professional ironist, if not indeed cynic. Critical theory, of course, invites us to take a step further, to move from irony to critique. Where phenomenological sociologies hone in on case studies, their critical counterparts are concerned with transforming such cases into "issues" (Mills 1945). If commonsense reflections on social phenomena tend to be reinforced by positivistic sociology in terms of "*this* is what's really going on," phenomenological social science tentatively hints that "well maybe *this* is what *appears* to be really going on." The critical approach on the other hand wishes to ask "*In whose interest is it that this appears* to be going on?" The differences could be expressed as "Telling it like it is—that's reality and we're stuck with it"; "Telling it like it is?— maybe we could construct a different narrative?"—"Telling it like it shouldn't be—though it could be different." In sociological thinking there is a persistent dilemma between discovery and invention. If positivism's commonsense thinking is concerned with telling the important stories, phenomenology is interested in the telling of different stories, or of telling the "same" stories differently. Critical sociology is at least partly concerned with the production of alternative stories and with promoting the audibility of alternative voices. It asks serious questions as to who holds custody of narratives and what the consequences might be. As Bauman (2000) puts it "truths" are "parts of the wall which the poets' mission is to crush"—"lies" undiscovered perhaps or more accurately ideologies? In fact Zygmunt Bauman had arrived in Leeds just before I did and it is a matter of some regret to me that I didn't try to pursue a doctorate under his supervision. Bauman's sociology (certainly over the last fifteen or so years) has influenced me a great deal. At the time I told myself I wanted to concentrate on "deviance"—though I also "knew" that Baumanesque high theory was beyond my capabilities.

I moved on to two other universities for doctoral studies, essentially dropping out of both of them. In the first I felt a fish out of water. It was an elite university and I found the faculty arrogant, dismissive, and certainly uninterested in me. A significant moment was when at a restaurant one evening one of Britain's best-known "cultural theorists" made a series of (ironic?) racist remarks about the Indian waiter in front of him. Naively I'd thought that academics were above that sort of thing. I'd not really been around them socially up to that point and it was an early indication to me of the distance which can exist between paper principles and live practices. At the second place I found myself "supervised" by a highly conservative criminologist who obviously loathed my perspectives and almost certainly my "style" (or lack of it). I got my first sense of petty jealousies and turf wars within academia during this period. Again the "glossy brochure" image of a community of scholars began to get somewhat matted. I concentrated on picking up part time teaching and discovered that whilst the "Leeds effect" was constantly in play, when I got into the sessions I rather enjoyed them. To my surprise I was offered my first full-time (temporary) post at Sheffield University to teach courses in social control and social theory. At Sheffield I became convinced that I could do this—that if I was engaged in Goffinanesque "impression management" then others probably were too and I could make a reasonable fist of it. Thank you Erving!

My next stop was at an Institute of Higher Education in South Wales. I was employed to teach "Organizational Theory" and I was the only sociologist in the college. Since my time in Leeds I'd had problems with the concept of "organization" (organic?—come on!) but institutional analysis could be rewarding, if rather bleak. I was working on a new degree in combined studies and I quickly took advantage of my singularity to adjust my job description. Soon I was teaching (to me) a pleasing combination of new criminology and the bits of social theory I found most interesting. By this time I'd come to the conclusion that the notion of a disciplinary "canon" was to say the least problematic. My interest in obtaining some understanding of how what passes for canons in sociology and criminology comes to be produced and reproduced stems from this time. I was thinking that Gouldner's (1970) notion of a sociology of sociology could and should be extended to criminology, in that in order to understand ideas we had to try to locate them in a variety of contexts. History I could do little about, but as that sole sociologist I found myself pretty much bereft of institutional peer pressure and hence able to create my own parameters and definitions of "the subject." My reference groups were primarily external, most concretely the European Group for the Study of Deviance and Social Control and more abstractly the Society for the Study of Social Problems. Within the context of combined studies, my students inevitably would have a selective experience of sociology—and one defined by myself. Of course my legitimate justification was that selections are always made, the key questions are who make them and how authoritarian is the level of enforcement? In other words are people encouraged to pursue other material/avenues of thought, to challenge the "official wisdom" regardless of who represents that "wisdom" I thought it hypocritical for a critical scholar to deny critique, and this remains an issue for me where some "critical" scholarship is concerned. I wanted to demonstrate the possibility of "alternative realities" but for me they were indeed alternative—rather than absolute. With Marcuse (1994) I found myself against "totalism" of all varieties. I discovered that I very much enjoyed working with nonsocial scientists. One was/is the film and media scholar Gill Branston with whom I've been involved in lively intellectual tussles ever since. The English literature scholar, Nick Potter, was another, still as close as I've come to a renaissance person. Both were radical in instinct but in no sense dogmatic. We could discuss and argue in a genuine spirit of intellectual inquiry, one free, as best I could tell, of hidden agendas or turf wars. I learned a number of things. I began to appreciate an interdisciplinary approach, becoming more convinced that divides were primarily institutional in character rather than endemic. I still think the idea of geographically separated departments is flawed, rendering less likely the cross fertilization of diverse minds in corridors and around coffee machines. In South Wales I became aware of the onset of managerialist entrepreneurship (and a crass version at that) which was starting to *manifestly* seep into "higher education." I saw blatant attempts at micromanagement and the "fine tuning" of statistical data. Members of faculty were bullied and manipulated, via a demoralizing mix of threats, bribes, and contrived divisions. At the same time as academics were being coerced into doing more and more with less and less, the senior management were creaming off vital resources on vacations masquerading as "recruitment initiatives." Aside from the white-collar crime though, the "legitimate" outcomes of the managerialist juggernaut were far more damaging. The new climate of "public accountability" (which public? for what?) led to what has become one of the banes of contemporary academic life—a tendency towards ludicrous and embarrassing self-aggrandizement in order to "justify" one's existence and that of one's institution.

I could see how things were going. Marcuse (1969) uses the analogy of a cyclist to describe the phenomena. Riding a cycle downhill is easy and on the level pretty much so. One just sits back, presses the pedal gently from time to time and enjoys progress. Going uphill, though, requires that one bend one's back (genuflecting before the powerful) whilst pedaling increasingly and intensely (stamping on the weak). It seemed unlikely that this process could be avoided, but it might be evaded for a while. I acquired a post in the sociology department at a traditional, rather than a new university—Bangor. For quite some time the academic culture was very different. I remember an administrator advising new faculty to develop their own research agenda rather than having it defined by external funding opportunities. I taught classes in social theory and social control, and worked with graduate students as an MA tutor and PhD supervisor. After a while I realized that three members of the department were actively specializing in criminologically related research and teaching. One was our head of department, a highly regarded, reform-minded specialist on imprisonment; another was a prominent ethnomethodologist, and then there was myself, representing critical criminology. It seemed to make sense to try to develop criminology as an undergraduate degree and eventually the "Centre of Criminology and Criminal Justice" was created. Names are important. At the time two of us were uncomfortable with the reference to "Criminal Justice." For us this smacked of catering (for me pandering) to the criminal justice system, rather than analyzing and/or critiquing it. My colleague preferred a simple "Centre of Criminology," whilst I, playfully alluding to the title of a book by Jason Ditton (1979), floated "Centre of Controlology." Our professor held out for "Criminal Justice," partly, I think, because he was genuinely committed to responding to administrative "needs" and partly because he rightly anticipated the way the ideological wind was blowing. Criminal Justice expanded, the number of incoming undergraduates rapidly outstripping those of sociology. Inevitably many of these students thought they were signing up for a vocationally orientated course, and specifically one which would prepare them for various "control" occupations. Some expressed impatience with what they saw as overly abstract theory, more found it interesting but questioned its "relevance." Others got as turned on as I had been by the critical and ethnomethodogical emphases and wanted more, many taking up places on our newly formed masters course and later registering for PhDs.

The changing balance of the department did not go unrecognized by the other sociologists, some of whom I think, suspected some kind of a putsch or at least takeover. More criminology/criminal justice students required more staff, and Bangor experienced the sort of expansion in these areas which became increasingly common worldwide. The new appointees were overwhelmingly criminal justice oriented and both the ethnomethodologist and I became doubly marginalized. The other sociologists distrusted our role in the CJ camp and the CJ people dismissed us as rather impractical, old-fashioned *über* theorists. Gradually the managerialist "realities" began to seep into the traditional universities. We criminologists were initially subtly and later more overtly encouraged to pursue research funds from wherever they were available and for seemingly any project providing it would bring in money. Internally an essentially cooperative culture came under strain from a more competitive one. Those willing and able to solicit, apply for, and acquire external funding were encouraged to see themselves as different from and superior to those who weren't or couldn't. I've never been professionally competitive, preferring to limit those impulses to places such as squash and tennis courts when the competition is of all the participants choosing. More relevantly, I believed that most of the sources of big budget funding were tainted in ways unacceptable to me. In short I concluded that the criminological agenda was being set by interests which were neither my own nor socially positive. The managerialist project, of course, by now was extended to various kinds of "evaluative" exercises. To this end our "accomplishments" were "bulled up" to a ludicrous degree. I recall almost squirming with embarrassment when the director of the relabeled "Centre of Comparative Criminology and Criminal Justice Studies" (who I knew by now thought of me very much as the flavor of many, many moons ago) made it sound as if I was one of the world's greatest experts. Such contrivances are, of course, the only logical response of an institution placed in an absurd situation. It is a consequence of the perceived obligation to represent "accountability" in both moral and fiscal terms. Into the university came an almost pathological obsession with monitoring everything and everybody. The inevitable result was that individual faculty spent a great deal of time trying to "creatively account" for what they did rather than just doing it; "witch-hunts" emerged seeking to spot and shame those "not carrying their weight." In classic "saints and sinners style," identifying the deviant helped to sanctify the hunters. It's important to note that the deviants were not unproductive. Productivity was just being defined in a narrow entrepreneurial sense, whereby reluctance to apply for dubious sources of funding was equated with letting the side down. This is especially important as it serves to channel and shape the direction of future criminological work. It was clear that the hitherto rather collegial and open-minded atmosphere was eroding. The CJ appointees enthusiastically endorsed the new ethos, manifestly in the name of "democracy" though I find it difficult to escape the conclusion that they recognized that their own interests would be best served by presenting themselves as (to coin a phrase) the new "zoo-keepers of deviancy" and *coincerned* university citizens! This didn't surprise me as anyone *aufait* with the emergence and history of criminology must surely realize it's primarily one-sided agenda. Looking back, given what I've come to understand about institutional life, I shouldn't have been too surprised by the response of some of the sociologists either.

We'd continually been presented with "top-down" initiatives of a seemingly increasingly ludicrous kind, framed within a form of discourse which was often simultaneously presumptuous, blatantly manipulative, and semi-literate. Even if one was in sympathy with the manifest objectives a sociologist should surely have seen the naivety in thinking the bureaucratic directives would accomplish them. Yet in department meetings colleagues seemed to switch their sociological brains off, take it as all on "the level" and suggest ways in which we could best comply. It seemed to me that one couldn't take this stuff seriously no matter which sociological tradition one came from and I found the meetings both irritating and stressful. My ethnomethodological colleague couldn't understand my reaction. His theoretical position allowed him to conclude that nothing of consequence would happen anyway! In the specific sense he may have been right, though my claim is that the framework within which we were encouraged to not necessarily initially *think* about the world but certainly to *talk* about it had an accumulative and corrosive general affect. Sometimes more and sometimes less subtly we were ourselves being manipulated by being invited to think that we had no choice but to dedicate time and energy into manipulating external agencies. If we accomplished this by for example "fixing" RAE criteria to make us look "good," we could clap each other on the back for being such effective impression managers.

With impeccable timing I moved to the United States in the first week of September 2001. I did so for personal reasons. At the University of Southern Maine I was/am employed in a criminology department. In one sense I've been most fortunate. The department was established, most unusually, as a criminology department rather than a CJ one, and the faculty members have always recognized the distinction. We give "health warnings" to prospective students (though with little obvious effect!). My colleagues have sociological backgrounds. All would probably self-identify as strongly influenced by critical criminology, though we've drawn different conclusions as to what this means. As with the vast majority of university departments, ours has not been free of conflicts. Egos, agendas, and on occasions even vendettas are or have been on display. In my view such is the character of institutional life. On the individual level people are instinctively supportive, collectively they are often toxic.

ANALYTICAL LEVEL, DISCIPLINARY BOUNDARIES, AND THEORY

Research of a butterfly and/or dinosaur

The purpose of this collection is to render clear the importance of acknowledging the role of foregrounding in the production of research and the "understanding" of it. The next section refers to my own gradually accumulating work. I've never had a "grand plan" or a sense of clear direction for my research. My investigations have been instigated by serendipity and opportunity. As with all research mine has come about from a convergence of structural and organizational location, and personal history, as well as being the result of relatively consistent theoretical perspectives. I would say that I've been somewhat of an academic butterfly that has floated onto something, considered it, and then moved on to something else. Yet, whilst landed, (whilst hopefully avoiding the wheels upon which crushing might occur) the butterfly regards the subjects/objects experienced via a certain kind of gaze or theoretical position. I'd self-interestedly argue the case for the butterfly—whose reluctance or inability to remain too long on any given flower may occasionally permit a broader vision as to how the ecosystem hangs together. The resulting diversity of topic is paralleled by diversity in method. I recognize that methods are always contestable and strongly suspect that often methodological challenges are really ideological ones in disguise. The practical environment of course means that in order to inaugurate much research one is expected to demonstrate methodological "rigor"—and curiously critical projects are often found wanting. Regardless of the methods one adopts I'm convinced that social scientists are engaged less in explaining the world than in constructing it. "Telling truth to power" may be a tad ambitious in what is surely the aftermath of empirical romantic naivety, but a persistent chipping away at the underpinnings of the self-interested and promoting definitions of the powerful should not be beyond the morals of even the run-of-the-mill academic. One can present alternative readings and facilitate alternative voices without having to conclusively endorse them as universally valid. We can invite people to read "nice" rather than "nasty" stories, though I engage some strategies to counteract the reader from being seduced into too easily accepting the story. For example I try to insert ironic, even flippant comments from time to time in order to fragment the text and invite the reader to hesitate and reflect before moving on. The convention in academic writing is to maintain a flow, to roll "logically" on from A to B to C. I'd prefer readers to stop and say "hey, but wait a minute." This is because 1) concepts in social science are essentially problematic with lots of unsettling parentheses, and 2) as a critical theorist I'm suspicious of totalist arguments. Totalist arguments imply "settlement" of issues which cannot be settled and "closure" of ones which cannot be closed. As sociologists, criminologists, and human beings, we have good grounds to fear the tyranny of consensus. I choose to offer persuasive invitations, but ones which can be refused.

My usual approach is to pick up on an often "small scale" event, to describe some of its features, and then suggest an "explanation" in terms of its location within a broader structural context. I assume that a micro occurrence both reflects structure and is an element in its reproduction. Concrete institutional analysis is essential as institutions are the points of conjuncture for the micro and the macro. Sociology should be concerned with outlining the acquisition of meaning and demonstrating connections with practices across differing social levels. In the final analysis though, one looks to "structure"—or more honestly to ones version of it. In my case, structure, and hence institutions and micro encounters alike, are all saturated with social domination.

I've indicated that as with so many others of my generation, I came into criminology via sociology. Nowadays my sociological interests are perhaps somewhat narrow, as I heavily focus on examining the establishment, maintenance, and reproduction of what passes for social "control/order." In respect of criminology, my concerns have been correspondingly broader. I have consistently attempted to reframe criminology in terms which go extensively beyond and against conventionally established administrative interests. As early as 1959 Mills was worrying that social scientific research as a whole was becoming bureaucratized, supervised by administrators, exercised by technicians, and accepting of the goals of social engineering imposed by funding agencies. Clarke and Critcher (1985) argue that this held true of the 1980s and the past twenty years has only intensified fiscal and ideological control over the research agenda. In my view wildly misnamed "ethical" committees have significantly functioned to maintain the relative invisibility of the crimes of the powerful. We can only understand the social (or antisocial) role of criminology by acknowledging the severe restraints which are now increasingly placed on its production. I must admit that I don't find it easy to recommend that critically minded students try to carve out a career in criminology. As I convinced myself perhaps the best I can say is that the alternatives for most people are probably worse.

Admittedly the critical criminological voice which emerged from the roots of 1960s deviancy theory has created at least some intellectual space and nourishment. It is accepted that the broadening of subject areas is legitimate within this branch of the discipline. However, within critical criminology, quite significant fissures have emerged. A few years ago this was framed in terms of "new realism" and "left idealism." Today I see it more as a divide between those of us with abolitionist and/or libertarian tendencies (who wish for the contraction of punitive sanctions) and those with more bureaucratic and/or authoritarian tendencies (who wish for their expansion). The difference can also be characterized as one between those who seek to promote their own "preferred victims" (and in so doing create more "crime") and those who wish to reduce knee-jerk claims for victim status (and hence limit "crime"). My claim is the zemiological one that "harms" may be negotiated, but "crime" is a counterproductive category which only serves to legitimate state control, vindictiveness, and the delivery of pain. Thus I much regret not only the intensified institutional fiscal and structural forces which serve to channel the work of criminologists ever more in an administrative technocratic and authoritarian direction, but also the interventionist/expansionist elements within "critical" criminology. Additionally I agree with Cohen's (1988) warning that our object of study needs to be other than just the behaviors we disapprove of. I recognize that I'm in danger of being thought somewhat of a dinosaur, though would playfully observe that whilst the brains of dinosaurs were tiny they were at least their own. I'll try to hold extinction at arms length for as long as I can too!

More seriously the obvious fact that the ideological climate is hostile to anti-interventionism makes it more important that that perspective continue to be articulated. There is a real danger of what Jacoby (1995) terms "social amnesia." As Kundera (1996) put it "the struggle of man against power is the struggle of memory against forgetting." Whilst academic "success" is clearly rendered more probable the more pragmatic and less skeptical the agenda, this isn't a route I've felt able to follow. Avoidance of such "practical" engagement might be thought self-indulgent, but for me it is the only ethical and intellectual choice. To endorse popular or fashionable bandwagons, even when the motives for doing so are authentically "humane" and the outcomes appear to be, is for me an act of bad faith as a "critical" theorist. R.E.M's line about declining offered solutions and alternatives has always been my reality. An authentically critical criminology is one which perpetually challenges "common sense" thinking rather than giving it sustenance. Critical criminology should, as Bauman (2000) puts it, "reopen the allegedly shut case of explanation." Though counselors seem to make a good living out of insisting that they can deliver it, there is really no "closure," nor should there be.

EXCLUSION, INCLUSION, AND DOMINATION

Most of my work has been concerned with issues of inclusion, exclusion, and domination. Exclusion is widely spoken of in negative terms, politicians wringing their hands over it and research funds made available in order to tackle it. Leaning on critical theory I've tried to argue that the kind of "social order" we "enjoy" requires the systematic reproduction of excluded populations. Acceptance of what passes for social order requires the continued presence of the "disorderly" (as with Christie and Bruuns' [1985] "good enemies" or Spitzers' [1975] "social junk and dynamite") as well as a corresponding and perpetually growing array of institutions and professionals whose official job it is to curtail their disorderliness. We have inclusionary rhetoric in the midst of exclusionary practices.

Inclusion is, however, not always just rhetoric. We have seen over the past decades, people from marginalized and subordinated groups being invited to the "party," and (on the surface at least) "accepted" within it. I think it necessary to address such key issues as "exclusion from what?" and "inclusion into what?" Which interests lie behind the selective inclusion and exclusion of varied social groups? It seems to me that one doesn't "celebrate diversity" by inviting a handful of the diverse to behave basically like you do. In some senses perhaps "inclusion" can be thought of as more dehumanizing than exclusion, especially given that the "really included" so often engage in dehumanizing activities. Inclusion generally means either the assimilation of a token, selected few, or the incorporation or "buying off" of potential threats.

"Incorporationist" theses, of course, have a bad press nowadays. Historically rooted in periods when for economic reasons larger numbers of people in the industrial world needed to be incorporated, they seem less credible in this millennium. More importantly, incorporationism is thought of as overly reductionist—of Marcuse at his most excessive. Indeed clearly people are to varying degrees self-reflective, adopting an ironic postmodern eye to the main chance in terms of opportunities for resisting and evading events not to their liking. Yet the key question is surely—what does it all amount to? Perhaps the satisfaction people derive from as they may see it "avoiding the madness" is at one and the same time the most which "dissent" is allowed to add up to, and is the guarantor of business as usual. I'd suggest that the different forms of exclusion and inclusion are exercises in social domination. The essential question is

who sets the terms by which people are in or excluded and in which circumstances? I've consistently attempted to ask questions of "domination," defining
it, identifying its sources and describing its processes, practices, and structures.
As a critical theorist "order" is an intellectual, a moral, an ideological, and a
personal problem. With Freire (1974) I'm interested in how dominators live
within the dominated. This includes myself, and the selective memories laid
out earlier in this article represent an exercise in self-reflection and awareness
as well as providing clues as to how to read past, present, and perhaps future
work.

SOCIOLOGY, CRITICAL THEORY, CRITICAL CRIMINOLOGY, AND ANARCHISM

There is another influence which pervades my work. That anarchist literature
I read in religion periods at school has influenced me all my life and I have
struggled to reconcile it with my "academic reality." Anarchism seems to be
a philosophical and political perspective which dares not speak its name in
respectable circles. There is no anarchist sociology which corresponds to or
competes with self or other proclaimed ideological sociologies—of Marxism
or conservative functionalism. It is rare for the word to be used in sociological
discourses, and in criminology it fares little better. Yet this is rather curious
since many if not most sociological perspectives in some senses can be said to
sit surprisingly comfortably alongside anarchist ones.

The difficulties a manifestly anarchist voice has in getting heard are fairly
obvious. Anarchist thinking has never had states or corporations to underpin
its credibility or to sponsor its research agenda as it poses a clear challenge
to current versions of "order" by providing moral and intellectual support
to those who are instinctively suspicious of "authority." "Authority" is dis-
avowed, only power recognized. Yet there are clear intellectual difficulties
also. Anarchism is justifiably conceived of as placing central emphasis on
"individuals" and individual autonomy. For most sociologists such an emphasis is misplaced if not indeed naive for at least two reasons. To begin with
individuals can only make sense of themselves in a social context mediated via
that most "social" of phenomena, that is, language. Secondly the assumption
is that those stressing individual autonomy are automatically opposed to, or
unsympathetic toward, collective interests—in other words are inherently antisocial. However anarchism does not deny the "social," it merely encourages

us to apply an extreme skepticism whenever the word is invoked, whether adjectively or normatively. Anarchism explicitly maintains what the skeptical sociologies implicitly do—that one should not be deceived into thinking that practices presented to us as "on the level"—that is, "social," "moral," "fair," or just "inevitable" and therefore "normal"—are unproblematically so. I'd claim that such is the essence of a sociology (or criminology) which is in any way worthwhile. The kinds of sociology which I think get by such a validity test are actually rather diverse. Indeed at some level most do. Even Parsonian functionalism provides us with a lens for seeing the world in a different, more quizzical way. His thesis for example on "illness as deviance" and his insights into professional legitimation (1951) are intensely radical in their implications. A very different kind of sociology, ethnomethodology, if it tends to reject the notion of power, certainly promotes a healthy degree of skepticism. Not without reason did Gouldner (1972) designate it, albeit contemptuously as "anarchist" sociology.

I have already indicated that it has persistently puzzled me how sociologists trained to look beneath the surface at every other institution, seem able and willing to suspend their various disbeliefs and intelligences where their own is concerned. The "problem" of late 1960s and early 1970s sociology and criminology was that significant numbers of "new" scholars seemed more than willing to declare the emperors naked. Sociology is essentially about laying things bare; or else clothing them differently. That is for me its great excitement and joy. Anarchism tries to do much the same thing. Right-wing attacks on sociology and critical versions of criminology made perfect sense. In a different context, so would left-wing ones.

Let's move to the contribution made by constructionist approaches to sociology generally but to criminology specifically. Certainly the aim was essentially to describe processes. Yet as soon as one goes beyond the telling of the tales of labeling, categorizing, and defining, and takes the perfectly reasonable, I'd maintain logical, next step of instigating inquiry into who seems to gain most from the successful application of such things; as soon as one recognizes the multifaceted nature of the power relations involved, one is implicitly pursuing an anarchist direction. Let's "play dinosaur" for a moment and recall the famous debate between Becker (1967) and Gouldner (1968). Gouldner had objected that Becker seemed reluctant to answer the question that he himself had posed as to "Whose side are we on?" Gouldner castigated Becker for electing to expose the brutal practices of mid-level "dirty workers" rather than their managers and ultimate employers. Probably rightly he implied that Becker benefited professionally from establishing such an apparently limited target. However Gouldner's real beef with Becker was surely because the latter was unwilling to align himself solely with Gouldner's preferred "proletarian" victims. Becker's hedging on "underdog" identification is at least partly because the underdogs in any given situation are not always so easy to identify. Yes, class, as well as gender and ethnicity are key factors, but the ubiquitous and diffuse character of power means that "underdog" identification needs to be provided situationally, and always necessitates a judgment call. Again the perspective which places most emphasis on such a version of power (one which arguably gives it both analytical strength and guarantees its political weakness) is anarchism. Put simply, anarchism draws attention to expressions of domination far beyond Gouldner's preferred victims. While light needs to be cast on the activities of those located in the higher echelons of states and corporations, we also need to reserve some rays for the array of "relative superordinates" who are "just" managers, officials, husbands, and everyday "schoolyard bullies." Midrange sociologies sensitize us to the "ironies" and contradictions of control within institutions. Using the problematic notion of "unintended consequences" and the slightly less problematic one of "latent function," they usually indicate how institutions may establish rather different priorities and accomplish different outcomes from those which provide them with their official *raison d'etre*. At the margins of criminology abolitionism has consistently attempted to identify these outcomes, and to present them as counterproductive with regards to an authentic sense of social harmony. Hence abolitionism has sought to withstand the extension of domination by arguing for the closure of prisons and mental "hospitals," and more recently has argued against their expansion and those of other "antisocial" alternatives. They warn against the abuse of power and the power to abuse which is deemed to be inextricably part and parcel of the process and structure of labeling and institutionalization. The preferred narrative of abolitionism is one of tolerance, compassion, and love, rather than the conventional criminal "justice" one of intolerance, vindictiveness, and punitiveness. Their romantic tales are the ones which most anarchists would prefer to hear. Admittedly anarchists would wish to say rather more about power. Human rights and civil liberties discourses on the "abuse of power" might perhaps be replaced by that of "power as abuse," and a conventional "inclusionist" buzzword such as "empowerment" might be replaced by that of "disempowerment." Critical theory has clearly had a fundamental influence on my thinking. Most commentators classify it as revisionist Marxism (Bottomore 1984). Whilst it's true that the Frankfurt school emerged in the course of a debate within and about Marxism, I'd suggest that there are grounds for saying that their accumulated "revisions" took them significantly in the direction of anarchism. Obviously a focus on class is fundamental in terms of any Marxist analysis. Class is of great importance for most anarchists also, but it does not hold an exclusively privileged status. Anarchists are equally as inclined to concentrate on the nature of states (international, national, and local), bureaucracies, and micropower. Critical theory shares in this variety of focus. The state is a key object for attention, the work on instrumental rationality renders it a natural resource for Green politics and the selective engagement of Freud of course attempts to address dimensions of micropower neglected within Marxism. Critical theorists have always been adamant that we should be willing to pay considerable attention to the construction of the "personality" and the ways in which personalities play out in concrete social situations (Marcuse, 1962; Adorno 1950). That the constructs were deemed to be ultimately determined by structure only made it even more important that we be willing and able to pay considerable attention to the specifics of that construction. Critical theory urged us to engage in archeological work in respect of the demolished and deep thinking with regards to the unbuilt. How do we come to forget things (Jacoby, 1975) or not learn them (Tester, 1997); how do we come to deny them (Cohen, 2001)? Critical theory was never quite as abstract as it is popularly believed to be. It was always to be applied to concrete social and institutional contexts. Whilst much Marxist work attempts a similar project, arguably there is a case to be made for the idea that it is insufficiently critical. The critical theory assault on instrumental rationality and its' advocacy of critical reason is similarly far more in tune with anarchist thinking. Marxism tends to see social progress occurring through the development of "rational" planning brought about by bureaucrats, technocrats, and scientists. Bauman (1989) characterizes their accumulative efforts as "gardening," whereby neateners and tidiers seek to eradicate a variety of social "weeds." It is not difficult to see administrative criminology as engaged in "gardening," nor in my opinion the expansionist elements of critical criminology. Essentially critical theory sees their activities as sources of and for the extension and intensification of social domination. Critical reason should be most rigorously applied to those processes, institutions, and structures which claim to represent reason.

Associated with this it is clear that Marxism provides us with both an analysis and a program. Marxists address the "what is to be done" question and have an agency in mind for doing it. Critical theorists, especially Marcuse (1994) have extreme skepticism regarding both program and agency. Whilst the working class is perceived as oppressed (contained within Marcuse's half garrison, half welfare world) it is not seen as a key agency of liberation. Perhaps it's difficult to formulate freedom in conditions of confinement? Critical theory and anarchism both decline to romanticize the working class. Emerging from it I share G. B. Shaw's (2001) line that the only people talking of the dignity of labor are those who haven't done any. Furthermore both critical theory and anarchism express antipathy to all "totalist" programs. There is a definite reluctance to propose or endorse prescriptions for human liberation. The best one can do, perhaps all one could or should do, is to "negate the negative" (Adorno, 1973). As Jarvis (1998) observes, this is not the same thing as nihilism. Rather, permanent critique is critical theory's ultimate expression, and this is anarchism's position also. Roy Harper once sang about how systems themselves are in and of themselves—by definition appalling and that accurately reflects a critical theory approach, an anarchist one, and in my opinion a genuinely critical criminological one. It seems to me that the positions I have come to adopt can well be described as "romantic pessimism."

My reflections in this article were intended to enable me to try to "make sense," not only of my academic career, but my life in general. Academic and other lives are the product of a huge variety of social forces. Perhaps it's important to try to articulate such self reflection from time to time, for one's self of course, but also to provide a few "archeological tools" for readers of one's own, and, more importantly, others' work.

REFERENCES

Adorno, A. (1950). *The Authoritarian Personality.* New York: Harper.

Adorno, A. (1973). *Negative Dialectics.* London: Routledge.

Bauman, Z. (1989). *Modernity and the Holocaust.* Oxford: Polity.

Bauman, Z. (1993). *Modernity and Ambivalence.* Oxford: Polity.

Bauman, Z. (2000). *Liquid Modernity.* Oxford: Polity.

Becker, H. (1967). "Whose side are we on?" *Social Problems* 14.

Bottomore, T. (1984). *Sociology and Socialism.* Brighton: Wheatsheaf.

Christie, N., and Bruun K. (1985). *Den Gode Fiende.* Oslo: Norwegian University Press.

Clarke, J., and Critcher, C. (1985). *The Devil Makes Work.* London: Macmillan.

Cohen, S. (1988). *Against Criminology.* New Brunswick: Transaction.

Cohen, S. (2001). *States of Denial.* Oxford: Polity.

Ditton, J. (1979). *Controlology.* London: Macmillan.

Friere, P. (1974). *Cultural Action for Freedom.* London: Penguin.

Garfinkel, H. (1967). *Studies in Ethnomethodology.* Englewood Cliffs: Prentice Hall.

Gouldner, A. (1968). "The sociologist as partisan." *The American Sociologist* 3.

Gouldner, A. (1970). *The Coming Crisis of Western Sociology.* London: Heinemann.

Jacoby, R. (1975). *Social Amnesia.* Sussex: Harvester.

Jarvis, S. (1998). *Adorno: A Critical Introduction.* Oxford: Polity.

Kundera, M. (1996). *A Book of Laughter and Forgetting.* London: Faber and Faber.

Marcuse, H. (1955). *Eros and Civilization.* Boston: Beacon.

Marcuse, H. (1962) *Eros and Civilization.* New York: Vintage.

Marcuse, H. (1994). *One Dimensional Man.* London: Routledge.

McKenzie, R., and Silver, A. (1968). *Angels in Marble.* London: Heinemann.

Mills, C. W. (1945). "The professional ideology of social pathologists" *American Journal of Sociology* 49.

Mills, C. W. (1959). *The Sociological Imagination.* Oxford: Penguin.

Parsons. T. (1951). *The Social System.* London: RKP.

Powell, C. (1984). "Control of criminology and legal policy; the case of Finnish neo-classicism." *Working Papers in European Criminology* 6.

Shaw, G. B. (2001). *Man and Superman.* London: Penguin.

Spitzer, S. (1975). "Towards a Marxian Theory of Crime." *Social Problems* 22.

Tester, K. (1997). *Moral Culture.* London: Sage.

2

Reflections of a Black Feminist Criminologist

HILLARY POTTER

My route from my birth to my present existence has been simultaneously privileged and marked with obstacles. I am not oblivious to the fact that I was afforded opportunities that many have not had. I was reared in a two-parent home with both of my biological parents, and doted on as the youngest of four children in a diverse working- to middle-class neighborhood in Denver. I wanted for (almost) nothing, as I was provided for with plenty of food to eat, a comfortable house in which to live, brand-name clothes to wear, an overabundance of toys to play with, and involvement in several extracurricular activities, including lessons in flute, dance, gymnastics, swimming, and tennis. As a *black* child, my life was relatively pleasant compared with the lives of many other black children. But beyond being provided love, stability, positive role modeling, and provisions, and though I have not experienced strife at the level that many other blacks have suffered, my encounters with sexist and racist experiences have directed me to the current juncture in my professional life. It has only been in the past few years that I have recognized that the path to my current ideology and chosen profession was not as disjointed and baseless as I thought. As I have recently tried to better define my overall area of study—the intersection of race, gender, class, and crime—I have reflected on my formative life experiences. It is my belief that as social scientists, we can practice objectivity even if we reflect on the way in which we situate ourselves in the research based on our life experiences that are mirrored in the work we do.

The nature of storytelling has supplemented me with fodder to trudge onward. Stories told by my parents about themselves, our family members, and faded memories of my personal experiences have affected my outlook. One of the stories often shared with me involved my parents' desire for me to start kindergarten at the age of four. Because I would not be five years old until a couple months after the academic year began, I had to be tested by a psychologist who worked for the school district. The 15-minute meeting—for which my mother was not allowed to be present—resulted in the conclusion that I had "ceased to develop" and that I did not function at the level I should have been for my age. The audaciousness of my mother would not allow her to rest on the psychologist's assessment, as my mother believed I was well-prepared for school because of the time she had spent teaching me to read and write. My mother spoke directly with (public) school district administrators and demanded that I be retested by an unharried and unbiased psychologist. My mother reasoned that the initial testing had been conducted by a (white) person who harbored racialized preconceptions that black children have a subordinate intellect compared with white children of the same age. While the second test found that I was especially shy and "had to be encouraged to be verbal," it revealed that I was ready to begin my formal education and that I had the mathematic and logical skills of children a few years older. It is frightening to think that I could have been held back before I was even allowed to get started—a fate that many black children suffer in the U.S. education system.[1] I *was privileged* as a black child because of the support of a tenacious and dedicated mother who spent much of her time in the home (as opposed to working outside the home) and an accommodating father, allowing them to protect me and to prepare me for the world I was to inevitably face.

LIFTING THE VEIL

Our identity is fluid. Not only does it develop and transform over the course of our lives, as we are confronted with various settings and audiences, we often shift our public behavior dependent on what is expected for us to successfully maneuver in the given environment.[2] This is not only the case for people of color, but for all people. However, this concept of shifting, arguably, is more prevalent among marginalized groups like people of color because we remain at the lower-end of the strata within U.S. society, with whites at the top (and in control). As we incorporate gender and socioeconomic class into these strata, the rungs become even more complicated. For people of color, in particular, it is regrettable that shifting becomes a conscious and habitual part of our lives. Being aware of this reality, my parents took great care in training me and my siblings accordingly. My mother regularly corrected the way in which we spoke English. While we could use some generational colloquialisms that we picked up in the neighborhood or at school (that is, the latest teenage slang), we were consistently instructed on the way in which we spoke English, with the focus being on the proper use of "standard" English.

This instruction by my parents was extended into the way in which my siblings and I carried ourselves as well. While my parents could not always control the influences we had outside the home, they did what they could while we were in the home. We were often forbade from watching certain television programs, such as "Good Times," which featured a hard-working, but struggling black family living in public housing ("the projects") in Chicago. My parents believed such programs (and movies in the same vein) were exploitative of blacks and only perpetuated a monolithic stereotype about how black people live and behave. This orientation to partiality in the way individuals are viewed based on their racial-ethnic identity has been confirmed for me in a variety of ways. For example, if future potential employers were not deterred by my gender, I was solely evaluated based on the merit of my formal education and work history. My especially Anglo-Saxon name has often found me mistaken for a white woman—among whites, Latinas/os, blacks, and others, alike. Although I have no solid evidence of racial bias, I was not blind to the slack-jawed and wide-eyed reactions I received when I showed up to job interviews. Because potential employers were aware of my gender, I knew this was not the reason for their reactions; I suspected my race is what caused the awe. In his book *The Souls of Black Folk*, published in 1903, renowned black scholar W. E. B. Du Bois used the concepts of the "veil" and a "double-consciousness" to describe these experiences of black people:

After the Egyptian and Indian, the Greek and Roman, the Teuton and Mongolian, the Negro is a sort of seventh son, born with a veil, and gifted with second-sight in this American world,—a world which yields him no true self-consciousness, but only lets him see himself through the revelation of the other world. It is a peculiar sensation, this double-consciousness, this sense of always looking at one's self through the eyes of others, of measuring one's soul by the tape of a world that looks on in amused contempt and pity. One ever feels his two-ness,—an American, a Negro; two souls, two thoughts, two unreconciled strivings; two warring ideals in one dark body, whose dogged strength alone keeps it from being torn asunder.[3]

Living in these two worlds taught me that regardless of the changing society in which we lived—particularly how different my childhood was from that of my father, who grew up in rural Alabama in the 1930s and 1940s—racial equality was a long time coming. This socialization and reality has continued to prove difficult for me when I present my research to a white audience. My goal is to enlighten others on the social forces that find blacks and other people of color with higher rates of crime victimization and criminal offending. I frequently worry about "airing the dirty laundry" about people of color and their experiences as victims and as offenders. But, ultimately, I know that I and my fellow race-and-crime researchers must continue in conducting and disseminating our work in order to effect change that will benefit communities of color. This is supported by Rhonda Baynes Jeffries and Gretchen Givens Generett's argument that "[a]s black female scholars, we are often the most stabilizing forces within our communities, whereas at the same time serving as agents of social change. And although we strive to meet the community's belief in our ability to create change, we encounter antithetical resistance from the same institutions that trained us to investigate, examine, analyze, and reform."[4]

AIN'T I A PROFESSOR?

A few years ago I located a fifth grade assignment I completed in which I was asked to ponder what "I want to be" at ages eighteen, twenty-one, twenty-five, thirty-five, and fifty. Since it has been instilled in me since a young age that I was expected to attend and complete college, I wrote that I would be a "college student" at age eighteen. For ages twenty-one, twenty-five, and thirty-five, I wrote that I wanted to be a "teacher." I always enjoyed being lost in my own world as a child and "playing school" with my stuffed animals and dolls. I developed numerous lesson plans for my "students" and, of course, I completed all the assignments in their names. Although I saw being a teacher as a noble position, I had aspirations to do what I considered to be upward mobility in the education field. At age fifty, I wrote that I wanted to be a "professor." Because I am a first-generation college student, my knowledge of higher education was minimal. I thought that in order to become a college professor, one had to first train as a kindergarten–twelfth grade teacher. While I have never forgotten about my endless hours of playing school during my childhood and my desire to be a teacher, it was not until the late 1990s that I returned to this ambition. To be sure, I was taken aback when I realized that I have found my way back to my childhood ambitions. However, on the predominantly white campus of the University of Colorado at Boulder, to most who do not know me I am invisible as a "professor." While I am grateful that I am recognized as being about ten years younger than my true age, I have come to believe that my relatively youthful appearance is only a small part of the reaction I often receive. Essentially, I do not represent what many continue to believe to be the image of a professor; that is, I am not white and I am not male.[5]

At the start of the mainstream feminist movement in the United States during the nineteenth century, black women were undeniably aware of their invisibility and began to speak in public forums on issues related to them. Although typically not included in standard depictions of the feminist movement, contemporary black feminist writers trace *organized* Black feminist efforts back to the nineteenth century when black women such as Maria Stewart, Anna Julia Cooper, and Sojourner Truth spoke openly of black women's affairs and breaking free from oppressive gender roles.[6] These women's public declarations of racism, as well as sexism—in particular, sexism by black men—did not go without criticism from men and other women in the black community.[7] Retractors in the black community did not want the general public to be privy to their in-group unrest and they felt more energy should be placed on securing freedom from slavery and on racial justice, in general, as opposed to trying to gain gender equality.

Fear of the black community's reaction to black women advocating for themselves was often not a concern for these revolutionary women. One of the most notable illustrations of this valiance was through the work of slavery abolitionist and woman suffragist Sojourner Truth. It was Truth's 1851 speech at the Ohio Women's Rights Convention that began to bring white women and all men in the abolitionist and women's rights movements to acknowledge black women in their struggles.[8] Although historian Nell Painter has critically questioned that Truth actually spoke the now legendary and widely used phrase "Ain't I a Woman?"[9] in her speech to the congregation, Painter recognizes that the *symbol* Truth has come to personify is important to black and white women feminists alike.[10] It is this symbol that I now realize I have held during my adult life. I was confronted with this matter during the only black studies course I took during my undergraduate education at CU–Boulder. The small class focused on black women fiction writers comprised of only women students, all of whom were white except for my roommate and me, and was taught by a white male. One day, as the lecture centered on what is now referred to as *intersectionality* of identity and status, a white student turned to me and asked, "What are you first: black or a woman?" I was stumped by this question and did not answer. Eventually the instructor recognized my discomfort with the inquiry and moved on with his lecture. In a subsequent discussion about the probe with my roommate, she and I decided that we were black first because of the all-white, frequently hostile, environment of Boulder. However, that declaration still did not feel completely accurate to what I believed my Self encompassed. Black feminist scholar bell hooks writes of a similar experience in her book *Feminist Theory: From Margin to Center*: "As a black woman interested in the feminist movement, I am often asked whether being black is more important than being a woman; whether the feminist struggle to end sexist oppression is more important than the struggle to end racism or vice versa. All such questions are rooted in competitive either/or thinking, the belief that the self is formed in opposition to another."[11]

This topic of representing one part of one's identity over another persists; only a small number of people are erudite in the subject of intersectionality. During the 2008 presidential campaign, I had regularly been questioned as to which Democratic nominee I supported because of my identity as a black woman. That is, before I would let it be known who I endorsed, I had often been asked if I supported Barack Obama because he is identified as black or Hillary Clinton because she is a woman.

As I continue to struggle with proving I can live up to the expectations of my faculty position, especially since I was not hired by means of an open search, I still feel as though I have to work twice as hard and produce twice as much to validate that I belong in academe. Joy James and Ruth Farmer write about black women faculty in the following way: "We simultaneously have power, and lack it, in paradoxical relationships in which power is sexualized and racialized. Our intellectual abilities are questioned. We are made into fetishes. While shut out of decisions and policy-making processes, we are held responsible for outcomes."[12]

I admit that I am what others refer to as a "workaholic"—though I prefer to refer to it as having a strong work ethic instead of pathologizing my work habits and drive. While some of the excess work I do has been self-imposed, recurrently the burden is placed on me by others. It is well-established—even if only anecdotally—that faculty of color at predominantly white colleges and universities have multiple advising or service duties (in addition to regular research and teaching responsibilities), both official and unofficial. Aside from serving as a tenure-track professor at CU–Boulder, being an alumna of the same institution provides me with the perspective of the "outsider within"[13] that makes it even more difficult to turn away any students of color who request my support, whether it be to serve on their honor's thesis committees, speak at a student-sponsored event, or to just chat. Likewise, I have found it difficult to refuse to participate in committees and forums related to gender and racial diversity. I do not often have to be asked how many hours I actually put into the job in one week because my devotion is not lost on my family, friends, mentors, and colleagues. And it is my family, friends, and mentors who beg of me to slow down and pull back. I have improved on this and am beginning to say "no" to the numerous requests of me, but, alas, I continue to struggle with fully heeding their advice.

SYNCING THE PAST WITH THE PRESENT

Indisputably, we all have life experiences that affect who we have become. It was only recently that I realized the potential impact of my curiosity during my multiple trips throughout my childhood to Leavenworth, Kansas. My great-great-grandfather George Augustus Hildebrandt, a second-generation white German, settled in Leavenworth in the mid-1800s with his biracial wife (a former slave belonging to my great-great-grandfather's father and a marriage that caused my grandfather to be disowned by his family). During my many visits to Leavenworth with my immediate family to visit my mother's parents, several of her siblings, and a slew of other relatives, we would regularly visit the farmland that has remained in the family since grandfather Hildebrandt settled there. In order to get to the farms from the family homes in town, we had to drive past the United States Penitentiary in Leavenworth. I always gazed in wonderment of the grandiose structure, curious as to who was stashed away behind the grey walls and what got them there.

Just as my desire to become a professor resurfaced well after my initial interest in the profession, it was only in the second semester of my junior year in undergrad that I decided to major in sociology because of the sociology department's offerings of criminology courses. This fifth change in my major was sparked by an interest in an academic subject that, to that point, had been unparalleled by my level of excitement for criminology and deviance studies. I originally ventured off to college with the objective of studying business administration and eventually owning my own business, like my parents. Taking courses leading to this goal did not hold my interest and, in time, I found myself majoring in subjects from international affairs to German to computer science. It was a sociology course on deviance that unearthed my suppressed fervor for the social construction of crime, criminal offenders, and the criminal justice system. A fervor that, no doubt, was based partially in my fascination with the Leavenworth federal penitentiary.

I was fortunate to be involved in a criminology internship program during the final year of my undergraduate education. Interning in a local halfway house and a secure youth corrections facility provided me with indispensable experiential learning and, more importantly, the opportunity to determine that my recent change in major was a sound decision. As I fast-tracked to graduation, I knew I had found my niche. Upon graduating I secured employment in the criminal justice field and soon after made my way to New York City to study for my master's degree at the John Jay College of Criminal Justice. Until I arrived in New York, I had lived only in Denver and Boulder. The boroughs and people of New York City offered me a priceless experience that was further enhanced by the diverse groups of people I encountered on a personal level at a school and job that inundated me with an astute education in the criminal justice system that I had not adequately acquired prior to my arrival in the city. My experiences in New York (and my other field experiences) find me regularly advising students to supplement what they read in their textbooks by getting away from campus, away from the brick-and-mortar traditional college environment, to truly experience the "crime-ridden society" they wish to understand.

Ultimately, I spent ten years working in community-based corrections, with such job positions as group home counselor, halfway house case manager and administrator, juvenile diversion counselor, and juvenile probation officer. My final years in the field found me pondering the effectiveness of the

U.S. criminal justice systems for youth and adults. During my time in the field I witnessed first-hand the extralegal workings of the system. I observed how the ability to hire private defense attorneys garnered less stigmatized charges (such as removing the term "sexual" from a misdemeanor assault charge) and lighter sentences. I observed that many of the individuals able to hire such attorneys were white. Even when economic class was not an issue, I often observed how white children were afforded more rehabilitative sentences, while brown and black children were ordered to serve more retributive sentences. Consequently, these furtive instances caused me to become increasingly dissuaded from working in a system that purported to be helping all victims and offenders on a justice-is-blind model, but, in effect, were meting out sanctions that kept poor black and brown adults and children in a cycle that set them up for failure and only exacerbated their lives. While I and others argue that the criminal justice system workforce needs to be increasingly diversified with more women and people of color—particularly in administrative positions[14]—I also advocate for a need to examine the use of retributive sanctions and the necessity of warehousing by way of imprisonment.[15]

Toward the end of my tenure of working in the criminal justice field, by which time I had returned to Colorado, I began an adjunct instructor position in a criminal justice and criminology department at a four-year state college in Denver. One of my professors at John Jay served as an essential component that led me to transitioning from criminal justice practitioner to criminology professor. While I did not share a gender identity with my young black professor, I saw in Ben Bowling someone I could become. I have had no role model educators in my likeness who have had a lasting effect on me. (Much of this is because of my upbringing in a state that has a minuscule black population; so my chance of being assigned a black teacher or professor was nominal.) Although Professor Bowling had watered the seed that had been sowed in my adolescent years about becoming ah educator, I maintained my jobs in the criminal justice field, and taught college courses on the side. But it was not long before I was offered a full-time visiting assistant professorship at the college, which forced me to make a decision about the next phase in my career. I eventually left the criminal justice field as a practitioner not as a form of abandonment of those who work in the system, but because I realized that my personal strengths were being depleted by working in the system and that I would better serve (and support) the system and its officials by focusing my efforts on research and education. I still have much work to do, but believe I have been more effective in how I contribute to the criminal justice field in my new role.

Soon after I began my visiting faculty position, I found my way back to CU–Boulder. My desire to educate and do research led me to pursue a doctorate degree but I was limited in my choices by remaining in Colorado. Originally, I wished to earn a doctorate in criminology, but my only and best option was to return to CU–Boulder for the advanced degree in sociology. Returning to the site that caused an inordinate amount of personal stress was difficult. But my determination to become a professor triumphed over any pain I endured during my late teens and early twenties.

TRANSFORMING THE PASSION

Another story told to me about my lived experience is one that involves a now-faded memory but that clearly signifies the person I have become. In my second grade of school a white girl in my class shoved me out of the lunch line and called me a "nigger." At the age of seven, I apparently understood the implications of this term and proceeded to challenge my classmate's derision by shoving her in return. As an advocate against the use of violence, I do not recount this experience to suggest that such behavior is acceptable, even to defend against the use of the most demeaning and connotatively harmful words, but to demonstrate that we all can improve the way in which we handle life's hardships. My mother delights in the fact that I had the fortitude to explain to the teacher who intervened that I shoved the girl because "I am not a nigger, I am a person." This is the only incident of which I am aware that I was engaged in an act of physical aggression (that is, violence) and I am thankful that I have developed a constructive outlet for expressing my contempt for sexism, racism, violence, and threats of violence, and any other forms of bias and hate.

It is not only *my* experiences that motivate my work. I recall the surplus of stories I have heard during my adult life about Aunt So-and-So and Cousin What's-Her-Name fighting off their abusive mates. I recall hearing of the struggles that family members and acquaintances had with criminal misconduct and with alcohol and other drugs. I recall the account of my mother's first time traveling to the South with my father and my two sisters to attend my paternal grandfather's funeral in Alabama in May 1963. This was during the anti-segregation protests that resulted in the use of fire hoses and dogs by police officers on black protestors in Birmingham and shortly after Martin Luther King, Jr., was arrested and held in the Birmingham jail for three days in April 1963. When my parents stopped at a gas station upon entering Tennessee, they were told that law enforcement officers were conducting searches of vehicles to discourage outside (Northern liberal) agitators from entering Mississippi and Alabama.

From Memphis, Tennessee, until they reached their destination of Wedowee, Alabama, my parents were told there were no keys available to unlock the "colored" restrooms. My father warned that he would not stop the car to let my mother and sisters relieve themselves at the side of road because he feared they would be arrested for indecent exposure. Fortunately, my maternal grandmother anticipated this dilemma. When my parents stopped in Leavenworth on their way to Alabama, my Grandma Nina Hildebrandt supplied my parents with a bucket to carry in the car to be used in lieu of a public toilet. When they *were* allowed to enter service stations operated by whites my father primed my mother with warnings about how to behave. This included only pointing to merchandise they wanted to purchase and then laying the money on the counter instead of handing it to the clerk. The concern of my parents being harmed by the violent detractors of the civil rights movement was exacerbated by my grandmother's and father's concern that my parents would appear to be an interracial couple because of my mother's fair skin.

I recall that through all this (and other harrowing tales of racism), my parents have still been able to recognize that "good white people" do exist; including those like my great-great grandfather Hildebrandt, who chose love over racial supremacy and bias from his own family, and like those individuals who have treated my parents with humanity and not on the basis of their African American heritage.

As I dedicated myself to completing my dissertation at the end of my doctoral studies, I was confronted with racism by unlikely sources. Without going into extensive detail that would "out" the responsible parties, I was accused of misrepresenting my data because during a presentation where I read narratives of some of the black women I interviewed, apparently I made them sound as though they were "middle-class white women." Essentially, I was accused of having translated my narratives from the so-called Ebonics to "standard" U.S. English. I refused to yield to this indictment and did not care if confronting the accusers would cause me to damage my chances of getting my degree. I certainly did not believe racism was a transgression of our pasts, but I must admit that I was gullible enough to believe that learned social scientists who had interactions with a variety of black students, including me, believed all black people spoke (and acted) alike. I was dismayed that such learned persons wore a set of rose-colored glasses through which they saw all black persons in a sole, typecast image—in spite of the repeated lessons from my mother during my childhood about using "standard" diction in public. Although a few years have passed since this incident, I continue to be incensed. While I have moved past this incident and similar events, I will not let it rest. It is not an issue of forgiveness; it is about using adverse life experiences to fuel our passion and do what we can, as individuals and collectively, to press on in our endeavors. Like many of the women and men I have interviewed in my research activities, I battle on and use this and other experiences as motivation to continue my work. I use all these experiences, whether they belong to me or to those who I respect and admire, to speak for those whose voices are not as loud as mine has become.

GOING NATIVE OR REPRESENTIN'?

It is the amalgamation of all that I have done and not done, have encountered and not encountered that has influenced my professional work and activism. With regard to my approach for researching the intersection of race, gender, class, and crime, a qualitative method for studying this area was a natural fit for me and my foci. Granted, we are taught in progressive research programs and we read in methods literature that, as prudent scholars, we should use the method that will best answer our research question. Further, Jeffries and Generett speak of how being a black woman scholar is complicated by choosing qualitative methods of conducting research:

> Attempts to remain connected to community, while simultaneously working within academia, have created barriers and challenges for many black women. Nonetheless, although qualitative research is a methodology where black women do not have to distance themselves from their research or lived experiences, there is an underlying fear that our work will not be taken seriously. . . . The fear of isolation from community and the academy force many black female researchers to question where and how our work fits within our respective discourses.[16]

I possessed this fear as I began to develop theoretical perspectives based on my dissertation research. As I began my research interviews with black women who had been in abusive intimate relationships, I realized that their life experiences were not defined by the abuse alone.[17] They were not ignorant to the connection between their life struggles and their social position as black women. In order to conceptualize the women's experiences with abuse, I could not simply consult standard theories of how intimate partner abuse is experienced by women. I had to situate the women's experiences within the greater context of the women's lives. To do so, I did not need to start from scratch. I knew I had to consult black feminist theory. Specifically, theory that places black women's experiences in the center of the analysis.[18] Black feminist theory situates black women as the focus of any investigation relating to black women, especially concerning the interlocking identities of black women (for example, race, ethnicity, gender, sexuality, etc.) and the social, cultural, and interpersonal subjugation they may endure as a result. In order to further appreciate what the women faced, I also relied on concepts from critical race feminist theory and feminist criminology to further refine a more adequate conceptualization of the women's experiences. Integrating these concepts and making attempts to explicate this functional understanding has led me to the notion of a black feminist criminology. Certainly, black feminist criminology does not necessitate focusing only on black women's issues, but on gendered, racialized, classed, and other stratified statuses from an intersecting identities and intersecting circumstances approach. Black feminist criminology considers *all* levels of societal impact, including social structural oppression, community and culture, and familial and intimate relations. Black feminist criminology can be used to address the intersectional identities of individuals and the way individuals become involved in crime or respond to being victims of crime as a result of intersecting identities. While I have initially utilized black feminist criminology to understand battered black women's reactions to the violence meted out on them by their intimate partners,[19] I argue that this standpoint can be extended to explain the victimization effects of other women of color, the involvement in criminal activity by women of color, and how other marginalized people, such as men of color and poverty-stricken individuals, become engaged in criminal offending and are affected by criminal victimization.

NO LONGER SILENT

It has been in only the past few years that I have not shied away from demonstrating my passion. With this passion, although I have an ethic of remaining respectful, I also do not temper that which is often stereotypically endemic of "the black woman": anger. With the support of my mother, from whom I initially learned this vociferous zeal, and the backing of other resolute individuals (like my father), I do not apologize for expressing my discontent over injustices, whether small or large, personal or professional. I have accepted that I will often be labeled as angry because of the persistent controlling images[20] of black women. Nevertheless, after years of being painfully shy, and even socially awkward at times, I am now unwilling to silence my voice.

NOTES

1. Orfield et al., *Losing Our Future.*

2. Jones and Shorter-Gooden, *Shifting: The Double Lives of Black Women in America.*

3. Du Bois, *The Souls of Black Folk,* 3.

4. Jeffries and Generett, "Black Women as Qualitative Researchers," 8.

5. See Howard S. Becker's examination on "master status" in his seminal work, *Outsiders: Studies in the Sociology of Deviance* (1963), where he specifically makes note of the difficulty for others to view nonwhites and females as doctors and professors.

6. Guy-Sheftall, *Words of Fire.*

7. Guy-Sheftall, *Words of Fire.*

8. Davis, *Women, Race, and Class.*

9. Sometimes worded as "Ar'n't I a woman?" (See Gilbert, *Narrative of Sojourner Truth.*)

10. Painter, *Sojourner Truth.* Painter has argued that convention secretary Marius Robinson's records of Truth's speech is closer to Truth's actual wording, which does not record any statements of "Ar'n't/Ain't I a woman?," than to Harriet Beecher Stowe and Frances Dana Gage's account written twelve years after the convention.

11. hooks, *Feminist Theory*, 31.

12. James and Farmer, *Spirit, Space and Survival*, 219.

13. Collins, *Fighting Words*.

14. Ward, "Race and the Justice Workforce."

15. Davis, *Are Prisons Obsolete?*

16. Jeffries and Generett, "Black Women as Qualitative Researchers," 5.

17. See Potter, *Battle Cries*.

18. hooks, *Feminist Theory*.

19. Potter, "An Argument for Black Feminist Criminology."

20. Collins, *Black Feminist Thought*.

BIBLIOGRAPHY

Collins, P. H. (1998). *Fighting Words: Black Women and the Search for Justice.* Minneapolis: University of Minnesota Press.

Collins, P. H. (2000). *Black Feminist Thought: Knowledge, Consciousness, and the Politics of Empowerment.* 2nd ed. New York: Routledge.

Davis, A. Y. (9183). *Women, Race and Class.* New York: Vintage Books.

Davis, A. Y. (2003). *Are Prisons Obsolete?* New York: Seven Stories Press.

DuBois, W. E. B. (1903). *The Souls of Black Folk.* Chicago: A. C. McClurg and Co.

Gilbert, O. (1998). *Narrative of Sojourner Truth.* New York: Penguin.

Guy-Sheftall, B., ed. (1995). *Words of Fire: An Anthology of African-American Feminist Thought.* New York: The New Press.

hooks, b. (2000). *Feminist Theory: From Margin to Center.* Cambridge, MA: South End Press.

James, J., and R. Farmer, eds. (1993). *Spirit, Space and Survival: African American Women in (White) Academe.* New York: Routledge.

Jeffries, R. B., and G. G. Generett. (2003). "Black Women as Qualitative Researchers: Performing Acts of Understanding and Survival—An Introduction." In *Black Women in the Field: Experiences Understanding Ourselves and Others Through*

Qualitative Research, eds. G. Givens G. and R. B. Jeffries, 1–10. Cresskill, NJ: Hampton Press, Inc.

Jones, C., and K. Shorter-Gooden. (2003). *Shifting: The Double Lives of Black Women in America.* New York: HarperCollins.

Orfield, G., D. L., J. Wald, and C. B. Swanson. (2004). *Losing Our Future: How Minority Youth are Being Left Behind by the Graduation Rate Crisis.* Cambridge, MA: The Civil Rights Project at Harvard University. Contributors: Urban Institute, Advocates for Children of New York, and The Civil Society Institute.

Painter, N. I. (1996). *Sojourner Truth: A Life, a Symbol.* New York: W.W. Norton.

Potter, H. (2006). "An argument for black feminist criminology: Understanding African American women's experiences with intimate partner abuse using an integrated approach." *Feminist Criminology* 1, 106–124.

Potter, H. (2008). *Battle Cries: Black Women and Intimate Partner Abuse.* New York: New York University Press.

Ward, G. K. (2006). "Race and the Justice Workforce: Toward a System Perspective." In *The Many Colors of Crime: Inequalities of Race, Ethnicity, and Crime in America,* eds. R. D. Peterson, L. J. Krivo, and J. Hagan, 67–87. New York: New York University Press.

3

An Accidental Criminologist

Luis Fernandez

"Cuando y cuando que se me antoja he de escribir lo que me de mi real gana; porque a mi nadie me manda, y es muy mia mi cabeza y muy mias mis manos"

—*Ruben Dario*

INTRODUCTION

My first reaction when asked to contribute to this volume as a "critical criminologist" was one of wonder. "Am I a criminologist," I asked myself? I work in a criminology program; I teach criminology courses; and I publish in criminology journals. Yet it is still difficult to see myself as a full-fledged criminologist, mainly because I never set out to become one and I am critical of the complicity of the discipline in working with the state.

After some thought, however, I have to admit that perhaps I am a criminologist, but if so, only accidentally. The reality is that, like most things in my life, I am a professor in criminology purely by happenstance and a little bit of luck. I never intended to be an academic, let alone a criminologist, critical or otherwise. Like other parts of my life, my intellectual and academic journey is convoluted, replete with false starts, blind alleys, and fortunate mistakes. So far, my career is evolving organically, following a trajectory guided by a combination of hard work and pure chance. In between dedication and happenstance live my hopes, desires, and passions, all constructed from my personal life history. In this chapter, I provide general guideposts describing how I became an accidental criminologist. While I can't promise to remain a criminologist for the rest of my life (which is too daunting a thought to consider at the moment), I present the following narrative as one of many ways to tell the story of how one Latino ended up in academia. As you read on, note that it is almost impossible to write about yourself without seeming self-centered, overindulgent, or a megalomaniac. With that said, what follows is an attempt at my partial confession.

ORIGINS

In the introduction to *The Archeology of Knowledge,* Michel Foucault (1972) writes: "Do not ask me who I am and do not ask me to remain the same: leave it to our bureaucrats and our police to see our papers are in order. At least spare us their morality when we write" (17). For Foucault the development of ideas is a deeply personal process, one that necessarily unfolds within multiple contradictions. A coherent intellectual project only exists in retrospect, as a form of fiction that one imposes on a life trajectory. Thus, if one reads Foucault's work, one finds an intellectual progress with twists and turns. Throughout his career, he exercised the right to change his mind, to follow divergent paths, to contradict himself in a constant quest to illuminate the functions of power, subjugation, and discipline. His spirit guides my work. Following Foucault, I also reserve the right to change my mind as I study revolutions, revolts, and state control. In the end, I'll let the bureaucrats and police worry about coherence.

By all accounts, I should not be where I am today, writing to you about academia and the field of criminology. Against the odds, I am a faculty member in the criminology and criminal justice department, where I teach, of all things, a course on law enforcement. How did I get here? And where is this all heading? How did I go from a child born in a small town in Nicaragua, to a teenager graffiti "bomber," "hip-hop b-boy," to a professor teaching future police officers? How could somebody possibly plan such a convoluted trajectory? You can't. This results only from historical circumstances that are, unfortunately, mostly beyond our control. Thus, the narrative connecting all this is, like Foucault intuited, mostly fictional, only coherent through a backward gaze.

In retrospect (and only in retrospect), it is no surprise that I am obsessed with revolution and social change. By chance, I was born in Managua, Nicaragua, ten years before the infamous *Sandinista* revolution. For those of you who don't remember, the Sandinistas launched a successful armed struggle against Anastacio Somoza, whose family had been in power for fifty-eight years in that country. Without doubt, this struggle significantly shaped the trajectory of my life.

My memories of the revolution are, like all memories really, a combination of what I experienced and what my mind constructed to build a coherent subjectivity. While I have many memories, the ones that stand out involve strife. For instance, I remember how *La Guardia National* (or Somoza's National Guard) patrolled our neighborhoods in military jeeps, dressed in full military attire, with rifles and high caliber weapons. Some thirty years later, I can still hear the sound of rapid gunfire that was present throughout my childhood. One of the most vivid childhood memories involves buying cherry bombs with a friend and throwing them at *La Guardia*, which in retrospect seems dangerous and dumb. In all honesty, I can't say why I did this. But I do have vague memories of believing that the dictatorship had to end. Eventually, my parents got word of my shenanigans and sent my brother and me out of town.

Another clear memory is of high school students taking over the school's grounds. Barely teenage kids, wearing red and black bandanas to cover their faces, the students confronted the well-armed *Guardia*. They shut the doors to the school, kicked out the faculty and the younger children (which included me), and declared the school liberated. After several intense hours, the National Guard stormed the school, beat the students, and placed them in jail.

Shortly after both of these incidents, the Sandinista *guerilleros*, together with university students, took control of our town, resulting in several days of intense warfare. Somoza ruthlessly bombed and attacked the town, killing *guerilleros* and civilians alike. By luck, my family was spared. (Some of our close family friends were not so lucky. A friend of my fathers was decapitated when a rocket hit his home.) To keep from being shot by random bullets, my family slept on the floor, stayed indoors for three days, and waited until the gunfire died down. When it did, they fled the city and months later the country.

I first became aware of revolution and state repression in this atmosphere, although the concepts were not clear until years after. As a young boy, the word revolution, and the reality of it, seemed both frightening and fascinating. While I never participated directly in any revolutionary action, this period changed me fundamentally. I rarely speak about these experiences and writing them here makes me uncomfortable, mainly because I fear that it sounds romanticized, fictitious. Yet these circumstances left a strong imprint, one that remains thirty years later and still influences what I read, study, and write about. It is no hyperbole to suggest that I study state control and social movements today only because some thirty years ago I was in Nicaragua and experienced the revolution.

MIGRATIONS

In 1980, my family fled Nicaragua and settled in Turlock, California. We were privileged enough to leave the country and immigrate to the United States. However, it was a relative and contextual privilege, because soon after our arrival to the United States we were economically bankrupt.

At my arrival to the United States, I spoke no English and neither did any of my family members. Entering the public schools not speaking English, in a part of the country riddled with racism against Mexican migrant labor, was not an easy task. For the first few years the school put me in English as a Second Language courses, with bilingual teachers in the classroom. My learning focused mostly on memorizing random words, such as "hamburger," "carrots," and "shoelaces" (which at first made it difficult to form full sentences, since it's rare when you need to put shoelaces on your hamburger). The rest of my school time I spent staring at the blackboard as my teacher taught the course in English. Yet, I somehow learned the language, not just shoelaces.

By the time I entered high school, I could carry a conversation in English, although with a thick Spanish accent. Having an accent in the California Central Valley is a racial demarcation dividing natives from "foreigners." Several times during this period I had to defend myself physically against people. In one instance, a young white male on a bike drove past me, kicked me, and said, "Go home you Mexican." At first I was puzzled, thinking that perhaps he confused me with somebody else, since I am not from Mexico. In time I understood the lesson; some people see no diversity within the Latino community. Regardless of your background, if you spoke Spanish and had an accent, then you were Mexican. However, none of these experiences made sense to me at the time. It was not until I read Gloria Azuldua's *The Borderlands/La Frontera* (Anzaldua, 1987) years later that the full implication of living in the metaphoric borderlands became clear and I began to see the racial implications of growing up Latino in the United States. Eventually, these experiences helped me build a Latino identity, and a strong solidarity with oppressed and marginalized people.

While discussions of politics and revolution were always present at the dinner table (mainly because of my families political migratory history), my intellectual focus did not start until I entered college. Unlike many (but not all) of the folks I encounter in academia, I started higher education at a community college, where I enrolled in remedial English, math, and writing courses. Soon I migrated to the social sciences, finding great radical, hippie professors with deep social consciousness.

To earn money, I took a job at as a cook at McDonalds, working the swing shift and taking classes in the late morning and early afternoon. My work mostly consisted of monotonous motions, coordinated between perfectly timed beeps (if you have worked at a fast-food restaurant then you are familiar with these sounds, if not, then listen for them next time you are at one). In retrospect, this was a key experience in building my intellectual backbone. That is, when I read Karl Marx his descriptions were not abstract. Rather, they were specific descriptions of my working life. As Marx describes, every moment was coordinated to extract the maximum labor from my body. But this understanding only came later. At the time all I knew was the work was miserable, it paid little, and that I hated the boss.

These kinds of working experiences and marginal backgrounds are central in creating critical thought. Having direct experience in exploitation makes abstract concepts like alienation and marginalization concrete. For those of us with this background, it becomes easier to see it elsewhere, among other people, making the intellectual leap from yourself to others much shorter.

In 1988, I transferred to California State University, Stanislaus. By then, Nicaragua and the Sandinista revolution were the darlings of the left. Professors from various disciplines (history, political science, sociology) discussed the revolution with utmost intimacy, as if it represented their only hope. Naturally, I gravitated towards political science and the leftist professors who were, by then, engaged in solidarity work in Nicaragua. It was in these courses that I began to read Karl Marx and to discuss why revolutions occur, presenting me with the first critique of capitalism. Marx's concepts of labor made such intuitive sense that I quit my job and promised always to be conscious of labor relations.

The experience with wage labor became, like my ethnic identity, a central part of my worldview. Later, when I entered graduate school, understanding complicated concepts about exploitation, marginalization, and racism was easy. This, I feel, made me different from most of my fellow graduate students, and eventually from some of my colleagues.

STUMBLING THROUGH

Not really knowing what I was doing, I applied and got probationary acceptance to the master's program in the political science department at Arizona State University. The academic environment felt foreign from the start. Student and faculty conduct made little intuitive sense. The inherent hierarchical social relations that exist in academia were mostly invisible to me, primarily because I was the first person in my family to attend college and graduate school in the United States. Unlike many of my fellow students, I had not been socialized in this environment. Not until years later did I figure out that students from more elite institutions were automatically more likely to get funding and the attention of the faculty; that some of these students came with social capital that related directly to academic success. At that time, however, I still believed that academia was mostly about producing knowledge and critically understanding and challenging the world. Needless to say, I was soon disappointed.

For the most part, the professors in the program ignored me. I didn't know enough to show up to their office hours and demand their attention. Nonetheless, I somehow managed to stumble my way through a master's thesis. While doing my research, I traveled back to Nicaragua two years after the Sandinistas left power (I couldn't travel back before then because the Sandinistas could have drafted me to fight in the *Contra* war). I interviewed the top tier of the Sandinista Party, including Daniel Ortega. My research focused on a simple question: how did Sandinista leadership start as committed revolutionaries and end up, by 1990, holding large plots of land and owning major factories? How could such revolutionaries turn into a new bourgeoisie?

After completing my master's degree, I was so disillusioned with graduate school that I promised not to return, a promise I did not keep, thankfully. My disappointment was common enough: academia was too political; the professors are careerist; it is a difficult place for working class people. Originally, I viewed academia as a place of thought, an idealized environment where individuals supported each other in their efforts to change the world. While there is space for some of this, the reality is more stark.

By yet another twist of fate, I was hired by a public policy research institute to conduct interviews with Spanish-speaking mothers. After a year, the institute received a federal grant to work with the Phoenix Police Department on an anti-gang initiative. For no other reason than availability, I was placed in charge of the project and began working closely with the Anti-Gang Unit. It was my first formal introduction to the criminological field, setting the stage for my career. I cannot stress enough how haphazard this was; it was utterly unplanned. Looking back, it is stunning that such random occurrences resulted in a criminology career.

PhD WORK

When I re-entered graduate school in the late 1990s, I came back with zero illusions. The goal, this time, was to refine my research skills so I could apply for better research jobs. I no longer sought to change the world or study revolutions, viewing academia as just another work environment. To achieve my new goal, I entered the Department of Justice Studies at Arizona State University, an interdisciplinary program with faculty who hold a diversity of views and embrace various approaches. Fortunately, my graduate cohort included several anarchists doing research on a variety of social justice issues, including animal rights, policing of homeless people, and restorative justice. It was refreshing meeting social justice people again. They reminded me of issues and ideas that I had neglected.

It is difficult to underestimate the role that my fellow graduate students played on my intellectual development. They, more than the faculty or courses in the program, introduced me to new ideas, theories, and ways of doing research. As anarchists and activists, they too had a skeptical view of academia. But the skepticism came with an appreciation for analysis and an engagement with what Hannah Arendt (1958) called the political. That is, they understood the importance of ongoing political activity, of people coming together to exercise their agency through free speech and persuasion, along with some agitation. They taught me that being a public intellectual required action, not just thought. For instance, while in graduate school we launched the "Save the Butte" campaign, which sought to take back a small mountain that the Tempe City Council had sold to developers. Using anarchist perspectives that favored decentralized modes of decision-making, we built a broad coalition of environmentalists, anarchists, Native American activists, and even Libertarians and Republicans. This ragtag of individuals, labeled "Goobers" by the local media, effectively used demonstrations to pressure the city council to buy back the mountain and make it a preserve. Simultaneously, other students were suing the city of Tempe for their attacks on the homeless, typified by the urban camping laws that forbade sleeping in parks, panhandling, and sitting on the sidewalk (for academic treatments of these struggles see Amster, 2004 and Ferrell, 2001).

At the same time these campaigns were developing in Tempe, 50,000 people gathered in Seattle, Washington, to protest the World Trade Organization (WTO) ministerial meetings. When the protests were over, demonstrators had shut down the city for four days and prevented the WTO from conducting business (Brecher, Costello& Smith, 2000; Shepard & Hayduck, 2002). This was, of course, the emergence of the Anti-Corporate Globalization Movement in the United States. Once again, unexpectedly, I became transfixed with revolt. This time, however, I realized that revolt, protest, and revolutions is a kind of life calling, a subject rooted so deeply in my history that it is unavoidable. Thus, I consciously embraced it as the subject of my work and turned my back to the world of public policy.

During the late 1990s and early 2000s, the anti-globalization movement was thriving in the United States. Demonstrations were periodic but constant. Every three or four months a group of activists put out an "action call" asking people to gather in a specific location to protest globalization, from Washington, D.C., to New York, San Francisco, and Sacramento. At first, the movement seemed scattered and unfocussed. Turning to the academic literature on globalization and social movements, however, showed that divergent groups of people were singling out corporate globalization as the enemy (Starr, 2000). What looked like incoherent tactics, such as defending animals, protecting the environment, or squatting in a dilapidated urban dwelling, were only different manifestations of the same movement. Suddenly a struggle to protect a small butte in Tempe, Arizona, was connected with larger struggles over the privatization of public space and the increasing encroachment of corporations.

While still in graduate school, I attended multiple large demonstrations across the United States. At first I was just curious about the movement, perhaps unconsciously revisiting my turbulent history. But soon these strange trips became a research project. Without consulting with faculty or forming a committee, I entered the field as a full participatory observer, hoping that I would stumble on an important research project. And I did.

Some of the most intense moments of my life were spent participating in the movement. But the seriousness of my research only came during a mass demonstration at the 2003 WTO protest in Cancun, Mexico. Because I speak Spanish, I was helping a friend interview *campesinos* from Chiapas, Mexico, who were protesting the WTO proposal to open world agricultural markets and eliminate farm subsidies. While conducting the interviews, thousands of other people had gathered near a fence erected by the Mexican police. Before long, the fence began to dance as protesters rhythmically picked it up and dropped it, eventually twisting it beyond recognition. Behind the fence were police in riot gear waiting with water cannons. As I interviewed *campesinos*, other protesters began throwing rocks above my head. From the corner of my eye I could see the rocks landing on police officers. Soon the rocks were returned as police officers picked them up and launched them back into the crowd of protestors, landing on unprotected heads. Trying to keep my composure, I could see bloodied people carried away from the protest.

While interviewing a middle-aged *campesino*, I realized just how serious and real corporate globalization is. I asked a *campesino* why he was protesting. He and his family were dying, he told me. Without farm subsidies he was unsure if he could survive on his land, perhaps he would have to sell it. Meanwhile, just beyond us, medics continued to find and move bloodied people past us. The man looked at one young woman holding her head, soaked with blood, and then looked back at me and said, "Somebody is going to die today. And it's going to be a good, honorable death." The truth of the statement almost knocked me over; somebody was going to die that day. More frightening, I realized, it could easily be me. On one hand, the *campesinos* were ready to die, living in a desperate situation that left no other alternative. I, on the other hand, was less sure about my mortality that day. I had understood the reality of human desperation, but only at an intellectual level, in a way that we academics understand things much of the time. That day I came face to face with that reality. I was also forced to recognize my privilege, the ability to travel to these protests, stand in solidarity with the wretched of the earth, and then travel back across the border, safe and protected. As the *campesino* foretold, somebody did died that day. And I carry that death close to my heart, as a reminder of the global struggle and the privilege I hold because of my migration and education.

When I arrived back from Cancun, some faculty in my department discouraged my work. The graduate director warned me against doing "activist research." According to the professor, students who engaged in activist research suffered three fates. They either failed to complete their projects; they finished but were unable to secure a faculty position; or they finished and are hired only at less prestigious teaching universities or community colleges. She thought I was smart and should not suffer that fate. I luckily ignored the advice, but it did worry me.

This type of pressure on young radical scholars seems common in academia, present beyond the departmental level. While presenting a paper at a national academic association, a prominent and well-established scholar took me aside for a conversation. After discussing his views on police tactics and mass demonstrations, the scholar asked me, "Are you trying to understand a phenomenon or are you trying to bring about the revolution?" Thinking carefully I responded earnestly, "In the end, I hope we can do a little bit of both." The scholar was visibly upset, walking away abruptly. These kinds of interactions with senior faculty can leave a young scholar shaken. If not careful, the fear of not getting a job, of not getting published, or of being labeled an "activist," and thus not a scholar, can derail good, thoughtful, and dedicated young people. Fortunately for those in my generation, other critical scholars have built institutions and support networks that provide alternatives to mainstream and careerist attitudes in academia. I encourage graduate students to seek out these people and institutions. Not only do they exist, but they are there to help and encourage good critical work. Take advantage of them if you can.

MENTORSHIP AND SUPPORT

After several false starts, my doctoral dissertation focused on the policing of protests, examining how the state (through various law enforcement agencies) managed, regulated, and pacified dissent. Rather than study activists, the dissertation took dead aim at police tactics dealing with social movements with no clearly identifiable leaders and whose organizations were fluid and flexible.

The completion of the dissertation, of course, was possible only because many scholars helped me and supported my work. The Society for the Study of Social Problems (SSSP), for instance, was instrumental in facilitating the completion of the dissertation. SSSP is an association of activist scholars who support the work of younger critical scholars, both economically and emotionally. I was lucky to receive a scholarship from the society that allowed me to stop teaching and work solely on writing.

However, the SSSP did more than provide financial support. Their very existence as a critical academic association made space for presenting work, developing ideas, and building social networks in academia. The association created a safe space for me and other scholars likely marginalized or dismissed by other institutions. I am grateful to the organization, and the scholars in it, for their mentoring, support, and guidance. But I am more thankful to them for having the foresight to start an institution guided by strong social justice values, an organization that is likely to play a strong role in fostering critical thought in graduate students and junior scholars in the future.

Equally important are the senior faculty with critical credentials who spent a lifetime opening spaces for other critical thinkers. Ray Michalowski, Nancy Wonders, Jeff Ferrell, and Peter Kraska are just a few examples of such individuals. Their work is critical and well respected, making room for other critical voices to enter the field. Several of these scholars have mentored me with great care, both as a graduate student and a faculty member. Their involvement has made all the difference.

For example, as a graduate student I was invited to speak at Northern Arizona University on the policing of protest. In the audience, by luck, was Ray Michalowski. After the talk he approached me and said, "When am I going to see a book proposal for the critical criminology series that I edit?" While at that time I was not thinking about a book, I kept Ray in the back of my mind for two years as I completed the dissertation. One week after defending it, I called Ray and told him I was ready for the book proposal. Three weeks later I had a proposal done and two months after that, only one month after my graduation, Rutgers University Press extended a book contract. This, of course, was only possible because a senior faculty created space for other critical scholars to publish their work.

Perhaps unlike the generation before us, it is easier now for younger scholars to exist, survive, and even thrive as critical criminologists. Those who have come before have made headway, forged entries into the academy, and opened avenues for the next generation. While there is still a lot of work to be done, these and other critical scholars have laid a strong foundation for future critical analysis.

CONCLUSION

As a junior faculty member, the methods and modes of the profession are still relatively new. However, those in my generation are lucky to have strong role models and a substantial legacy of critical scholarship. While gaining access to the mainstream of the field is still a challenge, the institutional support created for us makes our encounter with criminology less difficult. Yet, as entry into the academy is made less problematic, our gaze as critical criminologists must remain on social change and justice. Remembering Antonio Gramsci's (1999) concept of the organic intellectual, the next generation of critical scholars must remain dedicated to creating a counter-hegemony to capital, and must seek methods to remain connected to mass mobilizations. This may not produce the final just society, but the struggle for it must continue.

REFERENCES

Amster, R. (2004). *Street People and the Contested Realms of Public Space*. New York: LFB Scholarly Publishings.

Anzaldua, G. (1987). *Borderlands/La Frontera: the New Mestisa*. San Francisco: Spinsters.

Arendt, H. (1958). *The Human Condition*. Chicago: University of Chicago Press.

Brecher, J., T. Costello, B. Smith. (2000). *Globalization From Below: The Power of Solidarity*. Cambridge, MA: South End Press.

Dario, R. (2007). *Cuentos Completos de Ruben Dairo*. Managua, Nicaragua: Hispamer.

Ferrell, J. (2001). *Tearing Down the Streets: Adventures in Urban Anarchy*. New York: Palgrave.

Foucault, M. (1972). *The Archaeology of Knowledge*. New York: Pantheon Books.

Gramsci, A. (1999). *Selections From the Prison Notebooks of Antonio Gramsci.* Ed. Q. Hoare and G. N. Smith. New York: International Publishers.

Shepard, B., and R. Hayduk (eds.) (2002). *From ACT UP to the WTO: Urban Protest and Community Building in the Era of Globalization.* New York: Verso.

Starr, A. (2000). *Naming the Enemy: Anti-corporate Movements Confront Globalization.* New York: Pluto Press.

4

Traveling into Criminology

SHARON PICKERING

It was a relief to enter a lecture hall that was not full of flannel check shirts. I had come from engineering and hoped criminology was for me. I was the first person in my family to attend university, let alone be accepted to arguably Australia's most prestigious university. After explaining to the dean of engineering that I had made a mistake and wanted to transfer out it was made plain to me that as one of only ten women in my cohort he was not going to sign a transfer. According to him, if I wanted out I would need to leave the university, give up my position in college, return to regional life and reapply the following year. Instead of challenging this decision (which turned out to be entirely unfair) made by someone so senior and "all-knowing," I dutifully remained in engineering, not disturbing the faculty's gender ratios. I took the only available units from the arts faculty to someone adrift in the faculty of engineering: criminology. After wandering the halls of physics, chemistry, and mathematics (with their peculiar smells, challenging interpersonal behavior, and odd pastimes) criminology felt like home. After being attracted to the elegance of pure math and science and the cleanness of their calculations I yearned for the complexity of social and legal questions and answers. This was fortunate as no other discipline would take me. Criminologists spoke in complete sentences, did not need to draw diagrams to make a point, and seemed to be concerned with pressing social questions. I did not need to construct vector models, calculate the necessary dynamics of a cantilever bridge, or be concerned with how an underground car park does not collapse in on itself. There was every chance this might work out. I remember the first criminology lecture I attended concerned the difficulties of measuring crime. I could have listened to it all day. I was free.

I was to become a product of the University of Melbourne Criminology program. I was to benefit from the most prestigious and fastest growing criminology program in Australia. I was exposed to a wide-ranging selection of courses taught by passionate and well-placed academics. I was profoundly influenced by Christine Alder, Ken Polk, Rob White, Arie Frieberg, and Penny Green. I learned that criminology was concerned with the operation of the most extreme powers of the state and importantly could focus on the diverse ways people experience that power and control. As an undergraduate I did not have to endure empiricist, quantitative, or administrative criminology. Melbourne was home to criminologists who all took a critical bent of one form or another. When I first ventured to the ASC meetings in Chicago in 1996 I found the vast bulk of the ASC a peculiar breed. All those log linear regressions at first sent me into a deep sleep, followed by serious concern at the dominance of such conservative approaches within the discipline. Australia, while enduring plenty of mainstream criminological research, is seemingly home to a more ingrained critical tradition: one that takes as a starting point the importance of engaging with voices from below, the virtues of qualitative accounts, and the capacity to engage powerful agents along with those who have been dispossessed by the system. I never had to fight for such an approach to be heard. It was largely expected.

As an already committed feminist it was no surprise that my criminological concern initially focused on gender and gender inequities of the criminal justice system. I sharpened my critique of the system through the works of Stanko (1985), Heidensohn (1968, 1985), Smart (1976, 1986, 1989); and then I read Marcia Rice. Rice (1990) had argued that black women and women from developing countries were absent from feminist criminological discourse. I had that sinking feeling that I should have known this, that her critique was no surprise. For some time we had studied the difficulties of indigenous women in Australia, their gross overrepresentation in the criminal justice system. But I had not merged that concern with a reflection on feminist criminology. It was in the merging of a critical criminology with my feminist politics that I began to find my place within criminology. To this end I was particularly influenced by work on the power of the state, and the writing and teaching of Penny Green (1990). I was equally influenced by the ability of my mentors to accrue frequent flyer miles, a point to which I will return.

These early experiences of criminology guided my work toward the writings of not only broader feminist works but also those on the nature of society and particularly on experiences of women in conflict with the state. They all came to shape my ongoing concern with criminalization, particularly in relation to conflict. This concern has largely guided my career and continues to do so: from women and policing in Northern Ireland; to women and human rights in South-East Asia; to the criminalization of refugees in Australia and the contortion of sovereignty and borders in relation to the criminalization of mobility; and finally to return to issues of counterterrorism and culturally diverse communities.

Whilst undertaking postgraduate study in the United Kingdom I was struck by the peculiarity of the Northern Ireland situation and the lack of gendered analyses of policing. The political conflict in the North and the politics of women's contribution to the struggle seemed a good place to consider women in conflict with the state and the role of criminal justice agents and processes in that conflict. It was here that my broad concern with processes of criminalization developed into a concern with notions of resistance. It became clear that engaging women's accounts of struggle during the Northern Ireland conflict foregrounds a gendered critique of the state and its coercive agents, namely the police and the British Army. More importantly, it was through gathering and listening to these accounts that my methodological approach was refined—not through what I read but rather through living in a divided community in conflict.

I walked into my first interview at Falls Road the day after I first arrived in Belfast. It was in the Sinn Fein office. In the cramped waiting room filled with cigarette smoke and surrounded by mirrors etched with the names and pictures of Republican martyrs I waited to be ushered into a smaller room to conduct an interview with a woman who had served time for politically motivated offenses. It was a mild April day, but that interview was chilly due to the gaping hole in the wall that had been caused by a recent rocket attack on the building just before the first ceasefire in Northern Ireland in 2004. After another three interviews that day I gained greater access to the Republican community to conduct further interviews and research. It became apparent that such fieldwork was not only going to be rich but also emotionally taxing. This research not only taught me much about the importance of voice, but also of the role of the researcher who is insider and outsider all at once (Pickering, 2001b). Mostly it taught me that the most difficult (and often central) aspects of good fieldwork are often never resolved, but rather we reach a level of acceptable comfort in how we negotiate fieldwork situations. In an everyday sense, this meant yielding some control of your fieldwork to the situation, falling into cultures different from your own and being willing to work things out as you go along. Not terribly scientific.

My theoretical and empirical concerns were heavily influenced by where I was located during the early years of my career. In some part these concerns arose as a *result* of the importance travel has assumed in the development of my career. Driven by social inquiry and an antipodean need/desire to wander during my formative years this could be criminologically explained in a number of ways. First and foremost, criminology continues to be a discipline dominated by the Northern Hemisphere. As someone located south of the equator this requires a proactive approach to integrating work here (down under) with events in Europe and North America. In order for Australian criminologists to have currency they continue to need to make the links between their work and that which goes on in the international hubs of criminology half a world away. More often than not it requires a commitment to traveling vast distances. However, an interest in a criminology that goes beyond national borders has been an equally dominant influence on the theoretical and empirical questions of my research. Largely focused on domestic criminal justice, criminology has not traditionally applied its gaze to nationalist struggles, human rights, sovereignty, or cross-border mobility. As a result of a focus on gendered criminalization in Northern Ireland my work came to be preoccupied with all of these issues, which required extensive travel.

The next fieldwork site I ventured to was South-East Asia. Following activist work with Amnesty International, and in conjunction with that organization, my colleagues and I undertook research on how women in South-East Asia engaged with discourses of rights. Initially this project did not have a clear criminological angle but rather came out of intellectual concerns with international law and feminism. It was at this time that I was appointed to my first full-time academic position. A five-year contract secured my employment and, despite a heavy teaching load, which is seemingly the lot of new academics, I was able to carve out time for this new research project. This latest research concern had come directly out of our practice as women activists as well as our academic interest in human rights. When marking the fiftieth anniversary of the Universal Declaration of Human Rights we celebrated the lives of women who had advanced human rights. The response that we provoked in naming women who worked for social change as human rights activists included surprise, reluctance, and some outright resistance. This largely related to recognizing women who had valiantly worked around women's reproductive rights. We were interested in the fact that women's stories of activism in changing the lives of their communities could challenge some of the most polarized debates around human rights. Specifically we were concerned with how women's stories could shed new light on academic arguments with universality and cultural relativism. While we considered this to be important theoretical work it was a particularly challenging methodological undertaking. For white, Western women to undertake research in South-East Asia we had to acknowledge our privilege—this was unavoidable as we could feel it and hear it in every aspect of the project, from the questions we asked to the way we organized information. Indeed, "as we walked along streets, traveled in taxis and planes, sat on floors and waded in streams we felt our privilege— we also saw that our privilege was seen" (Lambert, Pickering, & Alder 2003, 35). Therefore we had to give over significant intellectual and personal time to working through the multifarious issues of representation with which researchers must engage when working in cultures other than their own. We were to benefit greatly from the insights of Narayan (1997), Alcoff (1991–92) and Ram (1998) in making sense of how culture, and particularly language, shapes such research endeavors. In doing so we came to see that our key concern with human rights discourse returned us to issues of criminalization. The women we spoke with had invariably encountered the state, and many had been the target of coercive state efforts. The criminalization of struggle was evident in the stories of women from Malaysia, Burma, the Philippines, and Hong Kong. The politicizing experience of criminalization was felt by many, and importantly for our work it was clearly gendered and had significant impact on how women in South-East Asia encountered the discourses and mechanisms of human rights.

This work, which was published as a book, continued to raise issues concerned with the North-South disinterest of a large body of criminology (and the associated industry) in work located outside the Northern Hemisphere. The publisher, who had commissioned a series on gender and criminal justice, sent through a proof of the book cover which was to be a map of South-East Asia. The proof sent through included a map of China and India. It took a number of e-mails to establish that these countries are not generally considered part of South-East Asia, that this was important considering the focus of the book, and that there was a clear need to correct the image.

Importantly the research in South-East Asia exposed me to many women who had been forced to migrate. I met many of these women on the Thai-Burma border in the border camps. Their accounts of fleeing Burma, and more importantly of their need to routinely re-enter Burma, their deportation by Thai officials, the absence of international refugee protection, their lack of status beyond the perimeter of the camps, and their fear of the Burmese regime radically changed my understanding of forced migration. Those forced to migrate do not move in a linear fashion; persecution occurs not only in countries of origin but en route and in countries of destination. The work of Saskia Sassen (1996, 1998, 1999) and Hannah Arendt (1966) informed how I made theoretical sense of this.

It was surprising that criminology had not engaged in the role of criminal justice and social control in the production of refugees, particularly the failure of the state in the country of origin to protect citizens from persecution as well as countries of the global north being unwilling to meet their obligations of refugee protection under international refugee law or international customary law. Most notable was the increasing tenacity of countries of the global south, such as Australia, in engaging in widespread practices of deionization and criminalization of refugees who arrive unauthorized. This clearly landed issues of refugees firmly within the criminological gaze. This research was initially concerned with how a criminological reading of refugee policy could shed light on the mobilization of "deviancy" that had ushered in a new era in the treatment of refugees (Pickering, 2005). While this in turn raised further issues of humanitarianism and state crime I was particularly interested in how the alleged crimes of those seeking asylum were amplified while those committed by countries of origin or destination were routinely diminished. This profoundly impacted the ability of refugees to gain meaningful protection from persecution. Theoretically it raised far broader questions, primarily around issues of state crime but more specifically with the reconceptualization of sovereignty and state legitimacy. Moving into critical work in the field of international relations (influenced by the work of Devetak [2001], Soguk [1999], and Weber [1995]) it became apparent that not only could criminology have something to say about the changing nature and use of territorial sovereignty but increasingly criminal justice agencies were key agents in its reshaping.

A focus on refugees inevitably insists on an examination of the border in one context or another. Recently, therefore, I have been examining the transformation of borders and the increasingly important and diverse roles that borders play in controlling populations. Under conditions of globalization the border has remained relatively unexplored in criminology (Pickering & Weber, 2006). Yet for large sections of the world's population the border is an everyday reality. In the first instance I was interested in the way policing agencies were reshaping their remit (and their political and material resources) in relation to concerns with the integrity of borders. Notably policing agencies are not only playing a prominent part in the fortification of borders (against some but not all populations) but are increasingly seeking to move beyond the territorial jurisdictional constraints traditionally used to demarcate their power and influence (Pickering, 2004).

Research on refugees and borders helped me develop methodological skills relating to the use of documentary sources and the ability to systematically critique the use of language (Pickering, 2001a). On the one hand this was because my concern with discourse from our work in South-East Asia had developed into a more specific interest in the use of language. However, it was also dictated by the difficulties of access to refugee populations—particularly those that do not reach countries of destination. Even in relation to conducting research on and with refugee populations there are significant gatekeeper issues to be negotiated, which routinely prove difficult if not impossible to resolve. Crucially such research meant that sensitive interaction with a range of stakeholders means that much research time is spent building and maintaining relationships to effect good research and meaningful outcomes.

Interaction with diverse stakeholders has been the central tenet of the most recent and most policy-oriented research I have undertaken: a wide-ranging project on counterterrorism policing and culturally diverse communities. Based on the premise that traditionally counterterrorism policing has been poorly calibrated and has alienated communities and resulted in counterproductive outcomes, this project seeks to develop approaches to counterterrorism that strengthen commitments to human rights and social cohesion. Running since 2004, it involves four lead researchers along with partner researchers at Victoria police, and over thirty-two community leaders from Victoria's multicultural communities. This project is emblematic of the changing research role I have come to play as I have progressed in the university system, as it has required dedicated time to its overall management of people and projects with less and less time for me to participate in the hands-on research. The most significant challenge for this project, and arguably for my career, was my decision to have a child in 2005. This turning point in my life has been critical in evaluating my career travels to date and their direction in the future.

A TRAVELER'S REFLECTIONS

My research career has been significantly shaped by the importance of what in Australia we call an ongoing position. This allows your time to be dedicated to the core tasks of your job rather than constantly applying and reapplying for positions, thereby taking away valuable intellectual and emotional time from my work. In this way I have been also privileged in that with an ongoing position comes the ability to attract nationally competitive research funding that makes resource-intensive research (such as that involving extensive travel) possible. Such funding is increasingly important to the evaluation of an academic's performance in the Australian university workplace. It is now also coupled with a concern with research quality as well as with well-developed teaching pedagogies and outcomes. These three elements in academic life are increasingly part of what I consider to be the university "game" with which all academics need to engage if they are to survive. Importantly, a focus on funding, publication, and teaching quality can be seen as supporting a well-rounded academic contribution, although in Australia there is ongoing debate as to what extent these moves reveal a more coercive intent on the functioning of the university workplace.

I began my full-time academic career at a regional university. This had significant benefits for my learning of the university "game." At a smaller institution it is much easier not only to learn how all the various parts of the system work, but also to gain far greater direct access to key decision-makers. This enables a more direct flow of information, and indeed in many ways increased accountability. At a smaller institution it is also more likely that academics will be placed in more challenging and responsible roles earlier, allowing them to climb the career ladder more quickly—that is if they find a way to balance the demands of research, teaching, and administration.

I am now very aware that this is my first mention of teaching. The challenges of teaching have been many and great in my career. I began teaching as I had experienced it: in short I emulated the teaching I had received. While this works to a point, before long I found I actually needed to study the practice of tertiary teaching myself. While at first this meant simply exposing myself to teaching scholarship eventually I came to focus on my teaching in the same systematic way as I approached my research. However, the greatest teaching challenge I have encountered is not the way to balance an informed approach to teaching along with the other demands placed on my time but in the internecine battles with colleagues over curriculum.

While I currently benefit from a very supportive and cooperative band of colleagues who routinely and collectively engage in productive curriculum discussions, throughout my career I have experienced significant tussles over the direction and content of curriculum with colleagues who seek to "hide" ideology or wish to refute the "politics" of doing criminology. At first I thought there could be accommodation between those who undertake a critical approach to their teaching in content and delivery and those who refute this position. Increasingly I found it integral for a curriculum to have an explicit identity in terms of where one sits in the broader school of criminology. Such an approach allows you to be clearer in your communication with students about what a given course can achieve, as well as creating greater internal coherence with the teaching of the unit. I also found that it means that you are not reduced to giving generalist courses ad nauseum, which seem to do neither teachers nor students any favors.

This approach brought me, together with colleagues in the United States, Nancy Wonders and Mona Danner, to undertake an online collaborative teaching venture with our students. Bringing together nearly 250 students across three sites to discuss their grounded experiences of culture and human rights in relation to criminal justice brought home the importance of bringing critical literature and approaches to the classroom. Orthodox criminology does not prepare students to locate themselves within local or global human rights landscapes in ways that more critical and interdisciplinary work can.

Significantly, an explicitly critical approach, in particular a feminist approach, to my teaching has been crucial in attracting graduate students interested in the research I conduct. I largely regard my work with graduate students as one of the most rewarding aspects of my career. Notably, the vast majority of my research students have turned out to be fellow criminology travelers who are also spending large chunks of time abroad in the pursuit of their research.

Equally important in shaping my approach to the classroom is that I was twenty-five when I was appointed to my first full-time position and it was easy to see the students smelled blood. Impression management is everything in the classroom, especially in large classes. After my first semester of teaching I took my class to the pub where one student revealed that when they saw me walk in they thought: "Great. She's too young, This is going to be straight from the books. I'm glad I was wrong." For some time thereafter I did my best to seem older than I was, regularly lying about any conversational markers that would give away my age. As it turned out I was thirty for about six years. But it wasn't only my students who were often preoccupied by age. Early in my career it was routine for colleagues, usually older male colleagues, to remark on my status as a junior academic, even after I received promotions. Rank it would seem was often still considered to be age—rather than merit—related.

I entered academia at a time when women had made many gains. I have greatly benefited from more senior women who have been part of the struggle in the university workplace to move through the glass ceiling that continues to see men clustered at the top of the university ladder. In particular I have been grateful to a range of fellow travelers in Europe and the United States with whom I come together at conferences and other international meetings to exchange ideas and experiences, and who have been a great source of support and inspiration, particularly when tackling the university system. The promotions system is one I have been through a number of times with the support of such colleagues. Indeed in order to move from a regional university to a leading Australian university I took a cut to the rank below where I had previously been employed, requiring me to repeat the promotion process a second time shortly thereafter. This was a difficult experience as I clearly lost ground in my career in sense of promotions. However, what I have now found is that as you move further up the career ladder the ways you can go about applying for promotion seemingly multiply. And while increased openings do not make gaining the promotion any easier it does indicate that ground lost at some points in your career can be made up for at other points.

The promotions process has also taught me about being careful in the administrative roles that become available. A colleague once pointed out to me that there is administration where you make a difference and there is "pattern holding" administration. To some extent we all need to do some of the latter if we are to be good workplace citizens; however, our focus should be on those administrative tasks that help our colleagues, students, communities, and institutions move forward to achieve positive social change. This advice has proved crucial in balancing my working life and ensuring that administration does not overwhelm, a particular risk if you are considered to be quickly rising through the ranks and in some ways vulnerable to being harnessed into administrative roles before you would ordinarily be expected to. Balancing leadership positions with the development of your research and teaching has proved critical in some of my recent decisions to maintain equilibrium in my working life.

The question of career balance is vexing because of course it involves far more than your career. The context in which my career has developed has radically changed over the last couple of years as I have gone from being a frequent flyer routinely attending at least a couple of international and half a dozen national conferences a year along with a stint of international fieldwork, to becoming a mother and scaling down my travel to one annual international trip and one annual domestic conference. It also means my nights and weekends are no longer my own. I was prepared for this change in working "rhythm," and I did not expect that it would not significantly impact on the amount I achieved. Yes there are more bags under my eyes, and yes getting to work can be compared to a military operation. But with supportive colleagues and work environment it can work. Most importantly a flexible and generous maternity leave policy meant that I could gradually return to work, as I was ready. This was coupled with on-campus child care where I was able to continue breastfeeding until the time that I chose to stop. As a sleep-deprived returning-to-work mum, this meant that control of my relationship with my baby was not shaped by the demands of the workplace but remained with me: a small but important point in feeling good about the institution, my career, and the new world of motherhood. In a recently released Australian study on when research works for women it was found that maternity leave policies have been crucial in the retention of senior female staff and their ability to continue their contribution to the university and their careers (Dever et al. 2006).

Wherever I have traveled in my career, across the lands and the disciplines traversed, I always come back to criminology. That is because at its core criminology continues to be concerned with what I consider to be the most pressing social questions of the day, and at its best it is increasingly responsive to the challenges of crossing borders, the opportunities of interdisciplinarity, and the possibilities of meaningful social change.

REFERENCES

Alcoff, L. (1991–1992). The problem of speaking for others. *Cultural Critiques.* Winter.

Arendt, H., (1966). *The Origins of Totalitarianism.* Florida: Harcourt.

Dever, M., Z. Morrison, B. Dalton, and S. Tayton. (2006). *When Research Works for Women.* Melbourne: Monash University.

Devetak, R. (1995). Incomplete States: theories and practices of statecraft. In *Boundaries in Question,* eds. J. Macmillan and A. Linklater. London: Pinter Publishers.

Devetak, R. (2001). Postmodernism. In *Theories of International Relations,* eds. Scott Burchill et al. New York: Palgrave.

Green, P. (1990). *The Enemy Within.* Buckingham: Open University Press.

Heidensohn, F. (1968). The deviance of women: a critique and an enquiry. *British Journal of Sociology* 19, 160–75.

Heidensohn, F. (1985). *Women and Crime.* Basingstoke: Macmillan.

Lambert, C., S. Pickering, and C. Alder. (2003). *Critical Chatter: Women and Human Rights in South East Asia.* Durham: Carolina Academic Press.

Narayan, U. (1997). *Dislocating Cultures.* New York: Routledge.

Pickering, S. (2001a). Common sense and original deviancy: News discourses and asylum seekers in Australia. *Journal of Refugee Studies* 14, 2: 169–186.

Pickering, S. (2001b). Undermining the sanitised account: Violence and emotionality in the field in Northern Ireland. *The British Journal of Criminology* 41, 485–501.

Pickering, S. (2004). The production of sovereignty and the rise of transversal policing: people smuggling and federal policing. *Australian and New Zealand Journal of Criminology* 37, 3: 340–358.

Pickering, S. (2005), *Refugees and State Crime*. Sydney: Federation Press.

Pickering, S. and L. Weber, eds. (2006). *Borders, Mobility and Technologies of Control.* Dordrecht: Springer.

Ram, K. (1998). Introduction: Migratory women, travelling feminisms, *Women's Studies International Forum* 21, 6: 571–579.

Rice, M. (1990). Challenging orthodoxies in feminist theory: a black feminist critique. In *Feminist Perspectives in Criminology*, eds. L. Gelsthorpe and A. Morris, Buckingham: Open University Press, 57–70.

Sassen, S. (1996). *Sovereignty in an Age of Globalisation*. New York: Columbia University Press.

Sassen, S. (1998). *Globalization and Its Discontents: Essays on the New Mobility of People and Money*. New York: The New Press.

Sassen, S. (1999). *Guests and Aliens*. New York: The New Press.

Smart, C. (1976). *Women, Crime and Criminology: A Feminist Critique*. London: Routledge and Kegan Paul.

Smart, C. (1986). Feminism and law: Some problems of analysis and strategy. *International Journal of the Sociology of the Law* 14: 109–123.

Smart, C. (1989). *Feminism and the Power of the Law*. London: Routledge.

Soguk, N. (1999). *States and Strangers: Refugees and Displacements of Statecraft*. Minneapolis: University of Minnesota Press.

Stanko, E. (1985). *Intimate Intrusions: Women's Experiences of Male Violence*. London: Virago.

Weber, C. (1995). *Simulating Sovereignty*. Cambridge: Cambridge University Press.

5

Convict Criminology: "Privileged Information" and the Authority of Experience

ALAN MOBLEY

For many years I have called myself an ethnographer. My way of pursuing social science research is to steep myself in the relevant literature and then go out into the world of human social relations and listen, speak with, and observe, people as they create and occupy places and participate in events. As an ethnographer I think it important to advance the craft and its acceptance as a valuable social science research methodology, particularly within criminology and the other policy sciences. Studies in criminal justice are largely concerned with the behaviors of marginalized persons. The ethnographic method has the capability to bring such persons into the research process, to "give them a voice," as it were, and to channel their lived experiences into the policy formation equation.

This chapter will offer an appreciative discussion of the ethnographic method with special attention to one of its more problematic components: how fieldworkers interpret and represent data. What follows is meant as constructive critique and as an opening to conversation, rather than a definitive last word.

The lens that I will use to analyze selected aspects of the ethnographic method is that of "Convict Criminology" (Ross & Richards, 2003). Convict criminology is said to provide a "new perspective" on criminology and criminal justice (Richards & Ross, 2001:180). This perspective is rooted in the experience of its practitioners—current prison inmates and former prisoners—now working as criminal justice researchers and (primarily) as critical criminologists.

Convict criminology lays claim to knowledge unknown to those who lack similar life experiences. In the words of its chief proponents:

> Ex-convict professors have endured years of lockup in penitentiaries and correctional institutions, lived in crowded, noisy, violent cellblocks, and emerged to complete graduate degrees and become professors of sociology, criminology, criminal justice, and related disciplines. They have an intimate knowledge of "penal harm," which they carry in their heads and hearts, and in some cases wear as scars and tattoos upon their skin. (Ross & Richards, 2001: 181)

Ross and Richards go on to declare the methodological "centrality of ethnography" to convict criminology (179). They acknowledge that criminology has a rich tradition of ethnographic research, but lament that the practice has fallen out of favor with the discipline. Decrying "armchair academics," convict criminologists encourage their peers to meet face to face with those persons whose lives are the objects of study. Such encounters, it is thought, might lead to a powerful transformation of the discipline and the policy sciences to which it contributes.

The practice of ethnography entails much more than simply conversing with research subjects. Issues of data interpretation and representation of research subjects remain to be dealt with. My goal for advancing fieldwork's methodological sophistication would be the proliferation of multidisciplinary research teams. Anthropologists, criminologists, social workers, and public health practitioners could join with researchers experienced in the ways of justice to form teams whose collective wisdom might best approach the complexities inherent in justice studies. It is my understanding, born of experience, that the harms currently visited upon society by the operation of the criminal justice system far outweigh the societal benefits. If we are to advance the broader cause of social justice by including the problematic operations of our systems of criminal justice, then we will need to find new, multidisciplinary, and collaborative ways forward. Consistent with this goal, convict criminology resists the temptation to insularity or simply "preaching to the choir." Instead the movement seeks to share with the broader criminological and policy-making mainstream insights gleaned from the insider perspective (see Ross & Richards, 2003). If criminology and related disciplines are to be effective at bringing the voices of the marginalized into the mainstream we need a reflexive ethnography that can serve as an invitation to dialogue. The traditional academic stance of arguing for the primacy of one's point of view may have to give way to a more collaborative, inclusive spirit.

My choice of the materials presented here for critique is based on exasperation. The works examined come to us from authors who have achieved some prominence within their fields of endeavor, and I would say deservedly so. They each got out of their armchairs and into the lifeworlds of their research subjects. Yet the convict criminology lens suggests that each has fallen prey to misusing their subject position as the teller of the tale. Such common problems as overstating conclusions, offering questionable interpretations as facts, and venturing underequipped into gaps in professional knowledge, lessen the utility of these well-meaning projects. Importantly, each writer claims the authority that comes from experience. This claim forms the basis of the difficulty I hope to highlight, for it provides the writer an authoritative authorial advantage that the reader has little choice but at least provisionally to accept.

Considered in this light, the claims of convict criminology to a type of rare or special knowledge are not so exclusive as they may appear. The position of "author" presupposes a privileged position of knowing, whether one claims to be directly and personally "experienced" in the subject matter or not. Authors who set about expressing their ideas and arguing for their validity (as I am doing here) are dealing in a very different intellectual currency than those who base their claims not on argument, but on direct experience. If convict criminologists and other ethnographers are to honor their privileged positions as authors, we might take extra care to let our data tell its story without embellishment. We as authors are always free to offer our opinions, and it is my contention that all of our work will be strengthened if such offerings are supported by cogent argument, rather than by claims to exclusive experiential knowledge.

ETHNOGRAPHY

Ethnography is interpretive social science (Geertz, 1983; Aunger, 1995). Ethnography requires trained observers who venture into the field, ask questions, witness and sometimes actively participate in events, and develop impressions. What is absorbed is a kind of "almost-knowledge," a provisional perspective that is then systematically tested against itself, against similar information, and compared with findings derived from alternative methodologies. The result is a composite, a multilayered representation of human actors in motion. Even with all its complex methodological twists, however, ethnography is a snapshot, a mere stab at explaining the virtually inexplicable. The aim is to learn something about different cultures or social situations, keeping in mind that our knowledge is always framed by our personal life experiences (Luhmann, 1990).

For all its limitations, ethnography undoubtedly provides insight (see esp. Van Maanen, 1988; Venkatesh, 2008). At its best, ethnographic description reveals shades of meaning, inviting the reader into worlds of sense and nonsense, where symbols and significations are defiantly displayed and carefully hidden, often simultaneously. The human subjects of ethnography are usually unfamiliar to readers, hence their interest in them. Patterns emerge in the depiction of even the most "foreign" situations, so that they soon begin to take familiar turns. Unique as we think we are, people everywhere engage in actions that lend themselves to categorization. Take headhunting in the Philippines, for example. For a Western reader, there could hardly be a more exotic activity. Still, headhunting was made intelligible to Western readers by its placement within the larger category of "male bonding rituals," like the more familiar deer hunting, or fishing (Rosaldo, 1989).

Besides the use of categories, the literary forms and styles of writing that ethnographers employ can also provide the unknown with an air of familiarity. Adopting the narrative style of a diary, for instance, allows the writer to position cultural expressions as personal experiences. By relating details and discoveries as if they occurred the way we are accustomed to hearing about them, in linear time, this technique imposes a comprehensible sense of order on an otherwise disorienting, foreign culture. The necessarily selective presentation of research data that is drawn from a vibrant, living context means that ethnography is always a creative act, an invention, and never the simple representation of a culture (Clifford, 1988).

Communication strategies are thus essential tools of the ethnographer. Ethnographers try to elicit complex responses in their readers by complicating as well as simplifying their portrayals of research subjects. Writing about, against, and among the culture under study provides a diversity of perspectives. "About" culture writing takes a stance that is detached: a "birds-eye view." The "bird" itself has a culture, a frame of reference or bias, so even this relatively objective telling is imbued with subjectivity. Writing "against" a culture means applying critical analysis to practices that are supported by conventions—a culture's set of "taken for granted" explanations for common events. Critical approaches are provocations that ignite a sort of chain reaction process leading, ideally, to the reinterpretation of familiar forms or "habits." Writing and thinking against culture is not a negating practice. It aims to question and thereby deepen our understanding of why people do what they do. "Among" the culture writing requires a more intimate brand of insider knowledge. Participants' rationales for what they do and why are explored for their convergences and contradictions. This type of analysis calls upon empathic skills, and both facilitates and is facilitated by a high level of mutual trust.

ETHNOGRAPHIC WAYS OF KNOWING: A SYMPATHETIC CRITIQUE

In what follows I will explore some of the strengths and weaknesses of different ways of obtaining information in the field and conveying it to audiences. Each methodological position falls under the rubric of ethnography. I start with a brief observation on an article written by part-time prison worker C. Fred Alford (2000) of the University of Maryland at College Park. I admire the piece for its substance and style. How its insights were obtained, however, is far from clear. Next we will visit the work of Philippe Bourgois (1995), which represents a multiyear project in observer-participant ethnography. Mona Lynch (1998) provides a fine example of the more invested stance of a participant-observer. Finally, I will review the "voice of experience" work of John Dilulio (1987, 1992, 1994, 1995, 1996a, 1996b). Dilulio uses the diversity of his lifeworlds—from South Philadelphia toughster to elite university professor—to bolster his authorial voice.

C. Fred Alford's *Discipline and Punish After Twenty Years*

Near the start of a provocative piece discussing the classic prison-oriented work of Michel Foucault, C. Fred Alford notes:

> Recently, I spent fourteen months doing research in a maximum-security state prison, Patuxent Institution in Jessup, Maryland. It is upon this experience that I draw, contrasting Foucault's account with my own experience (2000:126).

Through this statement Alford informs us that he intends to compare what he read in Foucault to what he experienced during his fourteen months of research. Alford uses his experience of Patuxent to refute much of what the French philosopher predicted would come to pass in the world of American-style prisons. Toward the end of the article, in a section titled "Research Appendix," Alford explains his experience, the source of this authority, in more detail:

"Friday was my prison day, and most of the time, about three hours, was spent with a group of about sixteen inmates" (142).

He continues:

For an hour or two on most Fridays I would accompany the prison psychologist on his "house calls" to administrative segregation, or the cellblocks. On the cellblocks I would try to come up with an excuse to sit in one of the day rooms for a while. If all else failed, I would come up with an excuse to walk around the tunnels, stopping here and there to chat with inmates. Many would not or could not talk with me, but a majority did (143).

Does it matter that in his "fourteen months doing research" Alford only visited the prison on Fridays, his "prison day," and that even on Fridays he was apparently only at the facility for half a day?

I think it does. Alford's initial claim to experience is misleading, and it lends an authority to his thoughts that they do not deserve. I will admit that as expressed in the article, his ideas make a good deal of sense. They are both provocative and illuminating. As an interested reader I am left wondering why the author felt that his ideas needed a validation beyond their intellectual merit? And although I applaud the inclusion of an ultimately more accurate depiction of his research period, I am still nagged by the knowledge that Alford knew what he was doing when he did it. It appears that, even in his off-hand way, Alford sought to bolster his credibility in the eyes of readers by laying claim to a temporal measure of experience that he did not actually possess.

For the convict criminologist, the concept and experience of time has profound personal and professional meaning (Mobley, 2003). The experience of imprisonment provides participants in the prison lifeworld an intimate knowledge of the transformational nature, the productive and destructive power, of serving time (Foucault, 1971). Besides misleading readers, casually misrepresenting one's experience of time is to transgress a core tenant of the prison convict code (Irwin, 2005), and perhaps put at-risk the perpetually fragile relationship between researcher and human subjects of research.

In Search of Respect: Selling Crack in El Barrio

The complicated mechanics implicit in ethnography produce rich and varied results, but not without some risks. To illustrate one such hazard I will introduce a segment from one of the most acclaimed ethnographies of recent times, Phillipe Bourgois' study, *In Search of Respect: Selling Crack in El Barrio* (1995). Bourgois spent three and one-half years researching the street scene of his East Harlem neighborhood. His account of Puerto Rican crack dealers has won many awards, and is reprinted widely. The point I wish to make by analyzing Bourgois' work relates to what is arguably its greatest strength, yet also its weakness. The issue is one of immediacy, and Bourgois succeeds brilliantly in capturing for his readers the thrill and tension of the moment. In so doing, however, he risks drawing his subjects in rather exaggerated tones. This differentiation certainly helps to separate and identify them, but it also risks idealizing or worse, demonizing actual human beings.

Who's Who?

In a chapter entitled, "School Days," Bourgois seeks to contrast the criminality of two of his principal informants, "Primo" and "Caesar." Among his intentions is to note how criminal subcultures produce people who engage in crime. Bourgois also reminds readers that neither all crime nor all criminals are the same. Individual choices and personal characteristics ensure that even tight-knit criminal peer groups that promote standardized personas and habitual practices still allow for ample individual diversification.

He begins: "Primo was more instrumentally criminal than Caesar." The assertion that Primo was perhaps more civilized and thoughtful in his choice of crimes is meant to make his threat more comprehensible, and therefore less severe, than that posed by his more impulsive and vicious compatriot. The vignettes that follow in Bougois' narrative, however, do not support this claim. While Primo explains his "thieving" in instrumental terms, as motivated by a desire to earn his own money his own way, his crimes are marked by rampant spontaneity, and failure. Primo offers the following description of stripping a car:

> Luis used to have me as a lookout because I was so inexperienced, so I wanted to graduate and do my own cars. . .
>
> That first time, it was too hard. I couldn't do it. As a matter of fact, I'm thinking now that probably Luis maybe gave me a radio that was hard to take out just to test me.
>
> So what I just did was, I took the long-nosed pliers—which is the basic tool that you need to steal the car radio—and since I couldn't have that radio, I pushed the pliers inside the cassette hole, and just started ramming it in there real hard, and fucked the whole car system up. And I kept the buttons [knobs], you know, the radio buttons, even though, I eventually just ended up throwing the buttons away (195–96).

Primo's criminality is certainly teleological, in that he sees his participation as a means to an end. When it is placed alongside Caesar's "heartless psychopathology" (203) however, the difference seems more a matter of quantity than kind:

> Caesar: When I was about sixteen, fifteen—something like that—I was with my cousin; he had just come back from P.R. [Puerto Rico] We was downtown in a shopping mall in Connecticut, in New Haven by Yale. We were kinda starving, and we needed some money. So my cousin had convinced me into robbing a purse.
>
> We noticed this old lady on a corner next to a hospital, but I was scared to do it. But then I said, "Fuck it. I'm gonna do it."
>
> I though it was a good spot, because she was waiting for a red light.
>
> So I snatched it; but she didn't want to let it go. So I dragged her for a half a block; but she held on.
>
> So I punched her in the head a couple of times, and she got real hurt, and finally let the purse go.
>
> Primo: Shut the fuck up Caesar.
>
> Caesar: Like I'm saying [thrusting his face into Primo's], I dragged her . . . dragged her for awhile. She didn't want to let go, so I punched her on the head. [demonstrating the motions]
>
> Then we ran about half a block into somebody's backyard, and we looked in the purse, and there was only forty dollars, and I gave my cousin half. I shoulda took it all, because he didn't want to do it, and I said, "Fuck it."
>
> We kil't [figurative] that fuckin' bitch. [contorting his face with an evil gleam that caused us all to laugh]

Primo: [irritably suppressing his laughter] I think mugging sucks.

Caesar: [retorting harshly to Primo] You know why I mugged her? Because I was desperate, and was in Connecticut, and I had been in New York, and I didn't have motherfuckin' shit.

We was going to kill that bitch, because I wanted money; 'cause I had been getting . . . dissed. . .

[raising his voice] I was Puerto Rican I was nightmarish. I kil't that fuckin' bitch, because I wanted money to get high, and food. 'Cause I was a crazy mother-erfucking Puerto Rican that didn't know shit. How about that? [shouting into Primo's face] (203–5).

Bourgois notes that he was shaken by the intensity of Caesar's story telling:

"Witnessing Caesar's celebration of violence and gratuitous cruelty was discon-certing, to say the least" (p. 205).

A close look at his telling, however, shows that rough language and bravado aside, Caesar's crime is a model of efficient, instrumental criminal violence. His teleology, in fact, is much more explicitly pronounced than Primo's.

Caesar was hungry, he wanted drugs, and needed money. To snatch a purse became his goal. His carefully chosen victim would not release her purse. Caesar used violence to force her to let it go. He then left the woman and ran off.

There is no indication that the violence employed was superfluous to the task. Nor is there any indication of anything other than a single-minded de-termination to achieve the goal. Caesar was "desperate," "starving," craving drugs, and out of money. His act was a calculated, reasoned response to his predicament.

The histrionic, perhaps cathartic story telling, obviously meant to im-press listeners, does nothing to alter the actual criminal act. Nor should it affect the ethnographer's characterization of the crime. Bourgois was upset, and my point is not to prove that he was wrong, but rather to show that readers of his ethnography cannot know if he is right. Is Caesar's criminal-ity less instrumental than Primo's? More violent, certainly. But less goal oriented?

Ambiguous or erroneous interpretations of lived events are common to the human condition. As an author, Bourgois himself has our sympathy and respect. He has certainly placed himself and his family in harm's way for the sake of understanding, and perhaps helping, a group of people caught up in a cycle of violence and self-destruction. His training and experience make him a thoughtful and authoritative guide. Bourgois realizes that "the anguish of growing up poor in the richest city in the world is compounded by the cultural assault that El Barrio youths often face when they venture out of their neighborhood" (p. 8). He is sensitive as well to the politics of representation. Not wishing to either condemn or sanitize his "characters," he labors to show us their good sides along with the bad. As a social scientist, Bourgois creates his categories. He then sets up contrasting characterizations, much like a novelist would, to provide flesh and bone testament to the validity of his constructions.

All ethnographic narrative is simplification. To accuse Bourgois of appropriating and simplifying the identities of his informants in order to pursue his theoretical points would be unfair. The ethnographer, however, like the autobiographer, has an added responsibility for accuracy that stems from an additional claim to expertise: s/he was there. Ethnographic authority is often difficult to argue against precisely because the data gathered and presented are unique. The situations represented on the page are, simply, slices of life. Arguments in favor of ethnography as a scientific way of knowing are limited by this same, replication-defying quality. Ethnographic analysis must wind its way between the interests of its author and the protection of its subjects, even as it attempts to illuminate for its readers both the seen and unseen reality of its world.

This not so brief look at one short passage in a monograph of three-hundred-plus pages is meant to augment a point Bourgois himself makes in his introduction: that the production of a text is selective; that the author situates his subjects, edits their words, filters their deeds, and, perhaps most importantly, assigns meanings, either directly or implicitly, to everything about them. An author both controls the presentation of context and the representation of research subjects. In the case of Bourgois, intimate knowledge may have inspired an interest to create the perception of an essential difference between Primo, his acknowledged "close friend," and Caesar, his "other major character" (p. ix).

Measuring the New Penology: Lynch's *Waste Managers?*

Now we turn to a study that has as its subject matter a situation that is closer to the immediate area of analysis. Mona Lynch worked alongside the parole agents of a particular field office for one year's time. Within the parole office she was a known researcher and a participant-observer. She served in the position of volunteer aide to the agents.

In an article derived from her research, Lynch sets out to test the validity of a leading contemporary concept known as "the new penology." Since I rely upon insights derived from the new penology in my own conceptual work, I find a discussion of Lynch's article useful for both its content, an examination of the new penology, and for its ethnographic form. Lynch contests the universal validity of the new penology framework, but she does so almost apologetically, as if she must do so if she is to be true to her data. I reinterpret the data in a way that will demonstrate both the explicit and the hidden power of the new penology.

The classic paradox posed by the participant-observer role is the risk that one might come to identify too closely with those one is present to observe. The presence of the researcher is intended to augment authenticity through immersion in place, but newly formed personal loyalties and the recently acquired ability to see the world through the eyes of research subjects may threaten to cancel out any insights gained from proximity. Lynch's goal in the article is to argue against a presumption of omnipresence for the new penology. She therefore uses her data, her interpretations of the actions of parole officers, to make a conceptual point aimed at her academic colleagues. To do so she deconstructs the laboriously constructed "images" of her worksite colleagues.

To introduce the new penology in seminal form, Lynch paraphrases its originators, Malcolm Feeley and Jonathan Simon. She writes:

> At the heart of what distinguishes the "old" from the "new" penology is the relative abandonment of the individual in defining and managing criminal populations. The individual, in old penology, is a volitional actor who can be reformed, treated, or punished; thus, his motivation for criminal behavior is an important element to determining appropriate penal action. While old penological policies may refer to aggregates and categories of criminals, the interventions are distinctly aimed at changing the criminal actors or "individuals." In contrast, new penological strategies . . . are not concerned with why criminals commit their illegal acts but rather with how to most efficiently manage the level of reoffending risk posed by them (p. 840).

In other words, under the new penology, crime is seen as largely incomprehensible and ultimately inevitable, but not as wholly unstoppable. With regard to paroled offenders, the pertinent question for crime fighters becomes, "Whose crime do we stop?"

Lynch examines the new penology as it relates to the conduct of parole officers. If the concept is to hold up, parole officers will be seen to rely increasingly on "actuarial practices," including "risk assessment scales," and "salient factor scores," to determine "dangerousness." Gone will be the practice of individual agents meeting, interrogating, and otherwise getting to know individual parolees. Instead, we should find technocrats: agents embedded within a highly structured, goal-driven bureaucracy. In the place of personal savvy and interpersonal skills, agents working under the new penology should show technical sophistication. In addition, knowledge of, or at least adherence to bureau policies should be in clear evidence.

Lynch identifies "level of supervision" as perhaps the key case management decision made by parole agents. More intensive parole supervision means more restrictive conditions for the offender to abide by, and less autonomy. Studies have shown that closer supervision results in a higher likelihood of rearrest (Petersilia, Turner, and Deschenes, 1992). Presumably, heightened monitoring also means that parolees have less opportunity to commit crimes. Those ex-offenders selected for higher intensity supervision effectively constitute the group of parolees whose crime is to be stopped.

The process by which parole agents come to designate particular parolees for supervision is therefore pivotal in determining the extent to which the so-called new penology influences parole. The new penology indicates that parolees will not be evaluated primarily by what they did, or even what they do. Their cases will be managed according to projections and profiles. In other words, they will be judged by what they are believed likely to do next.

Since agents are responsible for large caseloads, only those parolees who are deemed to be the most risky, the most dangerous, will receive close supervision. A majority of parolees, in fact, are assigned to the oxymoronic realm of "unsupervised caseloads." A case file relegated to unsupervised status does not represent an offender who is crime-free, only one whose criminality has become the responsibility of the police. Those worthy of watching by probation authorities are included in the risk management pool.

To answer the question of who exactly embodies the business of probation, we need to take a closer look at the process of determining reoffending risk and ask, "Risk to whom?" As Lynch points out, parole administrators order their officers to spend a great deal of time on paperwork, so that the office can skirt blame in the event of a horrible crime by one of that office's parolees. The category of risk, then, besides subsuming the familiar moniker, "dangerous to society," must include a category dictated by the internal needs of the organization, namely, minimizing the likelihood of *liability*.

Liability can be defined as vulnerability to blame. In the organizational context of social institutions such as parole, blame can constitute legal liability, but more often it is political harm that is at issue. Blame accruing to a parole office is most acute when a parolee commits a heinous crime, such as the infamous Richard Allen Davis killing of young Polly Klaas. Likewise, officials are exposed to blame when standard policies and procedures are not followed. Probation offices wishing to limit their liability must, one, invest considerable energy in supervising parolees with a history of or propensity for especially revolting crimes, and two, maintain more than adequate case files. In this way, the dangerousness or risk posed by the parolee, both to the community and to the parole office, can be mitigated.

Parole officers thus choose to supervise those parolees who pose the greatest risk to the parole mission. Run-of-the-mill criminal activity, the "can't be stopped" variety typical of irredeemable "career criminals," falls not upon parole officers, but to the justice system component best equipped to manage it: the police. On the other hand, those offenders deciding to opt-out of crime can do so at any time. Their interaction with law enforcement would thereby cease, with a minimum of wasted effort on both sides.

Far from viewing criminals as beyond repair, the new penology simply surmises that redemption flows from the self. Using the Alcoholics Anonymous model as an example, offenders must first bottom out before any meaningful change is possible. Since it is virtually impossible to determine what exactly constitutes "the bottom" for any given individual (that which constitutes rock bottom for one person, might for another be merely a ledge on the way down to further depths), universal, treatment-based case management as a behavioral change agent makes no therapeutic sense. Using probation and parole officers for intensive supervision, meanwhile, makes no sense financially. In the 1960s and 1970s, public budgets permitted a scattergun approach to rehabilitation/enforcement supervision. In the current era of fiscal limitations, social organizations are backing out of many areas where previously they were obligated. Redemption from crime, like participation in welfare programs, retirement planning, educational goals, and general self-improvement, has increasingly been framed as a matter of personal choice—the responsibility of each affected individual (Rose, 1996).

Lynch minimizes the importance of practices indicative of a new penology by maintaining that parole officers rely on tools other than actuarial practices to assess parolee dangerousness. Intuitive hunches, intricate conversational tricks, and proactive policing skills are mentioned. For example, "missed appointments and lying were viewed as signals of more serious transgressions among this potentially dangerous clientele" (p. 859). Although a close reading of the account makes it difficult to separate the systematically classifiable (lying, missed appointments as indicators of dangerousness) from the intuitive (lying and missed appointments as indicators of crimes not yet known), Lynch's informants maintain their autonomy from management systems dictated from above:

> Little faith was placed in making judgments based on any kind of scoring system; agents had their own system—one that relied heavily on actual interaction with the parolee—to decide who posed risks (p. 855).

This commentary on a version of parole officer methodology, one almost stereotypically in line with the macho, individualist worldview of the street cop, eschews the notion of parole officer as "street level bureaucrat." Instead, an idealized, "wannabe" law enforcement persona often displayed by corrections workers of all types is evinced. This interpretation of what they do diverges markedly from what Lynch actually reports as data, however. For example,

> The problem parolee may be marked [for assessment by parole agents] by his criminal history or past criminal allegations . . . Also, parolees who had been released from a high-security prison were treated with much suspicion and given little leeway for messing up (p. 860).

In other words, in constructing an assessment of a parolee, a parole agent ascertains the criminal history and current offense status of the parolee, either by reading the case file or from an interview. The agent then peruses the parolee's prison record, taking special note of where the prisoner was housed, and from where he was released.

Although each parole agent may have individualized foibles, prejudices, or simple likes and dislikes regarding specific crimes and prison facilities, Lynch's presentation suggests that prisoners who do time within maximum-security prisons get more attention from parole officers than do prisoners coming from minimum-security camps. What Lynch fails to discuss are the justice system procedures that result in inmates being placed in certain facilities.

In effect, scoring systems determine inmate placement, as do institutional needs regarding the management of inmate population characteristics. Scoring systems, such as salient factor tables, play a large role in sentencing. Criminal history documents, particularly those related to convictions, are influenced by decisions made by prosecutors that often reflect the internal dynamics of that justice system component.

Clearly, Lynch's listing of "cognitive shortcuts" employed by renegade/recalcitrant (one might say petulant) agents bears a striking similarity to standard risk classification norms, and constitutes an at least indirect application of actuarial practices. This, I would agrue, is the reflexive, internally-driven focus of contemporary penal agencies. It is the hidden power of the new penology.

Each component of the criminal justice system gets its chance to assess each client. Those assessments are then converted into data for subsequent assessments. As a case file grows it tends to become a self-fulfilling prophecy. Those most watched by parole agents come from the toughest joints. They are watched most intensively and so are violated more often. They went to tougher joints because of their records as assessed by probation officers prior to sentencing. If a probation officer assigns a high risk factor (based on schedules and guidelines reflective of the new actuarial penology) the offender tends to be sentenced to longer terms and be designated to higher security prisons. Upon completion of the incarceration segment of the sentence, parole authorities, fully believing that they are acting on gut feelings, hunches, and worldly knowledge/experience, place the parolee into the high surveillance category because of the "hard joint" experience of the offender, and their (the parole officers) personal experience with "those guys." The offender is then most likely to be violated and returned to custody, limiting the liability of the parole office and reducing danger to the public.

So much for the new penology model having "not yet trickled down to the front lines" (p. 861).

The Voice of Experience: A Dilulio Sampler

Now we move to the work of John Dilulio, a political scientist whose work as a criminologist has been very influential. Dilulio championed the movement in criminology to include the voices of justice system practitioners in prison evaluations. He implies that he speaks for practitioners, but also he has his own agenda. Dilulio begins his prison adventure near his (then) home base of Harvard University. He uses this preliminary research to sensitize himself for a larger project that results in a book, *Governing Prisons* (1987), that compares prison systems in three states:

> Before entering the maximum-security prison in Walpole, Massachusetts, I had read a fair amount of the scholarly literature on prisons, studied the reports of various blue-ribbon panels, and reviewed as many newspaper accounts, magazine articles, and even prison novels as I could digest. None of that prepared me, intellectually or otherwise, for what I observed at Walpole (p. 1).

Choosing to author a book on a particular prison or prisons is a bold move, certainly. Prisons are usually dirty and dangerous places filled with people who often act in loud, threatening, and obnoxious ways. By all accounts, a walk in the park it ain't. If one decides to undertake such a project with the intent of having it published, one ought to have an informed notion of what publishers expect. Media companies approve of sensational material such as that generated by tales from The Big House because they profit from it. Modern media giants play a prodigious role in manufacturing news of illicit sex, violence, and scandal. Promising more of the same virtually guarantees a receptive welcome. Dilulio researched his topic and found that maximum-security prisons are hothouses of scandal.

Dilulio chose to focus his research on "higher-custody" facilities. He defended his choice by noting that prisons designated medium-, close-, and maximum-security hold a majority of the nation's prisoners. They are also the best known, and "the most costly, violent, and troubled" (p. 4).

Dilulio is shrewd to note the celebrity status of our oldest and most infamous prisons. Their high name recognition means that he can drop monikers such as "Jackson, San Quentin, and Attica" (p. 4) and be assured a knowing response from the reading public. The trouble with Dilulio's formulation is that he can't leave well enough alone. As usual, he fudges a bit. By including medium-security prisons along with the "serious joints," he can create the claim that "higher-custody" institutions hold a majority of prisoners. But worlds of difference separate medium-custody from Max. In practice, medium-security facilities, usually called "correctional institutions," more closely resemble their lower custody counterparts than they do higher-level penitentiaries.

On a correctional continuum that stretches from lowest to highest, typical security designations are as follows:

Minimum

Low

Medium

Close/High

Maximum

As we can see (with the help of bold print), "Medium" is right where you might expect it: in the middle. States with large prison systems populate medium-security prisons with nonviolent offenders serving lengthy sentences. Mediums also house higher-security prisoners who are on the downward slope of their sentences, and lower-security folks who get into trouble at less-secure facilities. Smaller states use mediums prodigiously.

Convicts comprising all but the most extreme cases are eligible for placement there. Being a middling sort of designation serving a multiplicity of needs, medium-security holds the lion's share of prisoners. In California, one of the three systems Dilulio examines, around forty-five percent of the total inmate population is kept in medium-security. Minimum-security accounts for another twenty-four percent of that states' convicts (Austin, 2001). Another Dilulio target, Texas, houses over eighty percent of its prisoners in either minimum/low- or medium-security prisons (Austin, 2001). The final state Dilulio visits, Michigan, lists its medium-security population at forty-two percent, with another thirty-two percent in minimum custody.

Dilulio's grouping of medium-security correctional institutions along with the higher level penitentiaries is thus hardly a natural one, at least not so far as prisons are concerned. For an ambitious author striving to sound relevant, however, creating an illusion of significance is a vital trick of the trade.

Lest one think this an isolated incident, this habit of creating novel categories has been extended by Dilulio to other areas of crime analysis as well. In
an infamous op-ed piece published by the *Wall Street Journal*, entitled, "Let
'em Rot," he cites what would become one of his favorite statistics: "about 90
percent of prisoners are serious (two or more felony convictions) or violent
offenders." That figure, based on a 1991 survey of state prisoners by the Bureau of Justice Statistics, puts people arrested twice for drug offenses in the
same category as those arrested for serial bank robbery, rape, and murder.
Dilulio uses the opening paragraph of the *Journal* article to make the connection explicit, forming a homogeneous group of "criminals who assault,
rape, rob, murder and deal drugs." This is done in an effort to show that our
prisons are both cost effective and socially desirable, because they indeed hold
the "worst of the worst."

"Serious," of course, is a matter of perspective. During the 1980s and
1990s, a period of steep increases in drug war rhetoric and resource expenditure, Dilulio provided government drug warriors with legitimizing academic
verbiage. Drug offenses were then and still are considered "serious" by law enforcement, but the vast majority of drug offenses are hardly "violent" (Tonry,
1995; Irwin & Austin, 2003)

In articles for the *New York Times* (1996a) and *Washington Post* (1996b),
Dilulio performs an additional sleight of hand. He notes that a conviction for
"simple possession" of drugs such as marijuana is not always as simple as it
seems. The conviction of record does not imply the incarceration of a simple
hop-head, he claims, but the detention of a probable narcotics kingpin who
has plea-bargained his case down to a lesser charge. To buttress this position,
Dilulio cites statistics from the federal government regarding drug convictions. "And most Federal drug traffickers are not black kids caught with a little
crack cocaine or white executives arrested for a small stash of powder cocaine.
The average amount of drugs involved in Federal cocaine-trafficking cases is
183 pounds, and the average amount involved in Federal marijuana trafficking cases is 3.5 tons" (Dilulio, 1996b).

Here Dilulio conflates individual drug offenders, such as "black kids" and
"white executives," with federal "cases." One distinction between federal law
enforcement agencies, such as the FBI and DEA, and local police is that the
feds typically concern themselves with large conspiracy cases. Unlike local police departments that prioritize cleaning up neighborhoods with street corner

sting operations and sweeps of copping corners, it is not unusual for federal prosecutions to last several years. The goal of drug enforcement at the national level is to uncover, monitor, and eventually dismantle drug trafficking *organizations*. When arrests are finally made, dozens if not scores of people are taken into custody, from the men and women who load illicit cargoes onto ships and planes and conceal narcotics in their bodies, up to the actual decision-makers, the so-called kingpins.

A federal marijuana case that involves 3.5 tons of grass is likely to involve many separate seizures taking place over a long period of time. Alternatively, such a case might reflect the seizure of a single large vessel. In any event, each individual defendant could be said to be involved in a "federal marijuana trafficking" case, but most of the people under arrest are marginal participants, usually illegal migrants working the equivalent of brute manual labor for low wages. Dilulio either knows this or, as an expert, should know this. Either way, his scholarship is misleading and, I would suggest, irresponsible.

The average amount of marijuana per incarcerated person comes out to be quite high, presumably making his point. What Dilulio failed to mention, however, was that only a relatively small number of traffickers were responsible for the bulk of the seized drugs. A single convicted smuggler, for example, was caught with four hundred tons of high-grade reefer aboard an oceangoing ship. Upon how many innocent shoulders did Dilulio shift that load? Given his skill at "spin" and his tenuous association with the facts, it is hard to imagine that Dilulio's experience in criminal justice research failed to prepare him for what he saw at Walpole.

REFLEXIVE CRIMINOLOGY

Since ethnography purports to be in the service of science, one could surmise that a certain objectivity and detachment from outcomes would be required. Can such aloofness be reasonably expected from a researcher with prior knowledge of the situation under study? Certainly someone with a keen understanding of a given milieu would prove superior as an analyst than would a neophyte. Experience within a setting as contentious as prison brings with it biases, however, and these personal leanings must be taken into account.

Prisoners are well on the way to being once again the focus of prison research, this time through monetary necessity. Their subjective experiences are central to managing penality. As the subjects of research, prisoners are crucial to ethnography as well. They are at the heart of public policy discussions, even as they go unnamed. We can mock them, praise, demonize, or disparage them. Each has its effects, on them and on us. Alford, Lynch, Bourgois, and Dilulio each take the time to become acquainted with research subjects, but with varied results. Can we know those whom we study? Do we want to? Or do we want to hijack our constructions of their identities, and force them into service to our agendas? These are some of the questions raised in this work.

David Nelken (1994) has noted that reflexivity is a defining feature of modern systems. The inquisitive, evaluative gaze common to organs of social organization is turned back upon itself so that the movement of forward progress, or at least its outward appearance, can be maintained. Criminal justice system components, like the prison, are not immune from this tendency. Neither is criminology: the study of prisons, crime, and deviance.

Contemporary criminology has largely failed to recognize the subjectivity of prisoners and other felons, but this does not mean that their subjective perceptions have gone away. Opinions on crime, of course, are a street corner commodity; everybody has one, including those who reside in prison. Every criminal, in fact, is a criminologist: an expert in the manner, means, rationale, causes, and certainly the consequences of a certain order of crime. The criminal who is apprehended, sentenced, convicted, and incarcerated acquires an in-depth and extraordinarily vivid view of the criminal justice system. He, and it is usually a he, acquires substantial expertise across many dimensions of criminological discourse. Arguably an amateur, he lacks formal training in the cognate discipline. A possible indication of this amateurishness is his insistence on a positivist orientation. He can tell you where he committed his crime and why, and who talked him into it. If pressed he can narrate an account of the entire criminal decision-making process (see Maruna, 2001). Given time, he may provide a finely grained analysis of when and where he went astray: the family problems, neighborhood pressures, and personal shortcomings that brought him to his present state. Every prison inmate knows that he made mistakes, and that they finally caught up with him. And more than anyone else, he blames himself for his condition.

The convict who stumbles on to the formal study of crime and society often gets a surprise. It is called the sociological perspective (Mobley, 2003). He is still responsible for his crimes, but he finds that the responsibility is not his alone. Society, through intention or neglect, prepared a criminogenic stage upon which he was compelled to act. Society abused and discriminated against him, filled his head with materialistic desires, and instilled an urge for power. Society, in its often indiscriminate cruelty, told him in no uncertain terms that he could be whatever he wanted to be. He soon discovered, however, that he could not. If he was going to get what he desired, what he deserved, whether money or power or freedom from worry, he would have to step outside the lines. He knew where the borders lay and he sensed the depths that he would have to cross. The popular culture of consumption, that alluring damsel, led him to the water and bade him drink. And he drank.

The curtain falls and it rises again, and the third act of our drama involves the internal reconciliation of the man who loathes his own weakness and incompetence but understands that he is not solely to blame. How to reconcile the guilt of personal responsibility with the knowledge that his choices were few? How to square a nascent understanding of shared culpability with the certain knowledge that he will do the time alone? Hard to admit is that a working knowledge of injustice does little to lessen its sting. Convicts, especially those of color, know this viscerally. After all, the Emancipation Proclamation did not stop the Black Codes or Jim Crow. Such are the issues troubling the credentialed convict criminologist.

CONCLUSION

I hope the convict criminology lens has proved its usefulness here. I expect that as the number of convict criminologists grows and our sophistication deepens, our contributions will become more substantial. Especially as members of multidisciplinary research teams, convict criminology holds great promise. After all, our discipline addresses issues of life and death, truth and justice, harm and recovery. It needs all of our voices.

REFERENCES

Alford, C. F. (2000). What would it matter if everything Foucault said about prison were wrong? *Discipline and Punish* after twenty years. *Theory & Society 29*, 125–146.

Aunger, R. (1995). On ethnography: Storytelling or science? *Current Anthropology*, Vol. 36, No. 1. February.

Austin, J. (2001). Prisoner reentry: Current trends, practices, and issues. *Crime & Delinquency 47*, 314–334.

Bourgois, P. (1995). *In Search of Respect: Selling Crack in El Barrio.* Cambridge: Cambridge University Press.

Clifford, J. (1988). *The Predicament of Culture: Twentieth-Century Ethnography, Literature, And Art.* Cambridge: Harvard University Press.

Dilulio, J. (1987). *Governing Prisons.* New York: Free Press.

Dilulio, J. (1994). Let 'em rot. *Wall Street Journal* (January 26): A14.

Dilulio, J. (1996a). Prisons are a bargain by any measure. *New York Times* (January 16): A19.

Dilulio, J. (1996b). No angels fill those cells; the numbers don't lie: It's the hard core doing hard time. *Washington Post* (March 17): C3.

Foucault, M. (1971). *Discipline and Punish.* Translated by A. Sheridan. New York: Vintage.

Geertz, C. (1983). Local Knowledge. *Further Essays in Interpretive Anthropology.* New York: Basic Books.

Irwin, J. (2005). *The Warehouse Prison. Disposal of the New Dangerous Class.* Los Angeles: Roxbury Publishing.

Irwin, J., and J. Austin. (2003). *It's About Time: America's Imprisonment Binge.* Belmont, CA: Wadsworth.

Luhmann, N. (1990). *Essays on Self-Reference.* New York: Columbia University Press.

Lynch, M. (1998). Waste managers? The new penology, crime fighting, and parole agent identity. *Law & Society Review* 52, 839–869.

Maruna, S. (2001). *Making Good.* Washington, D.C.: American Psychological Association.

Mobley, A. (2003). The Two-Legged Data Dilemma. In *Convict Criminology.* Ross, J.I., and S. Richards (eds.). Belmont, CA: Wadsworth.

Nelken, D. (1994). Reflexive Criminology? In *The Futures of Criminology.* D. Nelkin, (ed.) London: Sage.

Petersilia J., S. Turner, and E.P. Deschenes. (1992). The costs and effects of intensive supervision for drug offenders. *Federal Probation 56,* 12–17.

Richards, S., and J.I. Ross. (2001) Introducing the new school of convict criminology. *Social Justice*, Vol. 28, No. 1.

Rosaldo, R. (1989). *Culture and Truth*. Boston: Beacon.

Rose, N. (1996). *Inventing Ourselves: Psychology, Power, and Personhood*. Cambridge: Cambridge University Press.

Ross, J.I., and S. Richards (eds.). (2003) *Convict Criminology*. Belmont, CA: Wadsworth.

Tonry, M. (1995). *Malign Neglect: Race, Crime, and Punishment in America*. New York: Oxford University Press.

Van Maanen, J. (1988). *Tales of the Field*. Chicago: University of Chicago Press.

Venkatesh, S. (2008) *Gang Leader for a Day: A Rouge Sociologist Takes to the Streets*. New York: Penguin.

6

Identity Matters: Cultivating a Critical Criminologist

NANCY A. WONDERS

I grew up on a small, self-sufficient family farm in rural Michigan. Like farm children everywhere, from the very start of life my three brothers and I were expected to do our share to keep the farm functioning. My job was to collect the eggs once a day, a job filled with pleasure and dread. Chickens may seem rather harmless, but for a small child trying to sneak a hand underneath a sitting hen's warm body, the fear of the random peck of a chicken's beak was at times overwhelming. Each day I had to overcome my fear if I wanted to seize the prize—a warm, fresh egg that would bring my family sustenance. Similarly, I learned early that the tasty treasures of the garden could only be harvested if I helped to fight the evil invaders that relentlessly sought to crowd out the crops. In the moist, humid Michigan growing season, the only things that grew faster than my brothers and I were the weeds. On the farm, it seemed that anything worth doing came at the cost of hardships and risks, both large and small. A swim in the creek meant risking the bloodsuckers; catching a glittering, elusive firefly meant suffering the bites of the far more numerous mosquitoes.

It seems appropriate to begin this essay on the farm since it is the place where I began. Indeed, so many of the characteristics that drew me to critical criminology stem from my deep roots in the farm country of the rural Midwest, including the recognition that change and success require hardship and risk. It should be no surprise that those who succeed as critical criminologists often come from backgrounds that are less advantaged. Critical criminology is unique and important because of its attention to difference, inequality, perspective, and power; it invites and welcomes critique of the status quo and change in the interest of a more democratic, inclusive, and just world. It offers a space within the academy for the voice of outsiders concerned with justice to be heard. Given the global forces that are daily linking diverse peoples ever more tightly together, such alternative voices are now particularly welcome (and needed) because of the unique vantage point their perspective brings to the discipline.

There is a value in exploring what C. Wright Mills called "the sociological imagination"—the link between biography and history. If history were destiny, I'd be living the farm life still since my current life as a critical criminologist was simply unimaginable to me as child. But the fact is that my ordinary farm girl childhood provided surprisingly fertile ground for the intellectual seeds of critical criminology to grow. Because of my farm roots, I believed that the personal was political well before I knew what the word feminist meant. I knew that the character of a person's labor shaped the character of that individual's life years before I read Marx. And I knew that social change was possible because I was witness to so many broad social changes in my own world. Of course, the fertilizer provided by key influences also hastened my development, and so the story of my growth is a story about them too. And though the harvest and yield certainly varies from year to year, I believe that there are ways that my experiences and work within the discipline might create the conditions for other critical criminologists to grow and flourish.

FERTILE GROUND

As a critical voice in criminology, I have come to appreciate the way that identity matters in shaping our life chances, experiences of injustice, and social world. In retrospect, it is easy to see that elements of my identity provided fertile ground for grasping and deeply integrating key features of critical criminology, particularly the importance of gender, race, and social class.

On Gender

For me, feminism is a not just a philosophy I discovered during graduate school; it represents a daily practice I discovered as a girl. My role model in this, and all things, is my mom. Married at the age of sixteen to my father, she was fortunate to finish high school, particularly since my father, the son of poor tenant farmers, had dropped out in the eighth grade. My mom had four children by the time she was twenty-five and when my youngest brother was still a toddler, she began her college education. A double major in math and political science, she graduated in three years at a time when women were still something of a rarity in university settings. All the while, she did the work of the farm alongside my father: bailing hay, tending the livestock, gardening, canning enough food for the entire winter, cooking, and maintaining a home.

As a child, I imagined that my mom must have been taught this wide range of skills by her own family—it wasn't until I was in my thirties that I discovered she taught these skills to herself by a creative combination of trial and error, combined with wise advice from a few generous neighbors. My mom's example has been a powerful lesson in pragmatism and the power of education. She could do anything she set her mind to with a little hard work and help. For me, this focus on "doing" as a path to "knowing" remains a core value and offers a strategic tool for reaching beyond the limits of biography and history.

Once my mom had her degree in hand, she became a teacher and, later, a librarian. Her love of teaching and books was infectious and laid essential groundwork for my future identity as an academic. This generational foundation, however, also taught me powerful lessons about the architecture of gender since none of my three brothers became readers, attended university, or pursued a professional career.

In the 1970s, my mom became the first woman ever admitted into a correctional facility as a regular worker in the state of Michigan, a story featured in newspapers across the state. She worked as the head librarian and as a math teacher. In a story not covered by the newspapers, two years later, my mother resigned from her position after experiencing sexual harassment, not by the prisoners, but her supervisor at the prison. As a recently divorced woman with custodial responsibility for three of her four children, I can only imagine how difficult it was for my mom to walk away from the highest paying job she had ever had. But at that moment, she taught her teenage sponge-of-a-daughter a great deal about injustice, self-respect, and the value of dignity over the dollar. I have no doubt that my work on gender and justice germinated from this very early event.

My mom still works in a prison and continues to be my most important role model. She runs a program that gives about thirty to forty long-term prisoners the opportunity to give something back to society—this prison program is the largest producer of Braille books for the blind in the nation. My mom struggles daily to treat those who are incarcerated with dignity and respect, to foster their personal and professional growth, and to provide them with meaningful work. She often works seven days a week to ensure that the men won't be trapped in their cells on the weekend. And she has frequently battled the prison administration to prevent efforts to move, downsize, and even eliminate the program in the current anti-rehabilitation environment. She brings both professionalism and humanity to her work. For many of the men, most of whom are lifers, she is their only link to the outside world. Her work humbles and inspires me.

Although her work in the prison has been transformative for the men who participate in the Braille program (and does much for blind students across the country), it does little to change the circumstances that bring people to prison in the first place. My mom's work led me to seek out strategies and tools that could cultivate significant social change, reduce inequality, and further the broad goal of harm prevention and social justice for all.

On Race

Because my mom worked as a librarian in a prison when I was in junior high school, she became a rich resource for my insatiable appetite for interesting reading material. Through her I accessed the books that populated the shelves in the prison library which, not surprisingly, centered on the concerns of those imprisoned there: race relations, social inequality, and injustice, particularly in the criminal justice system. I learned about race relations first from books. Piri Thomas in his classic work *Down These Mean Streets* revealed the realities of inner city life for Hispanic Street Kids; *Manchild in the Promised Land* taught me about the black experience in America, as did the fiction work *Five Smooth Stones* and nearly everything written by Richard Wright. I learned early that books could provide a powerful lens into the experiences of others and once I made that discovery, I never stopped reading.

The books I read as an adolescent convinced me that the United States was a hostile place for many social groups, but especially for the poor and those who had experienced discrimination based on racial identity. As if to reinforce these social lessons, my mom became involved in an interracial relationship with the person who was to later become my stepfather. Her relationship mirrored the social context of the time and exposed the way that social pressure and structural barriers could impede even the most powerful of human experiences—indeed, even the deepest love. For almost fifteen years, these two found only small ways to nurture their mutual affection, always far from the public gaze, while constantly testing the winds of social change. Finally, they decided to live together and marry.

My stepfather was born in Detroit and, as a teen, moved to Flint, Michigan—the town made famous by Michael Moore for its representation of the tragic decline and desperate poverty of post-industrial cities. As a young man, my stepfather served ten years in prison for two offenses that could have been scripted by Richard Wright. The first offense he was arrested for, he did not commit. He drove some acquaintances to a liquor store and, once his buddies were inside, they made an impulsive decision to rob the store. They jumped back into the car and told him to "drive!" Not surprisingly given their lack of planning, they were immediately caught by the police. A smart young man, my stepfather knew that his story sounded far too much like a novel to be believed, especially given his race, his social location, and the times. He was certain he would be convicted and sentenced to a long term in prison. And so, while out on bail for the first offense, his rage at racial injustice and the terrible impulsiveness of youth provoked him to commit his first (but the state's second) offense. As a result of the long sentence he received, he missed his young adulthood. He came into my life at a critical time in the formation of my identity and he remains one of the most important influences over my professional and personal trajectory as a critical criminologist. My stepfather never denied his mistakes as a youth, but his experience taught me the complex ways that race matters and shapes life circumstances. Given his parental influence in my life, he educated me through both example and exposure to his (and ultimately my) extended family to look beyond the surface of skin color. Because of him, I became intensely interested in understanding how cultural identities and racial and ethnic markers are formed, and also how they shape the character of (in)justice in our country.

A quiet man, both as a result of the silence enforced by his long incarceration and (perhaps) by nature, he surprised me a few years ago when he sat me down and sternly and urgently asked "Do you know why you do the work you do?" I told him that it was because of mom and because of him. I struggled as I tried to make my words re-create the ways that his life had influenced who I had become, and after several false starts and incomplete sentences said simply, "I'm your daughter." He held my eyes a long time, then said, "I know that. I just wanted to be sure that you did."

On Social Class

Looking back at my childhood, it is now evident to me that my family always struggled to make ends meet, although I did not realize it at the time. In large part this was because my biological dad frequently told stories of his own childhood that made our daily struggles seem modest and unremarkable. As a kid my dad woke up many mornings in the bed he shared with his brothers, brushing off the snow that covered his face because of the hole in the roof of their rented farmhouse. On cold days, he would have to get to school early, far ahead of the other children or teacher, to light the woodstove so that he could run a piece of coal back to his own home to keep his family warm. He became a carpenter before he was eighteen because his toolbox promised to help him build a life outside of the poverty he had suffered as a child. For me, the fact that dad could build or fix anything and that mom sewed our clothes, canned every last vegetable, and only went to the store for staples like flour and sugar, seemed more like a virtue than a struggle or challenge—for I was certain that my parents could make or grow what was needed to survive.

I gained perspective on poverty and hardship only after we left the farm. Then I learned that those without "the means of production"—land, resources, and control over their own labor—do truly risk immiseration. When my father could no longer work as a result of a heart problem, my mom's job in the public schools simply could not pay the bills. She began to pick up extra work, running a restaurant one summer, working at a community college library on top of her full-time librarian position the next year. When she and my father separated in my teenage years, I rarely saw my mom, though by now she had earned a master's degree. As a single woman with children living at home, her wages for forty hours of work simply could not pay the bills. She would spend several decades working multiple jobs just to make ends meet. In this way, I came to understand that social class is a set of structured inequalities unrelated to hard work and talent.

Because of these early lessons, by the time I was a teen, I understood that identity matters and shapes life chance, opportunities, and injustice. I knew that I wanted to work to affect change in the justice system, but especially to reduce the deep inequities in our culture that create the conditions for social harm and human suffering. I graduated a year early from high school, arguing to the local school board that I wanted to pursue a career in criminal justice so that I could go out into the world and change it.

SOWING AND FERTILIZING THE SEEDS

My childhood offered fertile ground for my development as a critical criminologist, but my undergraduate and graduate education, mentoring, hardship, and hard work helped to sow and fertilize the seeds for success within academia and the discipline.

On Education and Mentors

Given the struggle my mom faced as a single parent, I will be forever grateful that I entered college at a time when both merit and need-based scholarships still existed. Had I not benefited from these programs, I would never have been able to complete four years of university education, even at the relatively inexpensive state schools I attended. I went to Eastern Michigan University in the early years of its interdisciplinary criminal justice program. At Eastern, I had the good fortune to have two excellent internship experiences: one in adult probation and the other at a federal prison. Both experiences deepened my understanding of the justice system and offered invaluable lessons about justice careers I did *not* want to pursue since both prison and probation work seemed too late in the justice process to create significant and lasting social change.

In my senior year, I transferred to Western Michigan University where I graduated with a bachelor's degree, continuing on in the master's program after a brief reprieve to have a child and, subsequently, to end a ten-year relationship with my teenage sweetheart. At Western, I met two faculty members who literally changed my life and, as a result, brilliantly clarified the magical power of teaching as a vehicle for social change. Lou Junker, a radical institutional economist with powerful charisma in the classroom, introduced me to political economy, Marx, pragmatism, relational thinking, and sustainability (long before the word had currency). After his moving lecture on the symbiotic relationship between meat consumption in the West and world hunger, I became a vegetarian and have remained so to this day. Had he not died unexpectedly, I likely would have become an economist, but his intellectual influence has been lifelong. Because of Lou, I developed a deep belief that teaching is a powerful and enduring vehicle for social transformation, particularly when paired with carefully gathered knowledge and passionate delivery.

Ronald Kramer was a relatively new faculty member when I arrived at Western. As a brand new graduate student, I remember sitting across from him and informing him that I would like to be a teaching assistant if I could engage in "meaningful" work. To my amazement (and relief), he took my remark seriously and immediately incorporated me directly into his research project on the social regulation of corporations. This project financed one of my first out-of-state trips ever—to Washington, D.C. where I conducted several elite interviews, including one in the infamous Watergate building. For the first time, I had a taste of the excitement that could accompany research and I loved it. When Ron introduced me to the new and pioneering work of critical criminologists such as Bill Chambliss, Ray Michalowski, Drew Humphries, Marjorie Zatz, and Stephen Pfohl, I finally felt at home in the discipline. It is spine-tingling to me today that all of these individuals have since played key mentorship roles in my academic career, and that I now know all of these individuals as friends.

In the small town of Kalamazoo, Ron lived a very large life, not just at the university, but also in the community. Ron was an activist in the peace movement and in the sanctuary movement and, before I left Western, I was an activist in these movements as well. The annual Peace Week that Ron created on campus modeled a synergistic method for linking teaching and activism together. His daily life demonstrated to me that excellence in teaching and research, a passion for activism and social change, and a commitment to family and relationships are not incompatible. This model was crucial for me as a young single parent struggling to support a very small child, and made it possible for me to imagine myself as a future academic.

One of the best gifts the faculty at WMU gave me was the encouragement to pursue a doctoral degree at a different institution. Moving away from my home state and family, I headed to New Brunswick, New Jersey to pursue a PhD in sociology at Rutgers University. In addition to criminology, much of my coursework there focused on political sociology. It was at Rutgers that I explored social inequality (gender, race, and class) and global issues, such as development, social movements, and international labor relations. I had the very good fortune to enter with a strong and intellectually gifted cohort; several of my peers have gone on to become highly regarded critical sociologists. As a result of my experience at Rutgers, I remain convinced that excellent graduate programs depend as much on the quality of the students as the quality of the faculty.

On Hardships and Hard Work

During my time at Rutgers, the hardships of attending graduate school as a single parent were significant. Many students had the luxury of a singular focus on school work, but I immediately found myself juggling my academic load with parenting, political commitments and, importantly, the need to pay the bills. I have heard many students and junior faculty comment that they were "waiting" to have children until they had their degree, or their first job, or tenure. A parent at twenty-three, this choice was never one I faced. Because my first child, Brooke, was planned and wanted, I never struggled over the fact that I was a parent and believe still that going through graduate school with a child had its advantages. Because I was a parent, I was more focused on completion of my degree than many of my peers; I was also more focused on ensuring that each day was fun-filled since, for my daughter's sake, I couldn't afford to put off having a full life until after graduate school. However, as a *single* parent and financially challenged graduate student, I did experience my share of challenges.

Although I applied to and was accepted to a couple of other schools, the fact that graduate students at Rutgers are part of the faculty bargaining unit was probably the single most important reason for my choice to attend Rutgers over other programs; in addition to the stipend and tuition remission the program offered, my young daughter and I had excellent health benefits. Despite my stipend, I was constantly seeking other ways to make ends meet, including serving as acting assistant dean for a short time and working the last two years for the State of New Jersey on a statewide sentencing project. Although the additional work created hardship at the time, it was that hard work—and additional employment experience—that probably made the difference when I went on the job market. I have often said that I was not necessarily the best student in my program, but I do think that I was one of the hardest working and most persistent. These traits have carried me far as an academic.

While at Rutgers, I also discovered the intellectual excitement associated with interdisciplinary work. I became involved in women's studies and helped to organize a national graduate student conference on our campus, meeting many amazing feminist students and scholars in the process and creating a strong foundation for my later work on gender and justice. I also served as one of the first student fellows at the Center for the Critical Analysis of Contemporary Culture; that year, the ten faculty and students in attendance hosted lectures by Jacques Derrida, Stanley Fish, Robin Morgan, and many other intellectual giants. This rich experience ensured a lifelong commitment to interdisciplinary critical thinking and scholarship.

My interdisciplinary orientation was solidified when I met Fred Solop, a political science graduate student at Rutgers. We found friendship at the interdisciplinary boundary between sociology and political science and his intellectual insights and activist impulses still inspire me. He is one of the best activists and feminists I know, as well as an amazingly intelligent and progressive political scientist. His primary research interests are social movements, citizen participation, public interest polling, and digital democracy and, in all of this work, he seeks to understand how to foster inclusive participation and citizen engagement, a goal I share. Together we successfully navigated graduate school and the dissertation process, providing mutual support, critical reads, and encouragement. At the same time, we grew our friendship into an enduring relationship and decided to commit to each other for the long haul.

Fred and I worried that it would be impossible to find academic jobs together but, amazingly, when we went onto the job market, we both immediately landed jobs at Northern Arizona University, largely unaware that NAU's commitment to partner accommodation at the time was fairly rare and revolutionary within academia. I graduated with my PhD in May, already with a job in hand, but five days later it was old news, overshadowed by a much more important event—the birth of our son, Aaron.

My first year at NAU was a difficult one as the only woman on the faculty of a brand new department, so difficult that I considered leaving after only a few months given the hostility that the interim chair directed toward me. His hostility seemed especially harsh given that I was both a brand new faculty member and a new parent. Instead of exiting the institution, I made a decision to try to create change for myself, for the department, and for other women. I worked hard to connect to other women across campus, particularly through affiliation with women's studies and the Commission on the Status of Women. I also worked with others to pen the university's Safe Working and Learning Document, designed to prevent and respond to harassment and discrimination; this policy remains in force to this day.

Then, by a stroke of tremendous good fortune and a lot of hard recruitment work, we hired Raymond Michalowski to serve as the next chair of the department, a role he occupied for almost a decade. With his leadership, our department became one of the strongest critical criminology departments in the country and, over time, one of the most gender and diversity friendly. It is no exaggeration to say that when Ray arrived in Arizona, he brought water to the desert; he created a place where critical criminologists like myself could grow and flourish. Over the years, Ray has served as a colleague, intellectual compatriot, co-author, and friend. His commitment to democratic process and practice in academic departmental life made our department a particularly supportive, cooperative, intellectually charged, peaceful, and productive workplace, characteristics that continue to the present.

My colleagues at NAU have helped me to become a better criminologist by their willingness to share their own strategies, successes, and struggles as teachers, scholars, and activists. Although I have not worked at other institutions, I have yet to hear of an academic unit that can match the inclusive, democratic practice that governs ours, and I would now hesitate to work in a unit that does not incorporate similar practices. It was this spirit of cooperation that led the faculty to write a textbook together called *Investigating Difference* under the authorship of the "Criminal Justice Collective at Northern Arizona University." The proceeds from this book have generated a substantial scholarship fund for our students and have highlighted the depth of faculty commitment to fostering diversity within the justice system. Given my remarkable colleagues, it has been a particular honor in my professional career to serve as the current departmental chair and I consider many of my own professional successes to have emerged from seeds first sown in conversation or collaboration with my colleagues.

THE HARVEST

Perhaps because of my humble farm origins, I am still in awe at the gifts that accompany life as an academic and criminologist. While some of the bounty is the result of effort and hard work, some has to do with luck and circumstance. Of course, it's hard to know when you plant the seeds which fledglings will survive, but for those considering the academic life of a critical criminologist, I want to share some of the ways that my harvest has been exceedingly bountiful and well worth the effort.

On Research

As a student, I frequently viewed the academic focus on scholarship to be elitist and largely irrelevant to social change, but over the years, I have come to believe that scholarly work *is* a powerful way to further the broad agenda of critical criminology—for inclusive, democratic, and fair justice—and that applied research can genuinely help to further justice in the local community. Much of my scholarly work has focused on the relationship between inequality and (in)justice within the United States. This has included research on difference (gender, race, and class) and justice, feminist and postmodern theory, social class and justice (especially corporate crime and regulatory law), age, inequality and justice (especially focusing on school violence), and inequality in the justice system (especially in law, courts, and prisons). While much of this work has appeared in journals and books aimed at other academics, I have also participated in valuable applied research that has served my local community. In the process, I have learned a great deal about how justice works at the ground level, and have deeply enjoyed participating in research that has informed policy and practice in our local courts, tribal courts, domestic violence prevention and outreach, and youth violence prevention efforts.

Significantly, one of the most important catalysts for my current research agenda came entirely from outside of the university context. In the mid-1990s, Fred and I decided to invite a foreign exchange student to live with us for a year. When high school student Stephanie Maus stepped off the plane from Germany and into our lives, we simply could not have imagined how much she would change our futures. By the end of the year, Stephanie had already achieved the status of a family member. And when we went to visit her in Germany the following year, and the next year moved to the Netherlands while on sabbatical, her family and ours became committed to an enduring friendship and familial relationship that suddenly made the world seem smaller, more mattering, and more essential to understand.

Since meeting Stephanie, I have spent significant time in Europe. My decision to forgo heightened material consumption for annual travel is one of the best choices of my life. Each year, I spend about a month in Europe and have spent both of my sabbaticals there, living and conducting primary research in first the Netherlands and then Spain. My current work explores the impact of globalization (and the inequalities associated with globalization) on social justice, both in the United States and in Europe, but with implications for many other countries. My work examines the disproportionate impact of globalization on women, the poor, and developing countries, with a particular focus on changed "border performances" in the developed world. Through discussions with many friends and acquaintances in Europe, attendance at international conferences, visits to agencies, and via focus groups and participant observation, I have developed a deep concern about the strategies wealthy nation states are employing to ensure the continued exploitation of the world's most needy and the continued protection of the world's most privileged groups. This inequality is generating unparalleled social harm and, thus, will likely remain a focus of my research into the foreseeable future. My work on migration, borders, and human rights began more than a decade ago, but is more relevant than ever today. I am convinced that the future work of critical criminologists must be globally informed and globally relevant if it is to have impact.

As a critical criminologist, it is important to emphasize that my work internationally was first inspired by the personal connection that I developed with a student—and family—from another country. It is a unique gift of my research focus that I now count among my closest friends citizens from many different countries and I am endlessly grateful for the insight and honesty with which they have shared their lives.

On the Profession

There is no doubt that the field of criminology remains fairly conservative and that critical criminologists continue to struggle to redefine and reshape the discipline. While at times this reality is frustrating, through international travel and through my annual pilgrimages to professional conferences I have discovered many other like-minded souls who have inspired and deepened my commitment to critical and feminist criminology.

I am at heart both a sociologist and a criminologist and have remained professionally active in both fields. As a result of good mentoring, I first attended professional conferences as a master's student, including both the American Society of Criminology (ASC) and the Society for the Study of Social Problems (SSSP). These two organizations have both been important "homes" for me professionally, and it was through these associations that I met many luminaries in the field, several important mentors, all of my co-authors, and many of my very best friends. I cannot urge such professional involvement enough.

The division structure of professional organizations provides particularly valuable spaces for networking with other critical criminologists. Within the ASC, the first division that I became involved in was the Division on Critical Criminology (DCC) which initially provided an important space for me intellectually. At the same time, I became increasingly frustrated by the relatively narrow focus on social class that permeated much critical analysis within criminology. Like many others, I found that some critical criminologists could understand some of the intellectual arguments made by feminists, but they just didn't "get it" (perhaps didn't *want* to get it) when it came to the micro-politics of gender and racial inequality. Among both mainstream and critical criminologists, I observed an ongoing failure to integrate gender and race concerns into teaching or research and a relegation of service work to women, not just in departments and within the ASC, but also in their personal lives. It was at this time that I discovered the ASC's Division on Women and Crime (DWC).

At the first DWC meeting I attended, several women spoke about sexual harassment they were experiencing within their departments. We spontaneously organized an open forum about the issue for later in the day and immediately created a safe space for women to speak about the harassment and sexism (as well as racism and homophobia) they were experiencing in their work lives. The fifty-eight or so women who attended listened to one another, cared about each other, respected the diversity of identities and challenges faced by those present, and strategized to create change. These qualities so impressed me that I became deeply committed to the DWC, serving on numerous committees and eventually serving a term as its elected chair. I also developed enduring professional relationships and friendships with other feminist criminologists who serve as continuing inspiration. While my career has probably benefited most from the professional networks I developed with the DWC, I have also been involved in and valued the work of the Division on International Criminology and the Division on People of Color and Crime, as well as the excellent progressive networks that exist within the SSSP.

I have heard some say that service to such professional organizations is undervalued and therefore devalued work, but for me (and many others) such service has been the vehicle to profoundly important intellectual and personal relationships. It was through the ASC that I first met the amazing young scholar Mona Danner, who shared my rural background, deep passion for teaching, and commitment to social change and social justice. Like me, she became involved in ASC as a student, and so we had the enormous good fortune to meet fairly early in our careers. Over the years, we have written together, researched together, taught together, organized conferences together, traveled together, and interwoven our lives together in innumerable ways. My admiration for her is immense. I am better scholar and teacher—indeed, a better person—because of meeting Mona.

In a similar manner, I met Sharon Pickering—a dynamic, firecracker of a person whose research halfway around the world in Australia bore amazing parallels to my own. Her innovation and talent at bringing critical criminological voices together internationally has profoundly influenced my own trajectory. A few years ago, Sharon invited me to be part of the Prato Collective, an international group of critical criminologists whose work focuses on transnational crime and justice, as well as human rights. The creativity that has emerged from this group has been incredible and illustrates the synergy that can emerge from international collaborative relationships.

These are just two of the many powerful relationships that have resulted from my participation in professional associations, but they provide ample evidence of the value of professional networking for fostering success as a critical criminologist. For young scholars, it is important to realize that the community of critical criminologists is literally worldwide. Early participation in professional associations heightens opportunities to develop intellectually exciting partnerships, inspiring colleagues, and lifelong friends from all over the world!

On Teaching and Activism

As a critical criminologist, I believe that teaching and scholarly work are profoundly important vehicles of activism for social justice. Indeed, my own life was fundamentally changed by charismatic and knowledgeable teachers. I believe that it is not enough for people just to know more; they need to know how to use what they know for social change. For that reason, my goal in teaching is to empower students with the tools and strategies required for critical thinking and social action. In the classroom, I foster active learning and have enthusiastically embraced a teaching style that facilitates student engagement and empowerment. For example, I created several service learning initiatives that provide students with activist skills, including projects on school violence that allow students to make direct service contributions to elementary and secondary students in our local schools, while learning media and public relations skills, organizing strategies, and facilitation skills. Passing on the empowerment model I taught them, students in one of my classes organized high school students to engage in peer education regarding school violence; along with my students, the high school students created a public education event attended by over 250 students and covered by the local media. My classes have twice received Northern Arizona University's Service Learning Award for work they have done in the local community. I am very impressed by students' willingness to use what they are learning to achieve social change, and I can honestly say that their commitment and work have provided further inspiration to my teaching.

In addition to teaching a range of classes on difference, social inequality, and justice within my department, I have also taught interdisciplinary courses on building and strengthening communities. While critical criminology has played an important role critiquing mainstream criminology, it is my belief that it is ultimately essential for critical criminologists to advocate for positive social change and harm prevention by focusing on strategies to foster elements of good and sustainable communities. This work is now more urgently needed than ever before.

While I love writing and research, I am somewhat discouraged about the disciplinary quality of scholarly writing; bizarrely, it seems that the more esoteric the language and the more narrow the targeted audience of the publication, the more valued it is. For that reason, I think it is important to seek out more diverse and wide-reaching venues for written and expressive work on social justice. In addition to scholarly outlets, my writing has turned toward songs, poetry, and theater. For example, I participated in a project with a playwright who wrote an original script based on interviews with incarcerated women who killed their abusers. As part of the project, I participated in staged readings of the script to university students, the general public, shelter workers and, significantly, to inmates in the prison where the women on whose lives the play was based are incarcerated. After the script was read out loud, one of the incarcerated women stood and said "That's my life you read. That's it exactly. I have been embarrassed by my life, but your reading gives me hope that my life was not a waste." She went on to say that the knowledge that her life story would reach a wider audience gave her hope that other abused women would not suffer a similar fate.

Theater is a powerful medium because, unlike Western academic norms, it does not exclude emotion and values from discourse about justice. In order to reach a broader audience on socially relevant and justice-related themes, I have regularly directed plays at our community theater, including a play on stalking that was viewed by 1400 people who would not likely set foot in my college classroom. I have twice directed the *Vagina Monologues* as a way to educate the general public about violence against women and gender dispar- ity, and as a significant fundraiser for our local victim advocacy agency.

As a critical criminologist, I am constantly searching for more effective ways to educate and motivate a broad public to care about social inequality and social justice. In the process, I hope to redefine the boundaries of the discipline to incorporate and value alternative mediums that bring our work and ideas to a broader public.

On Living a Full Life

To fully explain my life as critical criminologist requires that I also high- light the necessity of living life fully—well beyond the at times distorting parameters of academia. It is a critical aspect of my intellectual and profes- sional existence that I share daily life with my soul mate and best friend, Fred Solop. We have published together, played together, parented together, and protested together. It is such a gift to live with someone who is exactly the same age, has exactly the same job, and who shares absolutely equally in all household tasks, and the bittersweet joys of everyday life. We also have shared the parenting of two wonderful and life-giving children, Aaron and Brooke. Both have enriched my world beyond measure—I consider my children to be among my best friends and favorite companions and I look forward to watch- ing how their futures unfold.

Although I work hard, my daily life integrates a lot of fun and reflects a vibrant quality of life. Virtually every day, I make time for an at-home coffee- hour with my partner and an end-of-the-evening glass of wine together. Over the past decade, I have taken classes or joined groups in modern dance, the Brazilian martial art capoeira, African drumming, Spanish, and art—among others. I exercise regularly and love outdoor activities that allow me to enjoy the remarkable beauty of the Southwest—hiking, mountain biking, and river running. I know that I think more clearly when my body is working efficiently and is in tune with the natural world. I am typically involved as a director, actor, stage manager (or in some other capacity) in a production at our local theater for two to three months each year. Some evenings I pick up my guitar and play a little music. It always sounds best when the room is filled with the voices and laughter of friends and family. My point is not to minimize the important work I do as an academic, but to emphasize in this narrative the rich bounty that comes from a life well lived.

CULTIVATING A CRITICAL CRIMINOLOGIST
On the farm, much of what made each harvest rich was given to us by nature— the soil, the sun, the rain, and even the worms. Similarly, we each enter the world with capacities, limits, and promises that shape who we will become; in this regard, identity matters. But just as the gifts of nature can be enhanced by hard work, deliberate care, wise planning, and a little creativity and imagination, so too can you cultivate the skills and talents needed to succeed as a critical criminologist.

7

From Dock to Doctor

ROGER YATES

In attempting to comply with the intentions behind this collection, to offer "original writings of personal and professional interest where authors can explore issues more generally subjected to self-censorship in other formal presentations," I must interweave the relevant interests and also investigate my past activities, especially those that led to a career in the social sciences. To this end I have initiated a novel epistemological and methodological move; namely, I have *interviewed my former self.* In the established traditions of qualitative research, I found in this exercise that the vexing issues of access and rapport were catered for with relative ease, while anticipating, of course, that on the issues of validity and reliability I may well be on much less stable ground. Both professionally and as a social movement participant in the area of animal protection, especially in animal rights theory and advocacy, my chief interest is in green criminology and zemiology. From the late 1980s onwards, especially after reading the likes of C. Wright Mills, Jürgen Habermas, and Stuart Hall, and having seen them described as "bridge figures" (Seidman, 1998: 172) who simultaneously engaged in academia and in debates in the public sphere, my intention has been to try to offer some sociological knowledge and theoretical clarity to the social movement I care about.

More of that later—first, to green criminology and zemiology. Both are marginalized issues in academia, but the former has fared rather better than the latter in recent years. Zemiology—or "harmology"—was launched in

1999 at a conference in Devon, England, and featured prominent British criminologists and sociologists such as Phil Scraton, Paddy Hillyard, Joe Sim, Tony Ward, and Steve Tombs.[1] Regretfully, the zemiological project has since largely floundered. As my own small contribution to the zemiological project, I characterized my doctoral thesis, *The Social Construction of Human Beings and Other Animals in Human-Nonhuman Relations* (Yates, 2005), as a work of non-speciesist zemiology. Although zemiology has somewhat stalled, green criminology—despite Halsey's (2004) attempt to "nip it in the bud" (Beirne, 2007: 60–61)—is now an established if still emerging discipline aligned with critical criminology's—and indeed zemiology's—aspirations of looking beyond street crimes where conventional criminology tends to languish. Green criminology has brought to us the concept of "green collar criminals" (O'Hear, 2004) to add to Sutherland's (1949) white collar variety. Michael Lynch (1990, 2001, 2004, 2004), who claims to have produced the first discussion of green criminology in 1990, argues that its purview incorporates the interests of studies in eco-critical criminology (for example, Barnett, 1999; Wilson, 1999), environmental justice (see Taylor, 2000), and non-speciesism in criminology, the latter taking its intellectual lead from Piers Beirne (1994, 1995, 1997, 1999, 2007, and see Cazaux, 1999). Eco-critical criminology (ECC) may encompass a philosophical position based on the notion of the "land ethic" which defines harms, rights, and ethics in relation to environmental issues. This ethic is utilized to investigate how human behavior impacts on the "biotic community." Therefore, those behaviors judged to preserve the environment are characterised as positive, while those behaviors that damage or act to disrupt environmental equilibrium are regarded as negative. Some recent work in this field has been ethnographic investigations of environmentalism and social movement mobilization in the Republic of Ireland (Kelly, 2007; Tovey, 2007).

The environmental justice movement places emphasis on "environmental racism," for example, in studies of population proximity to hazardous waste facilities, toxic dumps, and landfills. This movement is seen as distinct from the overwhelmingly white and middle-class environmental movement that emerged in the 1960s and grew in the 1970s as part of the shift toward so-called "new social movements," and forms part of the aftermath of the New Left students' mobilizations (see Gitlin, 1987; Freeman & Johnson, 1999). The non-speciesist approach in green and critical criminology may situate nonhuman harm at the center of study, whereas many orthodox criminological cal investigations involving nonhuman animal harm unreflexively regard animals as human property and concentrate on legal concepts such as criminal damage and the theft of private property (for example, in the case of "horse maiming," or the media's preferred phrase, "horse ripping" [Yates, Powell and Beirne, 2001]). A similar critique of the property status of nonhuman animals is at the centre of the re-invigorated abolitionist animal rights perspective, the foremost exponent of which is law professor and philosopher Gary Francione (see Francione 1995, 1996, 2000, 2008).[2] Of these major concerns in green criminology, my own principal interest is the non-speciesist approach to analysis. However, along with the spirit of animal rightist, "humanitarian" and "social reformer," Henry Salt (1980), and many contemporary eco-feminist writers (for example, Mies & Shiva, 1993; Adams, 2000, 2003), I accept that justice and exploitation issues are ontologically intertwined. While my route into the initial study of criminology was unconventional, it followed that of a limited number of scholars in the sense of my "being a convicted criminal" was soon to be followed by "being a criminologist"—or at least a sociologist in which the sociology of crime featured prominently in my studies. Stating the obvious, the academy is an excessively middle-class institution, so it is rather ironic perhaps that my introduction to it was facilitated by being sent along with lots of other working-class men into the British criminal justice and prison system. Without the opportunities afforded by the education department of a semi-open prison in Lancashire, England, I would simply not be teaching and working in the higher education sector at all. However, it certainly was not plain sailing when I attempted to move from a prison education tion unit to a "proper university."

My application to the sociology department at the University of Wales, Bangor, apparently sparked a minor security alert, prompting what was described to me later as a "special meeting" to discuss whether it was felt safe that I be admitted to the North Wales campus and, in particular, whether there was a threat to any of the university's animal laboratories. Yes, I was one of those "animal rights nutters" (Mann, 2007) and—even though it was still more than a decade away from the planes crashing into the Twin Towers in New York—"animal people" were already liable to be labelled as domestic terrorists, a label presumably taken seriously by some. Certainly, by the 1980s, the Hunt Saboteurs Association, which specialized in intervening between foxes, hares, minks, and those hunting them, were being characterized by police officers as, "terrorists not connected to the IRA."

And so—my journey from convict to criminology—or, from "dock to doctor" as I expressed it recently in a blog entry,[3] begins in the 1980s. In this decade I held a number of unpaid positions within the, then, revitalized British animal protection community: the mass mobilization that—with monotonous regularity—is mistakenly identified as the modern "animal rights movement."[4] Like most social movement advocates, or "protesters" as a general term, perhaps even one of Becker's (1963) "moral entrepreneurs," I had internalized the neutralizing message that, if one discovers an important issue in society, then one writes to one's Member of Parliament politely asking for change. If especially moved, then petition signing is required or, for the totally committed who risks verging on extremism, the actual *organizing* of a parliamentary petition is warranted. Like so many others I swallowed all this unquestioningly; so much so that I found myself in the 1980s at the constituency office of my local MP, meat eater, dairy drinker, and hunt supporter, Conservative Marcus Fox who smiled dismissively at the mention of nonhuman animal rights. It was clear that he felt that a concern for nonhuman animals beyond the usual lip service granted to conventional forms of animal welfarism was indication of a gross distortion of priorities and values. However, I persisted in engaging in orthodox and "authorized" modes of protest; joining groups, organizing jumble sales, going on sponsored walks, and several other *diverting* activities.

Exactly when the penny drops, of course, is different for different people. Eventually, however, most discover that they are rather wasting their time when they are "officially" protesting. I guess it took quite a time for my coin to drop: my "poor but decent" upbringing—my father was a coal miner but also a part-time "special constable" at the rank of inspector while my mother owned and ran a general store, the always-open shop in a very small Yorkshire village—certainly did not help. No scruffy inner city estate to radicalize me. Being white in England, no racist taunts. No police would kick down our door. After all, the local inspector in the special force had his own key.[5]

A couple of "jobs" I had once I'd liberated myself from petitions and jumble sales involved reporting to media contacts on some of the more "militant" styles of campaigning on behalf of nonhuman animals. This typically included passing on to journalists the details of the physical liberation of nonhuman animals from laboratories, farms, and other places of animal enslavement. Some actions involved "supergluing" locks or damaging windows with etching fluid and some involved the most controversial activities, such as arson or the mass release of minks from fur farms. As suggested above, my short time as press contact occurred at the very beginning of the process by which virtually all animal advocates became routinely and systematically dismissed as some form of "terrorists." In my day, however, in more general terms, those who wanted to see significant change in human–nonhuman relations were much more likely to be dismissed as harmless "cranks" (perhaps significantly, the name of the most famous vegetarian restaurant of the era) and more to be pitied than anything else. The change in the way modern-day animal activists are perceived is captured in the very title as well as the content of a recent collection of essays on contemporary animal activism, *Terrorists or Freedom Fighters?* (Best & Nocella II, 2004, and see Mann, 2007). There is a distinct seachange occurring when the slogans alter from "write to your MP" to "learn to burn" and "devastate to liberate" (Mann, 2007). As a consequence of this growing militancy, I quickly became associated through media work with acts of illegality in support of the perceived interests of nonhuman others.

There were *some* stirrings of changes with regard to media coverage during this period. My time engaged in press liaison in the early 1980s coincided with a marked shift in the way the invigorated animal movement was discussed, portrayed, and characterized by the international mass media. In essence, media coverage of campaigning had, to a significant degree, moved from being largely dismissive, neutral, or sometimes positive to being largely negative in tone. Of course, peaceful campaigning had continued throughout this period of change, with national organizations in Britain such as Animal Aid and then the British Union for the Abolition of Vivisection (BUAV) going to lengths to disassociate themselves from the most militant of animal liberationists. As ever, though, exclusively peaceful activity is generally ignored by the mass media rather than dismissed *or* championed, or it is sometimes characterized as a curious manifestation of irrelevant eccentricity (Miliband, 1969: 238). Campaign organizations may spend months on a project or protest march, expending a great deal of money and energy, only to find a virtual news blackout on their concerns unless and until something "newsworthy" occurs. This helps to explain if not excuse why modern social movement mobilizations such as People for the Ethical Treatment of Animals (PETA) and Fathers for

Justice have engaged in more and more outrageous publicity stunts involving "nude" female celebrities or activists dressed as "superheroes." In fact, understanding the media's concept of "the hook," one of the principal reasons I agreed to act as spokesperson for one of the more militant groups was the very fact that *their* activities were not consistently ignored by mass media industries, thereby facilitating some chance of elaborating on the motivation for the actions undertaken. In an MA thesis, *A Sociology of Compromise* (Yates, 1998), I cited research (Barnes, et al. 1979: 544–546) which, despite being dated, provides data on the relationship between militant and nonmilitant activities and mass media coverage. A five-nation study of "unconventional political action" revealed that the circulation of petitions and legal demonstrations represented protest activities with the highest public approval scores (85 percent and 67 percent respectively). This compared to "product boycotts" at 37 percent. Categories such as "rent strikes," "occupying buildings," "blocking traffic," "unofficial strikes," "painting slogans," "personal violence," and "damaging property" each achieved approval ratings below 20 percent. These data suggest that the activities most favored by the public are least likely to be considered newsworthy by a mass media industry whose "exacting criteria" are focused on issues such as campaign or protest size, drama, and novelty. Moreover, and in line with some social movement theorizing which conceptualizes the relationship between the mass media and social movements as a problematic and (for the movements) dangerous "media dance,"[6] I had noticed how media industries had seemed to "up the ante" in terms of what they were prepared to cover, be it on TV, radio, or in the national and regional press. For example, some journalists made it absolutely clear to me that I need not bother contact them about any "mere demonstration" or for coverage of some orthodox protest activity until at least one person had been arrested or (better still) injured.[7] In other words, and in concurrence with the findings of several scholars who have studied the relationship between social movements and the mass media, campaigners had to, or were made to feel that they must, engage in increased militancy—and preferably illegal activity—to ensure publicity for their cause.[8]

Even moderate forms of illegality seemed no longer to satisfy mass media interests by the mid-1980s. For example, where once photographs and descriptions of beagle-carrying activists exiting laboratories virtually guaranteed front page news and generally favorable copy, new criteria meant that substantial acts of damage and/or acts of arson were apparently "required" to achieve widespread and sizeable coverage. It was during this escalation of militancy that I unsurprisingly found myself on the wrong side of the criminal law and involved in what many regard as the first large "animal rights show-trial" prosecuted in Britain (see Mann, 2007: 139–143). In quick succession, after being in receipt of a four-year prison sentence, I encountered the realities of time "on remand" and as a convicted prisoner in several overcrowded English Victorian "local" jails in Hull, Liverpool, and Leeds, before a final move to a "semi-open" prison to serve out the majority of my term at Her Majesty's pleasure. While "education" was something of a hit and miss affair in the former settings, it was a full-time (but relatively low paid) option in the semi-open prison. And so, surrounded by fellow prisoners, probation officers, petty bureaucrats, overworked education staff members, and prison guards of differing temper, I had my first taste of the sociology of crime. I now rather Baumanesquely inform my students—without going into any of the gory (or any) details—that sociology really does seek to explain what one perfectly well knows about already!

Of course, as soon as I was taught a little social scientific methodology, I understood that I wasn't really paying off some "debt to society" after all—but instead taking part in an elaborate qualitative research project in British jails utilizing long-term participant observation techniques. Not that I was particularly successful in terms of integrating into general prison life. Never liable to "go native," I was clearly different compared with the average "con," which is a pretty dangerous position to be in inside a prison. As a marker of this outsider status, and although they were not really supposed to, some of the prison guards treated me as a "political prisoner" on the grounds that I did not profit by what I'd done. On the other hand, since I might get hundreds of birthday and Christmas cards as a result of being on the lists put out by Support Animal Rights Prisoners, I was told by prison officials that this "continuing involvement" with the issue by which I had "got into trouble" meant I was probably damaging my parole odds. The other cons, many of whom called me "Mr. Vegan"—marking another major difference between the general prison population and myself—were, by and large, mystified by my lack of payment for my troubles. They were more than pleased, however, that I always had a drawer full of vegan biscuits on hand for them when they were searching the prison wing to satisfy "the munchies" after a cannabis "party." Surely, though, they asked as a general matter, a payment must have been involved for attending a demonstration? [9] More than one casually wondered why these naive "animal people," myself included, didn't simply kidnap a few vivisectors, tie them to trees and break their hands with baseball bats. This is a sure way, I was told, to stop them re-entering the laboratory: obvious really. This reaction from fellow prisoners echoed the earlier experience of Ronnie Lee, the founder of the Animal Liberation Front, who was sentenced to three years imprisonment in 1975 for arson attacks on establishments associated with the vivisection industry. As animal protectionist Mark Gold (1998: 174) explains, "[Lee] was treated with a degree of sympathy by prison guards and prisoners alike, though the general response was one of disbelief that anybody could have risked their freedom for the cause of animals when they could have stolen "a hundred grand" and still faced the same sentence." Ronnie Lee was later to receive a ten year sentence in the same trial I received my four year term. The severity of his sentence, which coincided with the lenient terms handed down to some of the "Vicarage Rape Case" defendants,[10] led to questions being asked in the House of Commons in London. Once I had been exposed to critical criminological texts (for example, Box, 1989), I learnt more and more about the ideological nature of such sentence disparities and system biases.

For all the lack of social integration in my own prison situation, I realized later that my experience was rather sociologically rich, and was a deal more "valid," in a limited sense, than other accounts I heard when I left prison to begin a university undergraduate course that included sociology, social policy, and criminology. For example, I remember vividly my first taste of "university criminology" in which the professor delighted in shocking his young first year audience with the dramatic declaration that "some of my best friends are 'lifers.'" I had also met a number of prisoners "doing life" in my time behind bars and most—probably all—would have scoffed at the professor's confident assertion that he had the ear of all involved in every "level" of the prison system, from government ministers, administrators, and prison governors to general staff (the eponymous "screws"), "lifers," and the general prison population. I had seen the lifer inmates' tears and heard the psychologically relieving jokes after an emotional prison visit—"the missus brought my five-year-old for a visit this time. Problem is, I've been inside for eight years." I had witnessed the anxieties before another round of "psychological profiling," and the often intense forces that appeared to pull and push these men from apparent confidence to utter despair and back again. What they would rarely do—they admitted this to me as a trusted fellow con—was say very much at all to any of their arty-farty middle-class inquisitors that would not, in their perception, go down extremely favorably with the British government's Home Office department. In other words, they would regularly try to work out exactly what official interviewers wanted of them—whoever and whatever interviewers identified themselves as, especially those who attended on "special visits" as an academic might—and then attempt to provide it. Of course, not every single statement of prisoners in such circumstances would be designed to indirectly impress politicians and probation staff, as Laurie Taylor (1984) discovered when imprisoned respondents subsequently claimed that, in previous interviews, they had deliberately exaggerated and amplified accounts of their crimes and capers to test out his gullibility. For all the confidence in my professor's assertion, then, the likely truth is that "lifers"—of all people within a prison system—would be trying to feed him exactly the answers they believed he wanted to hear.

I believe that my own experience of confinement and subsequent tuition in the sociology of crime better equipped me in terms of understanding the nature and validity of sociological findings and also helped me adopt a reflexive attitude toward my past activities. If my criminological "participant observation" had led me to many revelations about parts of the British prison system, then my general education course in sociology taught me a lot about society quite apart from the rather black-and-white campaigner's image of social life and power relations I had relied on since at least the late 1970s. During my sociological studies I suddenly realized that the social sciences had a good deal to offer—and not least to social movement participants. This raises the issue of the "bridge figures" I mentioned at the beginning of this chapter. Sociology can help to explain the public and mass media reaction to social movements' campaigning messages, the nature of societal power relations, the origins and ideological maintenance of general attitudes about issues that concern them; and social scientific knowledge assists in the understanding of why certain of their arguments and claims meet with evasion and denial.[11] During my MA and doctoral period at Bangor University, I was able to explore this notion of bridge people with fellow PhD candidate (now) Dr. Alexandra Plows. We both entertained the idea that we may act as "bridges" between the animal protection movement, the radical environmental movements such as Earth First!, and academia. Alex's interests include investigations of the radical "green" movement in general terms, but especially social movement activists' identity politics and networking practices. Together we worked on a postgraduate dissertation project (Plows & Yates, 1997) on so-called New Age Travellers, especially those whose activities were frequently subject to media coverage, often in the form of a moral panic, in the 1990s in Britain. Since Alex had been "a campaigner" before becoming "an academic" like myself, we realized that, not only did this prior experience give us privileged access in terms of research opportunities, it also placed us in the role of "translator." For example, as said, it had rapidly occurred to me that advocates of nonhuman interests often held onto a rather crude picture of the forces that drive and resist social change. On the other hand, scholarship and the theoretical understanding of collective action had been poor and certainly unsophisticated until at least the 1980s and 1990s. We began to see our roles, then, as translating *our movements* to the academy and explaining relevant social forces and processes to movement participants.

Success in this endeavor has, for me, been extremely patchy at best. For, no longer able to see the world exclusively through a black and white campaigner's lens, it is often hard not to feel alienated from many of those one once had a great affinity with. A recent study of the animal protection movement by Bob Torres (2007), who approaches the issues of human–nonhuman relations and social movement advocacy from a political scientist's and a social anarchist's position, suggests that there is a great emphasis in the animal movement to do something—anything—so long as it is "for the animals." To some extent, this attitude is a result of the sheer size of the "problem" faced by animal advocates, for example, almost 100,000 nonhumans being killed every minute just for flesh consumption in 2003.[12] In this sense, many advocates feel they simply have not the time—let alone the inclination—to get embroiled in "abstract philosophical disputes" about human–nonhuman relations. Such attitudes—along with the dominance of Peter Singer's version of animal welfarism within the animal advocacy community—has left a considerable philosophical muddle at the center of the animal protection movement with its competing philosophies based on rights theory, eco-feminism, anarchism, utilitarianism, and traditional animal welfarism. There is so much resistance to "philosophizing," yet it is the philosophy of a social movement that directs and informs its campaigning claims as it acts as a claims-making enterprise in civil society (Jasper & Nelkin, 1992). It leaves a great deal of work to do for a "bridge person" like myself.

NOTES

1. www.radstats.org.uk/no070/conference2.htm.

2. Francione provides a contrast to Tom Regan's complex subject-of-a-life criteria for the basis of nonhuman animal rights (see Regan 1983; 2001; 2004) and suggests that all sentient animals need and deserve *one* right, the right not to be another's property.

3. http://human-nonhuman.blogspot.com/2007/07/from-dock-to-doctor.html

4. Francione (1996) describes the contemporary social movement that goes under the name "animal rights" as a "new welfarist" mobilization. It may not be the most diplomatic thing to thus characterize advocates who think of themselves as radicals and "hardcore," but that does not mean it is not an accurate characterization. It certainly seems to capture the progressive welfarist position of a movement inspired in the main by the writings of utilitarian animal welfarist Peter Singer. To add complexity, however, the modern animal protection movement also includes other non-rightists, describing themselves as influenced by anarchic or ecofeminist principles, who are wary or straightforwardly opposed to the notion of "bourgeois" or "male-minded" individual rights. Lawyer Lee Hall (2006) describes the sort of activists I used to represent as "animal-welfare militants."

5. During the 1980s, I was arrested on various demonstrations on a few occasions, and it wasn't until her son's contact with the police in this way that prompted my mother to "remember"' that my father had a special pair of brown leather gloves which he used when beating suspects at his police station, presumably a little time before the signing of the voluntary confession. My mother had previously—and wholly unproblematically—filed this information away, content that only "the wrong sort" and those who "deserved it" had been at the receiving end of my father's justice punches.

6. Rochon (1990) reports that it is common to find media coverage of "protest" focusing almost exclusively on issues of militancy and lawbreaking but with little or no articulation of the substantive or philosophical issues involved.

7. This explains why one of my busiest times with the press was during the staging of the notorious Waterloo Cup hare coursing event in Altcar, near Liverpool in 1984. Thirty-four-year-old Eddie Coulston, on his first outing as a hunt saboteur,

was attacked with a metal shooting stick by hare coursing supporter Paul Willingale and suffered a fractured skull requiring brain surgery. He was left afflicted with subsequent epileptic fits while Willingale was sentenced to six months in prison. On the same day, a fight among hare coursers left one of their number dead. Initial press reports speculated that a "sab" had been murdered. Details in Mann (2007: 231); and see his chapter entitled "The Sheffield Trial" (Mann, 2007: 139–143) for a fuller account of my trial.

8. Before the advent of the Internet, social movements were rather reliant on mass media coverage in terms of much of their public outreach opportunities. Most contemporary social movements, and indeed individual campaigners, have sophisticated websites featuring documents and video clips. However, although this provides them with an alternative to the formal media, it remains the case that the "mass" in mass media tempts contact with national and international media outlets.

9. In a similar way, when I first attended hunt "sabs" (the sabotage of foxhunts) in 1979, hunt supporters were convinced that the saboteurs were paid and organized by sinister forces. We played along with this, telling them that we received an envelope every Thursday complete with cash and a map of where the hunts will be on the following Saturdays. We told them that we had no idea who sent the money but had noticed that all the "Rs" were typed the wrong way round.

10. http://www.telegraph.co.uk/news/main.jhtml?hml=/news/2006/03/08/ nsaward08.xml&sSheet=/news/2006/03/08/ixhome.html

11. Cohen (2001) provides an excellent review of knowledge denial and techniques of neutralization, including his own "total denial" of animal issues.

12. According to Regan & Rowe (2003), this is a conservative estimate: "Forty-eight billion farm animals are killed each year around the world—nearly eight times the human population, more than 130 million a day, more than five million every hour, almost 100,000 a minute. These numbers do not include the billions of other animals whose lives are taken, bodies injured, and freedom stolen in the name of entertainment, sport or fashion."

BIBLIOGRAPHY

Adams, J. C. (2000). *The Sexual Politics of Meat: A Feminist-Vegetarian Critical Theory.* 10th anniversary ed. New York: Continuum.

Adams, J. C. (2004). *The Pornography of Meat.* New York: Continuum.

Barnes, S., M. Kaase, et al. (1979). *Political Action: Mass Participation in Five Western Democracies.* Beverley Hills: Sage.

Barnett, H. (1999). The land ethic and environmental criminology. *Criminal Justice Policy Review,* 10(2): 161–192.

Becker, H. (1963). *Outsiders: Studies in the Sociology of Deviance.* New York: Free Press.

Beirne, P. (1994). The law is an ass: Reading E.P. Evans' *The Medieval Prosecution and Capital Punishment of Animals. Society and Animals,* 2(1): 27–46.

Beirne, P. (1995). The use and abuse of animals in criminology: A brief history and current review. *Social Justice,* 22(1): 5–31.

Beirne, P. (1997). Rethinking bestiality: Towards a concept of interspecies sexual assault. *Theoretical Criminology,* 1(3): 317–40.

Beirne, P. (1999). For a non-speciesist criminology: Animal abuse as an object of study. *Criminology,* 37(1): 117–47.

Beirne, P. (2007). Animal rights, animal abuse and green criminology, in *Issues in Green Criminology: Confronting Harms Against Environments, Humanity and Other Animals.* ed. P. Beirne and N. South, 55–83. Cullompton: Willan.

Best, S., and A. J. Nocella II, eds. (2004). *Terrorists or Freedom Fighters: Reflections on the Liberation of Animals.* New York: Lantern.

Box, S. (1989). *Power, Crime and Mystification.* London: Routledge, 1989.

Cazaux, G. (1999). Beauty and the beast: Animal abuse from a non-speciesist criminological perspective. *Crime, Law & Social Change,* 31(2): 105–25.

Cohen, S. (2001). *States of Denial: Knowing About Atrocities and Suffering.* Cambridge: Polity.

Francione, L. G. (1995). *Animals, Property, and the Law.* Philadelphia: Temple University Press.

Francione, L. G. (1996). *Rain Without Thunder: The Ideology of the Animal Rights Movement.* Philadelphia: Temple University Press.

Francione, L. G. (2000). *Introduction to Animal Rights: Your Child or the Dog.* Philadelphia: Temple University Press.

Francione, L. G. (2008). *Animals As Persons: Essays on the Abolition of Animal Exploitation.* New York: Columbia University Press.

Freeman, J., and V. Johnson, eds. (1999). *Waves of Protest: Social Movements Since the Sixties*. Oxford: Rowman & Littlefield.

Gitlin, T. (1987). *The Sixties: Years of Hope, Days of Rage*. London: Bantam.

Gold, M. (1998). *Animal Century: A Celebration of Changing Attitudes to Animals*. Charlbury: Carpenter.

Hall, L. (2006). *Capers in the Graveyard: Animal Rights in the Age of Terror*. Darien, Conn: Nectar Bat Press.

Halsey, M. (2004). Against "green" criminology. *British Journal of Criminology*, 44(6): 833–853.

Jasper, M. J., and D. Nelkin. (1992). *The Animal Rights Crusade: The Growth of a Moral Protest*. New York: Free Press.

Kelly, M. (2007). *Environmental Debates and the Public in Ireland*. Dublin: Institute of Public Administration.

Lynch, J. M. (1990). The greening of criminology: A perspective on the 1990s. *The Critical Criminologist*, 2(3): 1–12.

Lynch, J. M. (2003). The meaning of green: Towards a green criminology. *Theoretical Criminology*, 7: 217–238.

Lynch J. M., D. McGurrin, and M. Fenwick. (2004). Disappearing act: The representation of corporate crime research in criminology journals and textbooks. *Journal of Criminal Justice*, 32(5): 389–398.

Lynch, J. M., and P. B. Stretesky. (2001). Toxic crimes: Examining corporate victimization of the general public employing medical and epidemiological evidence. *Critical Criminology*, 10(3): 153–172.

Mann, K. (2007). *From Dusk 'til Dawn: An Insider's View of the Growth of the Animal Liberation Movement*. London: Puppy Pincher Press.

Mies, M., and V. Shiva. (1993). *Ecofeminism*. London: Zed.

Miliband, R. (1969). *The State in Modern Society*. London: Weidenfeld & Nicolson.

O'Hear, M. M. (2004). Sentencing the green collar offender: Punishment, culpability and environmental crime. *The Journal of Criminal Law and Criminology*, 95(1): 133–276.

Plows, A., and R. Yates. (1997). *Break the Rules: Breaking the Stereotype of the "New Age Traveller,"* unpublished MA research project. Department of Sociology, University of Wales, Bangor.

Regan, T. (1983). *The Case for Animal Rights.* Berkeley: University of California Press.

Regan, T. (2001). *Defending Animal Rights.* Urbana and Chicago: University of Illinois Press.

Regan, T. (2004). *Empty Cages: Facing the Challenge of Animal Rights.* Oxford: Rowman & Littlefield.

Regan, T., and M. Rowe. (2003). What the Nobel Committee Also Failed to Notice. *International Herald Tribune* (Dec).

Rochon, T. (1990). The West European peace movement and the theory of New Social Movements. In *Challenging the Political Order: New Social and Political Movements in Western Democracies.* ed. R. J. Dalton and M. Kuechler. Cambridge: Polity.

Salt, H. (1980) [1922]. *Animals' Rights: Considered in Relation to Social Progress.* Fontwell, Sussex: The Centaur Press.

Seidman, S. (1998). *Contested Knowledge: Social Theory in the Postmodern Era.* (2nd ed.) Oxford: Blackwell.

Sutherland, H. E. (1949). *White Collar Crime.* New York: Dryden.

Taylor, E. D. (2000). The Rise of the environmental justice paradigm. *American Behavioral Scientist,* 43(4): 508–580.

Taylor, L. (1984). *In The Underworld.* London: Unwin.

Torres, B. (2007). *Making A Killing: The Political Economy of Animal Rights.* Edinburgh: AK Press.

Tovey, H. (2007). *Environmentalism in Ireland: Movement and Activists.* Dublin: Institute of Public Administration.

Wilson, K. N. (1999). Eco-critical criminology: An introduction. *Criminal Justice Policy Review,* 10(2): 155–160.

Yates, R. (1998). *A Sociology of Compromise: Social Movement Theory and the British Animal Protection Movement,* unpublished MA dissertation, School of Social Sciences, University of Wales, Bangor.

Yates, R. (2005). *The Social Construction of Human Beings and Other Animals in Human–Nonhuman Relations. Welfarism and Rights: A Contemporary Sociological Analysis,* Unpublished PhD thesis, Department of Sociology, University of Wales.

Yates, R., C. Powell, and P. Beirne. (2001). Horse maiming in the English countryside: Moral panic, human deviance, and the social construction of victimhood. *Society & Animals,* 9(1): 1–24.

8

Goody Two Shoes Meets the Bad Girls

RUTH WATERHOUSE

"Ungetatable, oddly cruel other people"

(Rhys, J., 1982)

My interest in norms and rules probably began with the experience of discovering I was left handed and that this placed me in a minority position; also that my family were "Non-Conformists"[1] though they seemed very correct and law abiding to me. I moved location a lot as a child and knew that how I spoke initially identified me as different from my new school mates. I quickly became very good at acquiring the local accent only to move on somewhere new and have to learn a new way of speaking. I was also an overweight child which was statistically less normal in those far from affluent days. Rationing had only just been abolished and most girls seemed to have Olive Oil legs but not me.

On the surface I was a very conforming child, polite, shy, and wanting to please authorities although I did have an eye quite early for social absurdities. It is hard to take social ceremonies seriously when you see your father cutting up the white, processed sliced loaf for communion bread; when during moments of silent, congregational prayer, The minister, who is also your Dad, catches your eye (which should have been firmly closed), winks and lets his false teeth slip on purpose to create a mischievous grimace. I was a great giggler and I think this was partly because quite early on I saw through the rules but also feared social ostracism for breaking them. Giggling was partly about irreverence but also a release of pent up social anxiety. A quiet child, I would hang back in so-cial situations and observe how others behaved. I somehow sensed that I wasn't quite a part of their world.

I was some kind of outsider but there again perhaps all children feel this since we are to some extent cultural outsiders during this period of our lives. There was a strong desire on my behalf to fit in but I remember feeling uncertain about the rules wherever we went. We never had the luxury of being local. In South West Wales, during the early 1960s, we were assured that one could live there for thirty years and never be fully accepted. This led to a kind of juvenile paranoia on my behalf. *They* were watching you. This was compounded by the fact that as minister's children we were "bearers of the community." A similar point has been recently made by the British Prime Minister Gordon Brown about his own childhood as a son of the manse. He notes how his every action was potentially perused by judgmental parishioners. In similar vein the behavior of myself and older brother was scrutinized. Small failings, Durkheim-like (Durkheim, 1964), were elevated to major misdemeanors by the congregation. I was not then the "only gay in the village"[2] but I shared with my best friend the dubious privilege of being the child of parents with a position of some moral authority in the community; mine the minister and hers the police officer. Not surprisingly we became friends, bearers of the moral culture; we subverted and avoided its burden whenever we could. It may be significant that my friend challenged the racism which permeated marriage in those days, marrying a man from Pakistan and converting to Islam whilst I rejected marriage and motherhood (though not children) and after over a decade of not unhappy heterosexual cohabitation chose lesbianism.

In my teenage years I eventually became more aware of the rules than each local community itself because I could never quite take them for granted. The paranoia went both ways. I watched them watching me. I had an early awareness then of the slippery, tangential feel to all social rules. They seemed powerful but fragile, slipping and sliding from my grasp. Rules and the practices arising from them seemed to be characterized by feelings of ambivalence and contradiction. As someone with a marginal status in whichever village or town we found ourselves in I came to regard rules and their observance with both curiosity and skepticism. This is not to explain my life and the directions I subsequently took by reference to a simplistic reaction to the norms, but that my position at the periphery of each new neighborhood led me to question rules rather than to accept them with deference. This questioning was almost invariably a theoretical rather than an empirical one as I was also searching for approval and inclusion. In early adulthood whilst researching the representation of female deviance in literature I came across the work of the author Jean Rhys (b.1890–d.1979). Her heroines scrutinize and are in turn scrutinized. In the following extract she captures exactly the timorous arrogance of the social outsider:

> I should like to laugh at her, but l am a well-behaved little girl. . . Too well behaved. . . I long to be like Other People! The extraordinary, ungetatable, oddly cruel Other People, with their way of wantonly hurting and then accusing you of being thin-skinned, sulky, vindictive or ridiculous. All because a hurt and puzzled little girl has retired into her shell." (Rhys, 1982, 25–26)

I too retreated inside myself when required to be part of the minister's public family. I was wary of being "out of step" in the social world of the chapel. Essentially liberal parents, my mother and father instilled in us a public politeness which was, however, relaxed in private. My father adhered to the very rule-bound nature of Methodism but always with an ironic twinkle in his eye. One of his hobbies was reading crime fiction and he delighted in a plot strewn with bodies. The more lawbreaking that took place, the better. Another pastime of his was pipe smoking and we were exhorted to clear the air by flapping newspapers whenever a member of the congregation appeared unexpectedly at the door. I quickly learnt that some division between the public and the private rules was a survival strategy and a more complex social device than simple hypocrisy. I note with some interest that Gordon Brown's father was not quite so relaxed although similar moral compromises were made:

> His father was the school chaplain and his Presbyterian writ ran at home as well as school, so Gordon and his brothers had to sneak out of the manse to buy the Sunday newspapers. Their father did not approve of shopping on the Sabbath, even though he read the newspapers himself on Wednesdays, when the guilt had faded. (The Daily Telegraph 2007)

I know from firsthand experience what impact such transgressions would have on Durkheim's Society of Saints. I was once spied upon as I came out of the sweetshop on a Sunday and could feel the disapproving whispers as I entered the chapel a few minutes later. My mother was a little concerned that I had let down the family side in public but not essentially exercised about the impact on my moral welfare. She was the epitome of the unpaid minister's wife dedicated to unsung public service but she also held down a paid job as a librarian. She quietly deflected public disapproval as she steadfastly issued library books and fixed fines for late returns. She was a working wife and mother which was relatively unusual in those days.

She welcomed people into the manse but she tried to ensure that as children we had ownership over a domestic space which was irredeemably tied to the chapel and the culture it represented. Our accommodation was tithed but our television viewing and comic reading went unpoliced.

We were never required to say our prayers before meal times although we were sometimes caught out by a religious guest who insisted on doing so. On such occasions we politely followed suit but privately thought the guest barmy and overzealous. A "right old holy Joe" was my Dad's pejorative judgment. I was strongly aware that the rules governing our behavior changed as we negotiated the difficult terrain between the public and the private worlds. Indeed since the Manse was both our home and a place of work the distinction between these spheres resembled a hair's breadth or perhaps more accurately a tightrope. As my school years came to a close I became increasingly fascinated by the stuff that binds societies and communities together and also what divides them. My chosen studies of history, English literature, and art enabled me to see that there were many ways to interpret the world and prepared me for the demands of the "sociological imagination" (Mills 1959, 1976) required by my undergraduate studies. Further my somewhat itinerant childhood had enabled me to see that whilst there were some absolute values such as "justice" and "fairness" there were also "different strokes for different folks." I was also becoming increasingly aware through news media coverage of the war in Vietnam and the civil rights movement in America that the apparent absolutes were disregarded if they got in the way of vested interests. But the USA was not the only liberal democracy intent on scuppering its own values. This was reinforced for me by the emergent "Troubles" in Northern Ireland. I watched the events in Derry and Belfast intensify during the summer of 1969 whilst on a holiday exchange visit to Holland. Watching the Dutch TV coverage of the conflict through the eyes of a liberal Catholic family

I had my first experience of seeing a political landscape without the distorted ideologies of the British Government.

ABSOLUTELY FABULOUS

Like many young women of my generation I benefited from a state grammar school single sex education. I was comfortable with the academic calendar with its ecclesiastical trimester rhythms. When I came to leave there was a kind of inevitability about going to what was then called a teacher training establishment. I had a love of literature and I thought I might be able to pass this on to other young people. I had not anticipated that the classrooms would be overfull, the children needy but not specifically for education, and my ability to respond to their wit, dependence, and defiance, nonexistent. Besides by then, amidst rumblings of social discord in higher education, I had met my first partner. Remote on our West Yorkshire campus in the hills we nevertheless picked up on the climate of dissent ("the crisis of authority") which was sweeping across the colleges and universities. We soon realized that this was an international movement of protest and subversion. The ability to protest an ironic outcome of our privileged position as postwar baby boomers, still heady on the healthy effects of state-subsidized orange juice and milk.

We were the future but we didn't want the future envisaged for us by the older generation. Students became trespassers in their own institutions; sitting in, occupying, and rifling through confidential files. We were minor thorns in the side of the academic flesh. This was exciting stuff. We gravitated toward the Young Socialists and attended folk evenings to sing about the world being turned upside down. We played hard at being political nonconformists but in reality we took very few risks. The attraction was the fantasy of being avant-garde and daring. Reading Gerard Manley Hopkins gave way to reading Engels, Marx, and Tressell's *Ragged Trousered Philanthropists* (2004). We encountered the discipline of sociology and found it asked the "right questions" whilst resisting dogmatic conclusions. We quickly abandoned teacher training for a more uncertain future with this fashionable, renegade subject. It offered a way of understanding some of the contradictions which seemed to surround being young and relatively privileged against the backdrop of social inequalities, nuclear proliferation, and the Vietnam War.

After just one term of sociological theory I abandoned the last remnants of my Christian beliefs in favor of Durkheim's functionalist analysis of the role of religion (1965). Religion was not it seemed about God. It was about social binds. It formed part of the glue of social cohesion. Morality and social norms were profane, not sacred.

Then there was Durkheim's revelation that through rule-breaking and the associated coming together of upright consciousnesses the moral boundaries were re-affirmed, strengthened, or transformed. An action gave rise to social outrage not because it was a crime but it became a crime because it created social outrage. It was the social reaction and the function of crime which mattered. In the hope that our deviancy represented a bid for social transformation we proceeded to join the street demonstrations. The carnivalesque had always attracted me and the street protests were akin to collective revelry and communal dance: a bit like a Whit Walk[3] but rougher, ruder, and more transgressive. It was a way of temporarily being included and the outsider in me was seduced into a fleeting feeling of inclusiveness. But this feeling of belonging quickly evaporated. I seemed to suffer from a kind of dyslexia of the rule book. I found it difficult to follow recipes of any kind.

Written technological manuals defeated me and I had a horror of car driving; an essentially rule-bound skill which provided a major status passage into the adult middle-class world. These failures intensified my fascination with the rule-governed nature of social life, especially the powerful and disquieting nature of the rule. Society was intrinsically rule governed but there was nothing intrinsic about any particular set of rules. I quickly saw that the rules were a social fabrication and could be changed by collective human action and will. I believed that moral absolutes were literally fabulous.

However, I wasn't a very convincing student rebel. I studied too hard and drank too little alcohol. I didn't touch hallucinogenic drugs at all and I had settled into a lasting and mutually supportive heterosexual relationship. The protestant ethic was deeply ingrained and despite my attraction to the nineteenth century writings of Kropotkin and Thoreau, I possessed a strong streak of moral conservatism. I was part of the radical youth movement but I was an alien within the student body. I was plagued by ill-defined guilt over minor misdemeanors and bemused by my colleagues' excesses. Rules were there to be broken but in their breaking I anticipated unknown social calamities. Rules may be insubstantial but the societal consequences for their infraction were only too real. I held back and immersed myself in my discipline. Sociology seemed to offer me a way of understanding the rule-governed nature of human life and society.

I began to identify with the ironies uncovered by writers such as Durkheim and later with social interactionists such as Becker (1964) and Scheff (1966). I had always found it difficult to grasp the complexities of social structure but I was drawn by the idea that society, including crime and deviance, arises out of a complex transaction between self and others. The social origins of the self, its transient nature and its vulnerability to social stigmatization made sense to me. From Durkheim I took the insight that deviance was not necessarily a social ill and conformity itself was a sociological problem in need of an explanation. From the interactionists I learnt that deviance is created by people as they negotiate their lives within a context of conflict. Sometime during my first year as an undergraduate we went to see a production of Arthur Miller's play *The Crucible*.[4] Performed inside a church in the Buckinghamshire town of High Wycombe its messages about the scapegoating power of communities came sharply home to me.

The condemnatory gaze of the zealous and the compulsion to denigrate the vulnerable out of a need for self-preservation reminded me of every small town I had ever lived in. Durkheim's recognition that deviance from the rules serves a boundary maintenance function began to make firm sense. I began to realize that the victims in social degradation ceremonies might be those accused of transgression rather than those offended against. I began to side with the outsider and found renewed sociological support for this position in the work of Becker (1964) and Erikson (1966). I began to center my thoughts on how people become outcasts in their own social worlds. The work of the interactionists fascinated me. Goffman's work on stigma showed me how people's identities can be spoiled by negative societal reactions (1968). Becker showed me how insiders create a safe space for themselves out of the social creation of outsiders. I looked with dismay at the criminal justice system which had the power to stigmatize and tag those who were already marginal in society. In humanizing the deviants I colluded with a process of dehumanizing conformers, especially those with authority. Becker's work gave me a way of understanding my own sense of not belonging.

It also served as a means of identifying romantically with the outsider. Becker exhorted us to take sides and declare whose side we were on. I had no doubts. I was on the side of the socially reviled, the misunderstood, the inept, and the cast aside. As a student of English literature I had always identified with those who were somehow "beyond the pale"; with Thomas Hardy's Tess and Jude; with Shakespeare's Shylock and Richard the Second. Even in child-hood I had been at one with Heidi as she suffered in the town, homesick for her alpine loft in the mountains. I empathized with those who were "out of place" just as I increasingly empathized with those who were "out of mind." For having no roots I was always "out of place" and beset by a thousand anxi-eties I sometimes felt "out of mind."

Ironically, Becker's work was not so far removed from the liberal phi-losophy of the particular branch of Methodism I grew up in. Here there was sympathy if not an empathy for the underdog. The manse was frequently visited by various itinerants some of whom were, in the parlance of the time, "old lags."[5] Methodism has a history of Home Missions and a concern for the "downtrodden" exemplified in the radicalism of people like Dr. Donald Soper (b. 1903–d.1998; Methodist minister, socialist, and pacifist). My father had been reared in the poverty of Ancoats, Manchester and was attracted by this social radicalism. In Methodism my mother found support for her pacifism and concern for animal welfare. Amongst some of the primitive Methodists[6] there was a refusal to collude with militarism. My first demonstration had been alongside two elderly parishioners who had been amongst the first to attend the Aldermaston marches (Campaign for Nuclear Disarmament). The Methodists seemed to stress the distinction between the sin (deviance) and the sinner (deviants). We should forebear from criticism because we are all sinners (deviants) now. We should therefore desist from throwing stones.

This was exactly what Becker seemed to be about: stone casting and the problems therein. We cannot condemn because given similar social circum-stances we may act in the same way. Who can tell?

Becker, however, came from a position of relativism and advocated an ap-preciative stance. This did not sit so easily with most branches of Christianity or indeed the other monotheistic religions. Even within the relatively liberal ethos of Methodism there were absolutes and sins were to be corrected not appreciated as cultural difference. There was a strong and rather rigid moral code especially where alcohol and gambling were concerned. Those that had social advantages but nevertheless crossed over the moral boundaries were subject to the most disapproval. They should know better. It was only the powerless (and grateful) who were worthy of pity and support. There was a social condescension here which undermined some of Methodism's radical potential.

Yet, given this background, Becker's message was sufficiently familiar for me to identify with his essential insight: that deviance is created via a complicated process of interaction between society and the labeled outsider; that those on the margins of society are more sinned against than sinning. This became increasingly clear to me when I embarked upon a postgraduate program in criminology at the University of Hull. As part of our studies we were required to visit various institutions within the criminal justice system. This included what were once known as Borstals (for young male offenders) and Hull Prison itself, then a maximum security facility. My memory of those visits is chiefly a visual one of a relentless and dismal gray; the grayness of casual brutality and hopelessness. I was particularly struck by the bleakness of the hospital wing and tried to imagine myself there, sick and powerless. This experience confirmed my belief in the futility of imprisonment and the need for abolition. A belief that was to have a personal significance many years later when a close friend was sentenced to a prison term for drunk driving. One of the first things I did was to send him a card of strong red hues to combat the gray.

Significantly it scarcely entered my head to consider the lives of the victims of those who had been incarcerated. Their experiences were not high on either the sociological or criminological agenda of the 1970s and 1980s. My concerns were for prisoners and the "pains of imprisonment" suffered both by them and their families. I did not think of the lives of the prison staff or about the long-term consequences of being burgled or subjected to assault.

AFTER ALL THESE YEARS—STILL CRAZY?

Looking back this omission may be partly explained by the fact that up until my mid-twenties I was insulated from any direct experience of criminal rule breaking by my middle-class privileges. However this could not protect me from an acquaintanceship with "mental illness." There was for example, "poor Jim," my 1950s childhood friend's father. Periodically he disappeared inside the institution on the hill which was spoken about only in hushed tones like cancer. He took his own life not long after suicide had become decriminalized in 1961. There was my own grandfather, shell-shocked from the First World War, who still shook whenever the sound of gunfire came from some TV Western. There were also the numerous parishioners who seemed to hover on either side of the mysterious divide between sanity and insanity. I sometimes wondered whether religion was the catalyst to their mental disturbance or a genuine source of spiritual solace. Whichever, the chapel seemed to provide some kind of sanctuary to those personalities who seemed extraordinarily diseased by the world.

During my time at Hull I happened to see Ken Loach's film *Family Life* featuring Sandy Ratcliffe as the family scapegoat.[7] Her distress is interpreted as a sign of "mental illness" and she is pathologized and medicalized. She is a tragic Laingian figure whose deviancy is interpreted as disease. I quickly became a convert to the radical interpretation of "madness" and "schizophrenia" as "breakthrough" rather than "breakdown"; as social deviancy rather than sickness (Laing, 1959, 1965, 1967, 1970; Szasz, 1960; Scheff, 1966).

I also came to see that there was a gender issue here. That the deviancy of girls and women was subjected to invalidation though medical labeling to a greater extent than that of men and boys. Laing's work provoked in me a deep desire to formulate an understanding of the complex meanings surrounding "mental illness" and to consider it as a reaction to the craziness of family life and wider society. It also provided me with a whole new category of social victims who could be empathized with and promoted beyond criticism. It became clear to me that not only was the criminal justice system a major source of oppression but so too was modern psychiatry. Whichever way you looked deviants were subjected to repressive state and community practices. This unquestioning empathy with the rule breaker was, however, somewhat strained by becoming a victim myself. The first time at the hands of a reckless driver and the second as the recipient of a sexual assault (neither seen, in effect, as serious offenses in the late 1970s). I dealt with this by subduing my emotions and regarding the two offenses as the result of the offenders' "hard luck stories." Sociology had primed me to regard the transgressors as "victims of social circumstance" whilst my religious education had encouraged me to see "there but for the Grace of God. . . ." I did not seek any retribution. I merely came to the view that victims like their assailants were well and truly stuffed.

I was by now teaching degree level sociology at a polytechnic (later to become a New University). I had responsibility for a new module in "Contemporary Social Problems" which quickly transformed into "The Sociology of Crime and Deviance." It drew a lot of students as such courses often do. Many such students had been radicalized by the same political movements as myself and were familiar with the various civil rights movements. Some had been members of the Mental Patients Union; some were part of the "Troops out Movement" (with reference to the "Troubles" in Northern Ireland) or the Anti-Nazi League. Several were linked to left-wing organizations such as The Socialist Worker's Party or Worker's Revolutionary Party. A growing number like myself were being drawn into sexual liberation movements as feminists and/or advocates for gay and lesbian rights. The teaching staff mirrored these political affiliations and a culture of critical thinking was encouraged. This is not to claim that everyone embraced radical political positions but teaching took place in a climate where the social norms and institutions were subjected to intense scrutiny. Conformity was a sociopolitical problem awaiting explanation. One of the contemporary political badges captured this dissenting mood by asking "What causes heterosexuality?" Prisons were regarded as dinosaurs incapable of dealing with the problems created by an unequal society. Most students were reluctant to advocate retributionist measures and were fired by creative alternatives to imprisonment.

GOODY TWO SHOES MEETS THE BAD GIRLS

This was felt most strongly when we considered female offenders. Following on from the work of Heidensohn (1985, 1989, 2000) we explored how mainstream criminology and sociology had largely ignored female offenders or had misrepresented their rule breaking through sexist ideologies. Our explorations led us to see how women's deviancy was sexualized and how women were criminalized for their poverty in a patriarchal society which denied them full citizenship. It was not difficult to empathize with the plight of most of these offenders.

We could understand why TV licenses might not get paid; why women might sell sex; why fraudulent benefit claims might be made and how shoplifting might be an innovatory way to become a proficient consumer. Some of us had done one or more of these things.

We explored how women were seen as the victims not of circumstance but of hormones; how they were denied agency; how women who seriously offended against the moral codes were "doubly deviant; doubly damned" (Lloyd, 1995). Then it became clear that many of the "bad girls" had been subjected to sexual and or physical victimization.[8] Further, that within patriarchal relationships "good girls" were also recipients of the "continuum of sexual violence" (Radford, Friedberg, & Harne, 2000) Indeed the distinction between "good" and "bad" girls was an illusion; an ideological device which divided women from each other.

In my role as personal tutor I found that when I wasn't teaching I was often asked to listen to the personal troubles of female students. These problems included rape, sexual assault, and harassment; childhood experiences of abuse, domestic violence, and forced marriage. My lectures emphasized that these private troubles were actually social harms (Howe, 1991) generated by patriarchal societies on an international scale. Male violence was not so much about the "hard luck stories" of the perpetrator as the oppression of women and girls. These crimes were an abuse and expression of power. I began to find that my long-held commitment to the values of relativism and the "appreciative stance" began to waver. As my feminism became more radical I moved toward an uneasy absolutism; male violence was unequivocally wrong.

It was the 1990s and as religious fundamentalism flourished so too did my political fundamentalism. All men benefited from violence against women; indeed all men were capable of this violence. There was nothing pathological about this violence. It was a normal feature of life within a patriarchal society. As such the problem did not lie with individual men thus an individual system of justice was redundant. I had always been critical of individualized justice. Despite this there was now a strong part of me that looked to this very system to ensure that male violence was subject to public censure and condemnation. I wanted the criminal justice system to secure justice for women and girls. That this system operated according to masculinist ideologies and practices was something we needed to oppose and challenge.

During this period I trained as a volunteer rape crisis counselor. This role necessitated that I took sides with the victim. My counseling training required that my empathy lay only with the client/ co-worker. Her story deserved and demanded an unquestioning acceptance. This was a social, political, and moral position. We took her side in order to facilitate the movement from victim to survivor to "thriver." I did not find this difficult. It was good to be able to take the high moral ground unequivocally for once. I was no longer dithering around with moral uncertainties, sitting on the liberal or radical edge.

I no longer sought to empathize with the perpetrator. I wanted him to be subjected to the formal moral indignation of the courts. Yet I also knew that the problem would not be resolved by individualistic solutions.

Retributionist principles intensified during this period and impacted on the criminal justice system. Though subject to fluctuations British rates of imprisonment outstripped and continued to outstrip most European counterparts.[9, 10] I found myself in a difficult position. I strongly believed that prison didn't work and that custodial punishment was inhumane.

Retribution was morally and politically bankrupt and reformation an unlikely outcome of incarceration. Yet from the early 1990s the students I taught increasingly expressed a desire to see offenders locked up or worse. It became increasingly difficult to represent offenders as people too. Demonization intensified alongside a call for ever tougher penal policies. As the victim took a more central position in the drama of crime and deviance the desire to pillory the offender grew deeper. Yet it remained clear to me that only certain victims were being heard. For instance whilst reportage of rape increased, conviction rates dropped.[11] Victims of state crime and crimes of the powerful still struggled, in the main, to gain public recognition of the harms done to them (for example. the survivors of the Bhopal disaster).

In my discussions with students I tried to make it clear that in criticizing the criminal justice system for failing to address the needs of many victims/ survivors I was not motivated by retributionism. This was not an easy position to take. As we approached the new millennium popular punitiveness was intensified alongside an increase in the fear of crime and terrorism. It was inevitable that attitudes toward crime and deviance hardened. Yet this process was not unequivocal. Perceptions of who the outsiders were shifted and changed. For example gays and lesbians experienced a cultural sea change as civil partnerships became a reality under the Civil Partnership Act of 2004 (with effect from 12/05/05).

Outsiders became increasingly associated with the renewed threat of terrorism which now seemed less involved with homegrown "Troubles" and more to do with international "fundamentalist movements." "Refugees" and "asylum seekers" took on the time honored role of "folk devils" alongside the "hoodies" and the "pedophiles." Sometimes these groups were conflated by claims that illegal immigrants had criminal records for child abuse. They served as double whammy "folk devils." Concerns about "civil liberties" were subdued in the face of increased surveillance, extension of police powers, and state crimes such as "extraordinary rendition." Although crime and deviance had always been political issues students were often less interested in what the state agencies were doing and more concerned about the incivilities they encountered in every day life. They simply wanted these incivilities to cease (a return to "correctionism") and for the perpetrators to pay for them. I too wanted them to cease but I also believed that those engaged in "antisocial" behavior had already paid the price of social exclusion.

The rise of a psychological worldview increased resistance to sociological explanations. It was frequently claimed that social problems could be reduced to individual proclivities. "It's all down to the individual isn't it?" Furthermore feminist approaches to male violence were countered by references to "women use violence too" thereby disinvesting feminism of some of its explanatory power. Indeed my work with survivors did reveal that women and girls could not always claim the high moral ground. Women did abuse their children, girls did engage in bullying, and domestic violence was not restricted to heterosexual partnerships.

That feminist research (Smart, 1990) had striven to register this too did not necessarily convince students of its theoretical integrity. In a rapidly privatizing society it was difficult to challenge the idea that private troubles were essentially social in origin. Five years into the twenty-first century, after nearly thirty years of teaching crime and deviance I felt I was losing my way. I simply did not know whose side to be on anymore. I knew I was against any fundamentalist interpretations of the world, secular or religious. Indeed I was once again fundamentally against fundamentalism. My belief that imprisonment was principally about the criminalization of the poor and not a solution remained unshaken. But I did want certain offenders removed from circulation and was genuinely perplexed by what should happen to them thereon. I continued to empathize with Jean Rhys' view that "humanity is never content just to differ from you and let it go at that" (1982, p. 25) but I no longer regarded those who upheld the status quo as simply or irredeemably "*oddly cruel Other People.*" I began to look back to where I had started out in my twenties. I returned to the work of Howard Becker and rediscovered his chapter entitled "The Study of Deviance: Problems and Sympathies." It was illuminating and even surprising. I had forgotten that he wrote:

> The characters in the sociological drama of deviance, even more than the characters in other sociological processes, seem to be either heroes or villains. We

expose the depravity of the deviants or we expose the depravity of those who enforce the rules on them. (1964, p. 175)

As the amnesia of decades fell away I remembered that it is ultimately a mistake to neglect the story of one side in favor of the other.

Politically, we may (perhaps should) identify more strongly with one side. However we must also continue to recognize that whatever else deviance is it involves transactions between social actors. Deviants and deviance; conformists and conformity are ultimately ordinary and commonplace. They are social creations and the property, wanted or not, of us all. As Becker says of deviance:

We ought not to view it as something special or in some magical way better than other kinds of behavior. Perhaps the best surety against either extreme is close contact with the people we study (1964, p. 176)

In some ways I had returned home after a long journey. I remembered that stone throwing comes from many sides. Being close to the stone throwing is rarely a comfortable position. But it is always important to chart the source and direction of the stones and their ultimate destination and consequence. Whatever the transgression we need to keep sight of the way in which it comes from us all and is not outside or beyond any one of us.

NOTES

1. Nonconformists belong to Protestant denominations that uphold a tradition of dissent from the Established Church.

2. "The only gay in the village" is the comedy catchphrase from the BBC comedy program "Little Britain." Daffyd ("the only gay in the village") is played by the actor Matt Lucas. In the series Daffyd lives in the Welsh town of Llandewi Brefi and ardently defends his right to this position.

3. Whit Walks are traditional street parades held in the North West of England during Whitsuntide.

4. Arthur Miller's play *The Crucible* (1952) first ran on Broadway in 1953 and was a response to Senator McCarthy's persecution of those deemed to be engaged in un-American activities.

5. "Old lags" is a term for ex-prisoners.

6. A radical branch of Methodism which originated in the North West of England.

7. Ken Loach's film *Family Life* was first screened in 1971 with a screenplay by David Mercer.

8. See www.Women in Prison.org.uk.

9. For details see http://news.bbc.co.Uk/l/hi/uk/4623404.stm, accessed 07/31/07.

10. According to www.homeoffice.gov.uk/rds/prisons, the UK prison population 06/30/07 was 80,205. This was 2 percent more than the previous year. By contrast in 1997 the year when the Labour administrations came in to power it was 62,000.

11. For details see article by Sandra Leville: "Rape conviction rate remain near record low" *Guardian Unlimited,* July 20, 2007.

REFERENCES
Becker, H. (1964). *Outsiders: Studies in the Sociology of Deviance.* New York: The Free Press.

Durkheim, E. (1964) (first published 1895). *The Rules of Sociological Method.* New York: The Free Press.

Erikson, K. T. (1966). *Wayward Puritans: A Study of the Sociology of Deviance.* New York: Wiley.

Goffman, E. (1968). *Stigma: Notes on the Management of Spoiled Identity.* Harmondsworth: Pelican Books.

Heidensohn, F. (1985). *Women and Crime.* London: Macmillan.

Heidensohn, F. (1989). *Crime and Society.* London: Macmillan.

Heidensohn, F. (2000). *Sexual Politics and Social Control.* Milton Keynes: Open University Press.

Howe, A. (1991). "The Problem of Privatised Injuries: Feminist Strategies for Litigation." In *At the Boundaries of the Law,* ed. N. S. Thomasden and M. Fineman, 135–149. New York and London: Routledge.

Laing, R. D. (1959, 1965) *The Divided Self: An Existential Study in Sanity.* London: Pelican Books.

Laing, R. D. (1967). *The Politics of Experience and the Bird of Paradise.* London: Penguin.

Laing, R. D., and Cooper, D. (1964, 1970). *Sanity, Madness and the Family—Families of Schizophrenics.* London: Penguin.

Lloyd, A. (1995). *Doubly Deviant, Doubly Damned: Society's Treatment of Violent Women.* London: Penguin Books.

Mills, C. W. (1959, 1976). *The Sociological Imagination.* New York: Oxford University Press.

Radford, J., and Friedberg, M., and Harne, L. eds. (2000). *Women, Violence and Strategies for Action.* Milton Keynes: Open University Press.

Rhys, J. (1982). *Tales of the Wide Caribbean: A New collection of Short Stories.* London: Heinemann Educational Books.

Scheff, T. (1966). *Being Mentally Ill.* Chicago: Aldine-Transaction.

Smart, C. (1990). "Feminist approaches to criminology or post modern woman meets atavistic man." In *Feminist Perspectives in Criminology,* ed. L. Gelsthorpe and A. Morris. 21–26. Buckingham: Open University Press.

Szasz, T. (1960). The myth of mental illness. *American Psychologist,* 15, 113–118.

9

"Hearing Voices, Bearing Witness": Reflections on Critical Analysis in Criminology

PHIL SCRATON

A PERSONAL JOURNEY

It was a happy childhood although my father never fully recovered from serious illness. I was four at the time and never knew him as a well man. Then again, I had no knowledge of any of his family. A Protestant, born in a workhouse, out of wedlock to a young mother in service, he was brought up by his grandparents as their son. To marry my mother he converted to Catholicism and his family severed all ties. It seems a conversion of convenience as he rarely went to church and gave no inclination of having a religion. My mother's family was second generation Irish and never missed Sunday mass. Despite our poverty the priest never missed Friday visits, collecting his money, tea, and a bun. We trooped to confession on Saturday and, being an altar boy who garbled Latin responses, as distant in meaning as they were in pronunciation, on Sundays I was hardly away from church.

While cleansing the soul was one mystery among many, corporal punishment troubled me from the first moment I met the infant school head-teacher, Miss Cassidy, who rapped knuckles with the sharp edge of a ruler for not knowing the catechism. I was five years old and had never been hit by an adult. School was part fun, part fear. It came to a head when I was nine. With the girls removed from assembly, I witnessed the public flogging, hands and backside, of a boy in my class who had been caught stealing food from a shop close by the school. Eighteen lashes. The head-teacher, accompanied by the parish priest, delivered his verdict: "You have let yourself down. You have let your family down. You have let the school down. But most of all you have let God down."

From that morning I doubt I trusted authority again. For the first time I had witnessed the full, violent potential of adult power—its authority carrying dual legitimacy of state and church. In school we had a "black babies" league table. Each week we gave money and our names moved up the table. At two shillings and sixpence, or half a crown, we wrote a chosen name on an envelope containing the money. It was sent to the missionaries. Primary school children bought the right to name African children. While saving money, we were saving souls. In the words of a Paul Doran song made famous by Christy Moore: "Missionaries and pioneers are soldiers in disguise" (Moore 2003, p. 15). I was a model altar boy and was soon accompanying my favorite priest to vocations exhibitions. Unlike us he had a car and I felt special. I was eleven years old and the missionaries were keen to recruit.

I decided against the missions and went for the secular priesthood. Aged twelve, I headed north to a seminary, locked in a form of custody for forty-six weeks of the year. It was on one of my brief sojourns home that our local church became the focus of an international scandal. A popular, East European Catholic doctor in the parish had been prescribing contraception to women patients who attended the church. She had been outed and excommunicated, the case making headlines in the national press. Ten o'clock mass was always packed to the rafters and as I led the priest onto the altar I could see the doctor kneeling alone in a pew while others stood along the back of the church. At communion she stood in line and at her turn she knelt at the altar to receive the host. I held the communion plate beneath her chin and the priest passed her by. Head bowed, tears flowing, she returned to the isolation of an empty pew. She was ostracized.

Why are these stories relevant here? Cumulatively they represent a quiet, growing awakening that, for all its certainty and absolutism, the faith into which I had been born seemingly condoned social injustice and imposed its authority by combining physical and ideological forces. In the seminary I read Don Camillo and the struggles between the Italian parish priest and the Communist mayor. I aligned immediately with the politics of worker priests and nuns in their work against poverty in Latin America. In my seventeenth year I left the seminary, and within a short time I left religion. I studied contemporary history, politics, law, and economics at the local college of further education and thought about teacher training. According to my dad, university was not a place for "the likes of us." He wanted me to "get a trade" and a "proper job." My intention to study sociology was met with incredulity: "What's that? Sounds like common sense!" Yet my mum stood by me, telling me that secretly he was "really proud."

By now I was living in Toxteth, which butts up to the University of Liverpool on its south side. There had been major controversy over house clearances to accommodate ever-expanding faculties and schools. During the first few days we met with tutors on the top floor of the Roxby Building, looking down on the rows of terraced houses—home to the Liverpool-born black community. A young ethnographer, Owen Gill, pointed across the rooftops: "You won't find sociology in here" he said, "that's were you need to be, down there in the community." I said, in my then strong Liverpool accent, "I've spent ages tryin' to get into here an' now I'm here you're tellin' me I should be out there!"

Of course, Owen was right and his work, particularly his *Luke Street* ethnography (Gill, 1974), was testimony to the "view from below." My time at university demonstrated how far removed were sociology and the other social sciences from the lives and experiences of those they purported to study. Further, I was a fish out of water. Many times in the early days I thought my dad had been correct. So many students had public school and privileged backgrounds. Their vocabulary, their way of talking, and their confidence were so intimidating, especially in small group tutorials. Despite being from a highly talkative family, university silenced me. I felt an outsider in my own city. Then came the University Senate House occupation.

On March 9, 1970 a mass meeting of students was held in Liverpool University's Students Union, Mountford Hall. It was the culmination of a range of issues: the racism of the chancellor, Lord Salisbury; the university's involvement in chemical and biological warfare contracts; university investments; the holding of secret files on students particularly following anti-apartheid demonstrations. Denial without substance came from the vice-chancellor and he and his associates left an increasingly hostile meeting. Spontaneously a group of several hundred marched on the Senate House. An eleven-day occupation began, the red flag hoisted above the building. A month later the university suspended nine students for up to two years and expelled a tenth. Nearly 200 signed a declaration of equal responsibility. Eventually, following considerable national criticism of the university, the disciplinary charges were revoked but new rules were issued to students focusing on disruption, obstruction, willful damage, and defacement of university property.

The occupation paralleled resistance among black youth in Toxteth directed primarily against police racism. Barricades were regularly built to prevent police incursions into the community. In the university classroom, with a few notable exceptions, structural functionalist sociology—in its various forms—seemed to interpret a different world to that which dominated the news. Poverty, racism, Vietnam, apartheid, violence against women were the focus of consolidating mass movements for rights and liberties internationally while our tutorials mulled over the "founding fathers," "social surveys," and the relationship between "work and leisure." Yet there were modules on class and "race," social and political theory, encouraging a more critical and relevant perspective. In my third year I became absorbed in reading Frantz Fanon and Paulo Freire, determined to explore the political relevance of the writings of Eldridge Cleaver, Huey Newton, Angela Davis, George Jackson, and James Baldwin to my experiences of Toxteth. Then I met a newly appointed senior lecturer recently arrived from Hong Kong. It was a defining moment. He asked me what I intended to do on completion of my degree: "Research" I replied, "Research into social justice." He laughed dismissively, "Be realistic, you'll never get a First, you'll never make a researcher." He was right about the degree.

RESEARCH AT THE MARGINS

I registered part-time for a Masters by research. These were the days before postgraduate taught courses. Initially the only project for which I could gain supervision was on leisure and class in Netherley, a white working class estate of medium-rise blocks on the southern extremity of Liverpool. It was a dreadful development in two-tone grey, without character, without infrastructure, and without jobs; planned and designed by people who would never live there. Reassured by false promises, people were lifted from long-established moorings in the inner-city and dumped on the periphery. The estate was built on the flatlands beneath Woolton, one of the most affluent areas of the city. Researching leisure exposed the contradiction. While the "folks who live on the hill," as they were characterized, competed over the size of their indoor swimming pools, in Netherley there was neither swimming pool nor leisure center.

Given the structural functionalist perspective and survey methods un-derpinning the project I was a reluctant researcher, constantly drawn back to work on neocolonialism. Out of the blue a priest from the university's Catholic chaplaincy invited me to witness, as civil liberties observer, a local council eviction of Irish Travellers from wasteland in the heart of the city. I had no knowledge of Gypsies or Travellers but agreed to monitor the actions of the bailiffs and police. The violence of the early hours eviction, the willful disregard for families, their trailers (caravans), and their possessions, was overwhelming as bailiffs, hired by the council and protected by the police, drove men, women, and children from the land. Deposited on the public highway, the police escorted the convoy of defeated and demoralized Travel-lers to the force boundary. What I witnessed that morning marked me pro-foundly. Years later Fergal Keane (1996, pp. 225–26) wrote about his first visit to Rwanda in the 1990s:

I leaned over the bridge and noticed that two bodies had become lodged in the rocks at the side of the gorge. One was that of a man. The other that of a baby, between six and twelve months old . . . killed with a machete, a gash across its skull. It did not seem like a real child. It looked like a doll. . . . I looked again and of course knew that further back along the river, perhaps fifty to one hundred miles further back, an adult had taken a knife and ended the life of this child and then hurled it into the water. I stepped back from the bridge and felt like being sick. . . . I kept asking myself the same question: What kind of man would kill a baby? What kind of man?"

Keane reflected on genocide in Africa as "tribalism," a "crazy African thing" on people "prone to this kind of behavior." He left like many of my colleagues believing that the short stocky ones had simply decided to turn on the tall thin ones because that was the way it had always been." Yet once he had reached "beneath the surface" of assumptions about tribal hatreds he discovered a "complex web of politics, economics, history, psychology and a struggle for identity." Two years after bearing witness to the dead child in the river he had the answer to his question:

Anyone, anyone at all. A man like you or me. Not a psychopath. Not a natural-born killer. A man born without prejudice or hatred . . . conditioned by the preachings of powerful men. (Keane, 1996, p. 226)

These few words gain authority from the abandonment of simple explanations of causation in favor of a deeper grasp of context. They encapsulate exactly my first responses when witnessing the violence and cruelty delivered on the Irish Travelling community and my deficit in knowledge and understanding.

On the windswept site of urban dereliction that was Everton Brow I began working with Irish Travelling families. Under the 1959 Caravan Sites Act the city was obliged to provide a site for Travellers unless it could gain exemption by demonstrating that there had been no history of encampments within its boundaries. As Liverpool was the apex of Travellers' movement between Ireland and Britain a case for exemption was impossible to sustain. Yet the council had stalled provision for two decades. While its officials talked of "illegal encampments," and continually attempted to prosecute Travellers under public health legislation, it was their employer that contravened the law. I helped raise funds for the Liverpool Travellers' Free School: a part-time teacher in a local church hall.

As a researcher I faced the realities and difficulties of being an insider–outsider. I was on the site daily, spending more time there than most of the men. Eventually, the school gained local authority funding. It comprised of two on-site trailers without heating and five teachers offering a three session day to accommodate the Travellers' workdays. As I taught in the school, advised on imminent evictions and read and wrote letters for families, I became an "insider" in terms of trust. Yet, in every other way, I was an outsider struggling with the seemingly implicit contradictions of my research. I experienced the temporariness of an ever-changing "community" and developed an understanding of its historical and contemporary realities but also I witnessed the direct impact of unremitting interpersonal and institutionalized racism that comprised its daily reality.

I visited the West Midlands where, during a technically unlawful eviction, three children had been burned to death as a trailer (caravan) had been ripped from its jacks. The moment I met with the families will never leave me. Writing from jail, Johnny "Pops" Connors (1973, p. 167) illustrates the experience of being an Irish Traveller in mid-1970s West Midlands: "my wife kicked black and blue by the police in her own trailer three days before the baby was born; my little son very badly injured and my trailer smashed to pieces; the hospital refused to treat us; the councilors [elected local government representatives] said kick them out at all costs." The questions were obvious. What kind of people could be so reckless as to cause the deaths of children?

How could such brutality by state officials be justified or rationalized? On what basis could a coroner's inquest rule such deaths as accidental? Why were journalists and academic researchers unconcerned?

Back in Liverpool, a leaflet was circulating the local estates. It demanded that the local authority evict the "Irish tinkers," the "dirty parasites," threatening: "Get the tinkers out or else." Within months, in Warrington, a leading councilor called for a "final solution" to the "gypsy problem." Given the genocide directed against Roma in the Holocaust, the comment was calculated to instill fear within the local travelling population. Gypsies, classified as genetic asocials by the Nazis, have remained the ultimate, collective illustration of "otherness." Even their mass deaths have been erased, "their suffering largely absent from discussions of the Holocaust, as they are absent from the monuments which memorialize it" (Clendinnen, 1998, pp. 10–11).

In this climate of hate Howard Becker's (1963) portrayal of "outsider" is literal. There is no adoption of, or adaptation to, a chosen lifestyle, no room for a negotiated acceptance. The daily reality of life on Everton Brow was local authority harassment, local community attacks, and police brutality. Evictions happened at first light and the self-styled, private hire bailiffs were undiscriminating and unremitting in their use of force. While men and women defended their homes and families, their children screamed in fear. There were no case studies, ethical guidelines, or briefing papers to advise the fledgling researcher on her/his place and role in such circumstances. Academic conferences were as distant in their analyses of such events as were their contributors from the action. At the launch of a report into the deterioration in relations between house-dwellers and Travellers and flanked by academics and policy makers, Roy Wells, then president of the National Gypsy Council, gave an insight into his community's view of academic research:

> Your clever academics befriend us for a few months, they come down to our site, eats our food and drinks our tea. Some of them even lives amongst us. Then they disappear to their nice homes and university libraries. Next thing we know they're giving lectures on us, writing books about us . . . what do they know about our struggles? How can they know our pain? We live it all the time. Our persecution lasts a life-time, not just a few months. Give us the tools to say it right and we'll tell you like it is. You know what we call them on our site? Plastic gypsies (in Scraton, 1976, p. 76).

INSTITUTIONALIZED RACISM

Throughout the twentieth century Liverpool's black population, born and brought up in the city, endured persistent and uncompromising victimization. Formerly a small fishing village, Liverpool grew to international prominence on the proceeds of the lucrative and pernicious slave trade, on the wage slavery of northern England's "dark and satanic mills" and on handling Europe's "people trade"—the port was a conduit for international emigration. Throughout the late nineteenth and early twentieth centuries the city received, into its back-to-back, condemned houses and tenements, immigrants from Ireland, Wales, China, Africa, and the Caribbean. It became a city of diversity, of gradual decline and of segregation. Its reputation, fuelled by authoritarian local politicians, exploitative industrialists, and a severe police force, was that of a once-proud and successful port eroded by a militant, violent, and criminal underclass. This ideological construction became imbedded in the collective psyche of those who lived and worked in middle class and white, "respectable" working class areas. It is well illustrated by the Merseyside police chief constable's report to a Home Office inquiry into civil disorder in the early 1980s:

> it is a matter of historical fact that Liverpool has been beset by problems of violence and public disorder throughout the centuries. Constant reference is made by Muir (1907) to the turbulent character of the Liverpool populace, its related dangers, problems which were multiplied and were aggravated during the 18th and 19th centuries by large-scale immigration of Irish, with more than 400,000 entering Liverpool in 1846 and 1847, in the aftermath of the great potato famine. Most travelled on to America but enough remained to aggravate the problems of poverty, unemployment and overcrowding which then, as now, were the breeding ground for violence. Add to this the appreciable number of Welsh rural labourers . . . To enumerate other foreign nationalities would be a daunting task . . . After the 1st World War, there was a remarkable increase in the number of coloured immigrants to Liverpool, initially seamen who stayed and married white girls . . . The black community, like the Chinese, has been a feature of Liverpool life for generations. Each of these new communities brought with them associated problems, disputes and tensions which, on occasion, spilled over into out breaks of violence. (Oxford, 1981, pp. 3–4)

There is absolute certainty in the chief constable's interpretation of the pathology inherent in the relationship between incomers, violence, and social malaise. Liverpool's "inhabitants" had long been reputed to be proportionately tougher, more violent, and more "pugnacious" than found in other seaports. The "aggressive nature" of the "true Liverpudlian" was fixed, culturally endemic, its pervasive manifestation apparent in a "belligerent attitude" inspiring "violent disturbances" thus "fulfill[ing] her [sic] reputation as a tough, violent City, to the present day" (Oxford, 1981, pp. 4–5). In his portrayal the chief constable confirmed what social geographers refer to as a "cognitive map" in which identifiable problem populations were matched to specific neighborhoods; dangerous places, threatening spaces. On streets that "bred" violence, where there was scant respect for the rule of law, no quarter was given. Differential, discriminatory policing was adopted as the only appropriate response to the community's "decline in standards of self-discipline . . . manifested in the ever spiraling increase in crime of all classifications, particularly crimes of violence" (Oxford, 1981, p. 6).

How was this represented in the assumptions shared by those who policed the streets and interacted with Liverpool's diverse communities? A police sergeant interviewed by McLure (1980, p. 10) provides a tellingly graphic illustration:

> To his left, the North Sub (sub-division), and it's a bit of a desert island on that side. All those cliff-dwellers in high rise flats; the bucks running wild and a few buckesses too . . . then straight in front of him the market-place: all that glitters, merchants and moneylenders, beggars and meths-drinkers lying about legless! Then to his right, the South Sub: the jungle noises and even more the jungle behaviour of clubland; then yellow country, Chinatown; then, up in the right-hand top corner, black people country, Upper Parliament Street . . . if he's coming on nights, he'll probably see five sort of stockades with campfires burning; places he can get in out of the cold and safe from a hiding . . .

The shared ideological construction and public representation within the police reflected assumptions about marginalization that were profoundly cultural, undoubtedly inherited, and persistently pathological. It manifested in a propensity to violence associated with territory, the occupancy of sinister neighborhoods—"jungle land," "black people country," the yellow peril."

> No-one escaped this inner-city patchwork of lawlessness posing an ever-present threat to the law-abiding middle classes. Hardline policing was the established antidote to hard communities. The "war zone" imagery was not restricted to

the custom and practice of differential policing on the street but underpinned operational policies and priorities. There were "stand-offs" throughout the 1970s between the Black community and the police. Streets were barricaded to keep out police patrols. (Scraton, 2007, p. 19)

My experience of living and researching in Toxteth in the 1970s and 1980s provides a contrasting account from a quite different perspective. It was a community of high unemployment, poor housing, few facilities, and little hope of significant change. Youths walking into the city were met by police officers who turned them back. In word and deed the police were abusive, intimidating, and racist. On night shift at the local police station officers pooled money and organized "coon races"—the first police officer to bring in an arrested black person won the jackpot. The few black people to join the police were hounded out by appalling racism within the force. These acts and events could be rationalized as the unacceptable behavior of a minority of rogue cops—the comment most often used was "racism is everywhere so we're bound to have a few." Not so.

Following the unprecedented uprisings of Liverpool's black community throughout the summer of 1981 I wrote the following:

Racism is a long endured inhumanity in Liverpool's black community. The picture painted by [local] politicians is of a harmonious, integrated, cosmo-politan city. This ignores the brutal reality of the inter-war period when the first generation black community was the butt of white racism. Importantly, it also veils the institutionalisation of that racism within the practices of local government and state agencies. There has never been any realistic attempt to alleviate poverty, poor housing, casual employment and unemployment which has trapped the black community . . . Recession, in terms of disproportionate levels of unemployment, discrimination in schools, work and housing, minimal social amenities and heavy policing, is the established way of life in the com-munity. (Scraton, 1981, p. 25)

My work with Irish Travellers and in Liverpool's black community pro-vided clear evidence that racism was deeply entrenched in the fabric of public and private institutions. I adopted Stokely Carmichael's conceptualization of "institutional" racism as systemic. In 1981 the Scarman Report into the Brixton "riots" denied that there was evidence of institutional racism in contemporary policing. It took another twelve years, and the Macpherson Report into the racist killing of Stephen Lawrence in London, before "institutional racism" was given public recognition by an official inquiry. Without becoming trapped in semantics, interpreting institutional racism in the post-Macpherson period becomes little more than accepting that racism exists across an institution. "Institutionalized racism," however, more accurately and acutely identifies racism as part of the fabric, the culture, and the ideology of an organization. It is so profoundly imbedded that it is not necessarily apparent in policies and practices.

RESEARCHING DEATHS IN CUSTODY

In the late 1970s my research focus shifted from the regulation of the Irish Travelling community simultaneously to the policing of the Liverpool-born black community and to police operations in Knowsley, a predominantly white working class area of the city. In June 1979 a drunken fifty-six-year old man with a serious a heart condition died in custody having been arrested in controversial circumstances. He had been drinking in a public house and, singing loudly, was returning home across derelict land. Two police officers attempted to push him into the back seat of their two-door police car. He lurched forward onto the rubble-strewn ground. Other police officers arrived and eventually he was carried semi-conscious to a police minibus. While being unloaded at the police station he was dropped onto his head. Now unconscious, he was carried into the charge room, laid on his back on the floor where he urinated and died. Jimmy Kelly's injuries were extensive including a fractured jaw. According to one pathologist, they were consistent with a severe beating.

Following a major community-based campaign and extensive media coverage, including a prime time documentary based around testimonies of civilian eyewitnesses, the inquest into Jimmy Kelly's death was held. Researching the case as part of a study of Merseyside policing, I attended the entire inquest. Many civilian witnesses had difficulty remembering sequentially the precise details of events recorded in their initial statements, yet they were adamant that the police had used unacceptable levels of force during the arrest. Most recalled witnessing assault by the police after Jimmy Kelly had been subdued. The first officers at the scene admitted using force. As he lay on the uneven ground an officer sat astride his body punching him "three or four times" in the stomach. Under cross-examination a fellow officer agreed that the punches were probably to the face because the officer was sitting on Jimmy Kelly's chest. It was admitted that in attempting to put him into the car they had grabbed him by the testicles and somehow he had somersaulted out of the car onto his head. Having requested backup the officers restrained Jimmy Kelly; one officer stood on his feet while another knelt on his chest. Handcuffed, he was transported on the floor of the minibus. The police considered the force used, given the circumstances, had been reasonable. Their actions after arrest were uncontested other than inconsequential points. Summarizing the evidence, the coroner instructed the jury that for a verdict of unlawful killing they "should have to be satisfied beyond all reasonable doubt that . . . unreasonable force had been used . . . [and] that the deceased had sustained injuries which were the consequence of that unreasonable force and . . . such injuries effectively caused the death." The jury returned a unanimous verdict of "death by misadventure" caused by heart failure with alcoholic intoxication and exertion as contributory factors. Jimmy Kelly's family interpreted the verdict as amounting to self-inflicted death—that by drinking heavily in the full knowledge of his heart complaint and resisting arrest Jimmy Kelly had brought death on himself. The chief constable welcomed the verdict stating that it "cleared the individual officers involved and the Merseyside Police from the many allegations and criticisms which were made after this incident occurred which have now found to be without substance" (*The Guardian*, April 18, 1980). A decade later in an article written for *New Society* I made a passing reference to the case and, together with the journal and its editor, was sued for libel by four police officers.

Researching and writing about this case and others, the lack of in-depth research into deaths in custody, the problems regarding inquests into deaths in controversial circumstances, and the problems facing bereaved families in accessing disclosure of documents, became apparent. In 1980 I became a founder member of INQUEST: United Campaigns for Justice. During this period I was working in Milton Keynes with Stuart Hall, Greg McLennan, Joe Sim, John Muncie, and Mike Fitzgerald on the Open University's first criminology module, *Issues in Crime and Society*. Filming for the new social sciences' foundation course, we were the first television crew into St. Paul's, Bristol after the 1980 black community uprising. Again it was clear that the violent protests were the direct consequence of institutionalized racism endured by the community, particularly at the hands of the police. The Open University modules developed at that time remain some of the most critical scholarship of the 1980s, significantly influencing the development of critical criminology. *Crime and Society: Readings in History and Theory* (Fitzgerald, et al., 1981), the course text, remains in publication.

By 1982 I had returned to Merseyside and was teaching at Edge Hill College of Higher Education, now Edge Hill University. Two years later, with Kathryn Chadwick, we founded the Centre for Studies in Crime and Social Justice as a forum for critical analysis that took its lead from colleagues at Berkeley. At the time we offered only two undergraduate modules in criminology and there were no higher degree programs in the institution. After battles against elitism with the validating body, the University of Lancaster, we introduced a Masters in Crime, Deviance and Social Policy and, two years later, a second Masters in Human Rights and Equal Opportunities. These later amalgamated to become a consolidated Masters in Criminology, Rights and Justice. During the 1990s we introduced an undergraduate degree in Critical Criminology and a doctoral program. Over seventy of our graduates went on to teach and research in universities and associated institutions. Central to the ethos of our work was a commitment to research-led teaching, the close association of investigative research, critical pedagogy, and diverse publication. In the early days of the Centre our research into deaths in controversial circumstances was focal (see Scraton and Chadwick, 1986, 1987a, 1987b).

This emergent body of work showed empirically how authoritarianism underpinned the rule of law and how, politically and ideologically, it was manifested and experienced at the personal, social, and institutional levels. We researched the deaths of eight boys and young men in the Glenochil Detention Complex. In one year there had been twenty-five serious suicide attempts and 180 boys placed on strict suicide observation. The detention center was the site of the military-based "short, sharp, shock" initiative introduced by Thatcherite Home Secretary William Whitelaw. Bullying was rife in the Young Offenders' Centre. On the landings we found the disabled, the mentally ill, the unassertive, the weak, the sex offenders, and the loners subjected to a relentless barrage of physical and mental torment. They were extorted, verbally harassed, and physically beaten. The complex exemplified the institutionalization of male violence. The so-called "inmate culture" and its hierarchy of violence was actively utilized by staff to control, contain, and manage the jail.

brief contacts with relatives and friends are in stark contrast to the daily routine which begins at 5:45 A.M with slopping-out the contents of the plastic chamber pot . . . prisoners are under a rule of silence with commands shouted at them, army style, by prison officers . . . prisoners are marched to breakfast, marched back to their cells, change their clothes, inspected for work, marched to work, marched to tea-break, marched to their cells, change their clothes, inspected on parade and marched back to work. The time is now only 1 P.M, the prisoners have changed their clothes three times, been inspected twice, marched everywhere and remained in total silence. (Scraton and Chadwick, 1986, pp. 148–49)

"Failure to cope" was seen as a problem within the individual rather than symptomatic of a harsh regime. Individuals expressing rationality and sensitivity learnt to cry alone. Those who disclosed their pain were placed on strict suicide observation: solitary confinement in strip cells; extreme cold; constant electric light; coarse canvas blankets; coarse canvas pinafore dresses; no underwear. We concluded:

On the other side of the cell door the isolated, cold, bored individual sits in a rough canvas gown, one paperback book and a bible. Seventy-two times a day an eye appears at the spy-hole reminding the child that there is life outside. This is the treatment afforded to those children and young people considered to have such a serious mental condition that their lives are at risk. A medical model defines the risk, a punishment model defines the treatment. (Scraton and Chadwick, 1986)

The primary research into a range of cases, often working closely with bereaved families and ex-prisoners, revealed the negative imagery and established ideologies, "deeply institutionalized in the British State." They provided "the ready justification for the marginalization of identifiable groups," successfully deflecting responsibility away from state institutions (Scraton and Chadwick, 1987b, p. 220). The political management of identity constituted "a process of categorization which suggests that the 'violent,' the 'dangerous,' the 'political extremist,' the 'alien,' the 'inadequate,' the 'mentally ill,'" contribute to their own deaths either by their pathological condition or their personal choice." (Scraton and Chadwick, 1987b, p. 233)

Our analysis suggested that advanced capitalism, neocolonialism, and patriarchy comprised interrelated political forms while generating ideological constructions of reality justifying, defending, and reinforcing political-economic relations of dominance. Societal consensus, particularly in the context of a receding economy or in the protection of more broadly drawn frontiers (i.e., Fortress Europe), we argued, was sought through the rhetoric of liberal pluralism. Social forces within democracy's civil society, however, were backed by the constant presence and occasional use of physical coercion. Draconian legislation and policy, the uncompromising products of successive Thatcherite administrations, depended on the exercise of state-sanctioned violence. They also required internalization through ideological appeal and acceptance or—for those resisting authoritarianism—through what Poulantzas (1978, p. 83) refers to as "mechanisms of fear." Since that period, successive Labour administrations have assumed the authoritarian mantle, not least in their introduction of "anti-terrorism" legislation. The moralisms implicit in this inherited political project remain firmly in place: good versus evil; civilized versus chaos; moral authority versus permissiveness.

Throughout the 1990s, deaths in custody leading to unlawful killing or neglect verdicts at inquests represented the sharp end of a continuum of state violence directed toward black communities. The United Nations Committee Against Torture reported on its extensive United Kingdom investigation into custody deaths. It concluded that a significant cause for concern was the number of deaths in police custody and the apparent failure by the state party (U.K.) to provide an effective investigative mechanism to "deal with allegations of police and prison authorities abuse" (*Statewatch*,1998). Concern over the investigation of and inquiry into controversial deaths was not confined to the deaths of black people. A spate of suicides of young women in Cornton Vale prison in Scotland, and of children and young men in custody throughout Britain, raised serious questions concerning the escalating incarceration of children, young women, and young men for relatively minor offenses. Concerns about harsh regimes, violent bullying, and staff complacency were overshadowed by official explanations and internal inquiries which focused on individual pathology, personal inadequacy, and fractured family lives. If victims did not bring death on themselves by their aggression and refusal to conform, the "problem" lay with character weakness and failure to adjust.

What emerged from two decades of campaigns and resistance regarding deaths in custody was evidence of a yawning gap between official discourse, inquiries or verdicts and alternative accounts provided by bereaved families, regime survivors, rights lawyers, community workers, and critical researchers (see Goldson and Coles, 2005; Sandler and Coles, 2008). If official discourse—manifested through public inquiries, in-house government reports and so on—is to succeed it has to negotiate (at best) or deny (at worst) the material conditions out of which it arises. The political purpose of official discourse is never a full and open inquiry. Rather, it is intended to reaffirm public confidence in a deeply flawed and much criticized criminal justice system, reconstruct new forms of operational legitimacy and secure strategies ostensibly which demonstrate a willingness to respond to public concern.

The mid-1980s was also a period of considerable disruption in Scottish prisons. In November 1986, following a rooftop protest at Peterhead Prison in North-East Scotland, Edinburgh's Gateway Exchange held a series of public meetings to consider prisoners' persistent allegations of brutality. Prison protests soon extended throughout the Scottish prison system, escalating to hostage-taking and a further rooftop protest at Peterhead. Former life-sentenced prisoner and director of the Gateway Exchange, Jimmy Boyle, commissioned me, along with Joe Sim, to conduct independent research into the protests. The research revealed prison regimes in which violence, including assaults on prisoners by prison officers, was endemic, reflecting a long history of confrontation and abuse. Conditions, particularly in the Victorian jails, were inhuman and degrading. Regimes amounted to little more than warehousing, with prisoners often locked in their cells for most of the day.

Prison managers and officers used threats and intimidation in their attempts to prevent prisoners participating in the research and the researchers were prohibited from entering prisons. Despite these inhibitions many prisoners wrote detailed and verifiable accounts of their experiences. As Jimmy Boyle stated, the research was "unequivocally about the unheard voice of the underdog" providing a "powerful indictment of our so-called democracy . . . vividly reminding us that there is another story which, until now, has remained untold—that of the prisoner" (Scraton, Sim, and Skidmore, 1991, p. vii). The research into custody deaths and prison protests heard and projected the voices of those silenced and vilified within total institutions. It challenged the pathologization of prisoners, so much the stock-in-trade of media sensationalism and politicians' sound-bites. And it contributed significantly to long-term, fundamental reform within the Scottish Prison Service.

RESEARCHING HILLSBOROUGH

In the 1989 Hillsborough disaster in Sheffield, England, ninety-six men, women, and children were crushed to death at a major football match watched by police, stewards, and a worldwide television audience. It occurred as a consequence of exit gates being opened by the police to relieve congestion at entry turnstiles. Over 2000 fans walked into the stadium unstewarded down a steep tunnel and into the back of already overcrowded pens. While fans were dying on the steps of the terraces the police commander reported that fans had forced entry into the stadium, causing an inrush. His lie was immediately broadcast live around the world supported by further police allegations of fans' drunkenness and violence (see Scraton, 2000/09). This led to the coroner recording the blood alcohol levels of all who died, including children, the appalling treatment of the bereaved by the police in the immediate aftermath, a deceitful police briefing of Prime Minister Thatcher and her Home Secretary, and vilification of fans in the media.

Within four months of the Hillsborough disaster Lord Justice Taylor produced an interim report for the Home Office concluding that the "main cause" of the disaster was "overcrowding" and the "main reason" was a "failure of police control." He also criticized Sheffield Wednesday Football Club, their safety engineers, and the local authority which had failed to issue an up-to-date license for the stadium. He directed his most damning conclusions towards South Yorkshire police. Senior officers had been "defensive and evasive." In "handling of problems on the day" and in giving evidence they had failed to show "qualities of leadership to be expected of their rank" (Taylor, 1989, p. 50). The police commander's "capacity to take decisions and give orders seemed to collapse." He had failed "to exert any control." Worse still, he lied; his "lack of candor" triggering "a widely reported allegation" against fans (Taylor, 1989, p. 50). The severity of Taylor's criticisms, alongside his exoneration of the fans' behavior, took many commentators by surprise.

The director of public prosecutions, however, decided there was "no evidence to justify any criminal proceedings" against any organization involved and "insufficient evidence to justify proceedings against any officer of the South Yorkshire Police or any other person for any offence" (letter from the head of the police complaints division to the chief constable, August 30, 1990). After the longest inquests in English legal history and two days of deliberation by the jury the majority verdict returned was accidental death.

Given our previous research into controversial deaths and our knowledge of public inquiries and coroners' inquests, the Centre for Studies in
Crime and Social Justice was commissioned by the Liverpool City Council
to research the aftermath of the disaster. I was familiar with football and its
policing having been a Liverpool supporter since I was a child. Sheila Coleman, Anne Jemphrey, Paula Skidmore, and I established The Hillsborough
Project. In 1990 we published *Hillsborough and After: The Liverpool Experience* (Coleman, et al., 1990), covering the Home Office Inquiry under Lord
Justice Taylor, the media coverage of the disaster, and the appalling treatment
endured by bereaved families and survivors in the immediate aftermath. This
was followed in 1995 by *No Last Rights: The Promotion of Myth and the Denial
of Justice in the Aftermath of the Hillsborough Disaster* (Scraton, Jemphrey, and
Coleman, 1995).

Eight years after the disaster a former police officer who had been on duty
at Hillsborough was interviewed for a late-evening television documentary
on disasters. I happened to be watching. He commented that police accounts
had been embellished to "make it a more hygienic day for all concerned"; he
"could never be clean again." After many months I made contact with the
officer and we met:

> on a cold early winter's day high in the hills above Hathersage, the former officer
> recalled the dreadful moments in the pens as he fought to save lives. He remem-
> bered the pain and sorrow, the anger and insults, the sense of failure. But he
> also detailed the aftermath. The moment when a young officer with eight years'
> service was asked to change his statement . . . Walking through the first snows
> of winter [he] recounted how he received back a word-processed version of his
> recollections [of the day]. It was annotated, sentences scored out, words altered.
> His most personal comments, his experiences, deleted. (Scraton, 2000, p. 185)

Fifty-seven of the original 154 sentences in his original statement had a
line through them and a further twenty-eight were significantly altered. This
was how I discovered that in the immediate aftermath of the disaster the chief
constable of the South Yorkshire Police appointed a team of six senior officers
to work with the head of management services and a prestigious law firm who
"review and alter" police statements. Police investigators, the judicial inquiry,
the coroner, and Home Office officials were parties to this procedure. Between
1989 and 2000 a Home Office inquiry, a criminal investigation, civil litigation,

inquests, judicial reviews, a judicial scrutiny of evidence, and a private prosecution failed to reveal the precise circumstances of the deaths or full details concerning deeply disturbing information-gathering processes. In 1999 I wrote *Hillsborough: The Truth*, updating it a year later to include the private prosecution. The scale and duration of the project had a formative impact on the work of the center eventually leading to an ESRC-funded seminar series on disasters and their aftermath and a Nuffield-funded disasters' research archive (see also Scraton, 2005, 2007). The book was updated again in 2009.

Researching Hillsborough confirmed the institutionalized deficiencies and inadequacies evident in our research into deaths in custody. The medico-legal frame of reference and procedures were consistent in their limitations and powerful state institutions—particularly the police—used privileged access to evidence, investigations, and inquiries in serving their interests and protecting their reputation. The systematic review and alteration of police statements after Hillsborough remains the most visible example of inappropriate manipulation, nondisclosure, and evidence management. Cumulatively, the cases raised profound disquiet regarding the institutional and structural deficiencies embedded in medical inquiry and the administration of the law. The bereaved and survivors discovered to their financial and emotional cost that the theatre of the law has minimal relevance to the discovery of truth and the realization of justice.

In 1996 sixteen children and their teacher were shot dead at Dunblane Primary School in Scotland. My research with bereaved families overlapped the Hillsborough Project. The perpetrator was portrayed as a "pathological loner" who had an "unhealthy interest" in young boys. Within hours the explanation for the deaths of sixteen young children and their teacher was summarized in two words: "pervert" and "monster." Soon after, a public inquiry was conducted. It touched only briefly on an issue that had long-term consequences for the bereaved: their treatment by the Central Scotland Police on the day of the shootings. In June 1997 I interviewed many of the families and discovered that from the time of their mid-morning arrival at the school until mid-afternoon they had been held by police officers in a staff room without receiving any information about the incident or their children. It became apparent much later that the senior officers were concerned that gun licenses had been issued and renewed to a man who had been investigated and was considered by an internal assessment an unfit person to have guns and ammunition in his possession. A decade on, the disturbing issues raised by the case remain unanswered (North, 2000; Scraton, 2007).

DEMONIZING CHILDREN

Within media and political discourse Dunblane provided a counterpoint to another tragedy involving children. Three years earlier, caught on camera, two young children led a toddler by the hand; a frozen CCTV image transmitted throughout the world. James Bulger, aged two, was taken from a shopping mall and killed by his ten-year old abductors. While Dunblane was ascribed the imagery of lost innocence, Jon Venables and Robert Thompson became personifications of pathological evil. The public outrage directed on the streets and in the media toward two young children, their prosecution and conviction for murder in an adult court, and the disclosure of their identities and photographs at the conclusion of the case elevated a rare event to one illustrative of a crisis in childhood. Opportunist Conservative and Labour politicians projected an atypical, complex case as evidence of a generation deficient in basic morality, discipline, and responsibility. Prime Minister John Major's called to "condemn a little more and understand a little less" (*The Mail on Sunday*, February 21, 1993). Opposition Home Secretary Tony Blair stated what had occurred fell "like hammer blows against the sleeping conscience of the country" (*The Guardian*, February 20, 1993). It was an unfortunate metaphor. The "crisis," as these responses suggest, was not confined to serious crime but was projected to include a spectrum of behaviors labeled antisocial or offensive.

The Centre for Studies in Crime and Social Justice was located nine miles from the Bootle shopping precinct from where James Bulger was taken. Collectively we were deeply concerned at the public reaction and media coverage surrounding the case, not least how an exceptional case so quickly was portrayed as emblematic of growing lawlessness among children and young people. We formed the Young People, Power and Justice Research Group and in 1997 published *"Childhood" in "Crisis"?* (Scraton, 1997). It mapped the regulation and criminalization of children and young people that followed the case, including the backlash against children's rights, the moral panic regarding "feral" children, persistent young offenders, and antisocial behavior. In the year the book was published I was invited to a public meeting convened to discuss crime, particularly involving young people, in Skelmersdale New

Town. It was part of a rushed "consultation process" initiated by the recently elected Labour Government to discuss the contents of a proposed Crime and Disorder Bill. The meeting was chaired by the local Member of Parliament. Children and young people were not invited. The evening soon turned into an unrelenting attack on "yobs" and "thugs." A youth worker and I raised the problems and issues faced by children and young people in the community, including the easy availability of drugs and alcohol and police harassment. We were shouted down and roundly condemned as being "soft on crime" and neglectful of victims. Any attempt to discuss the media-infused public outcry around children and young people was mocked. It was a clear warning of the gathering backlash against children's rights.

The James Bulger case and its aftermath had major consequences for policy and law reform regarding children. It was the catalyst for a moral panic regarding feral children, persistent young offenders, and antisocial behavior that hardened the regulation and criminalization of children and young people (Haydon and Scraton, 2000). The Labour Government, led by Prime Minister Tony Blair, assumed the mantle of authoritarianism from its predecessors and the consequences were profound. A moral imperative drove the agenda, based on an unsubstantiated assumption that there previously existed a "Golden Age" of personal hardship but collective benevolence when hardworking, dedicated families were the bedrock upon which community spirit and civic responsibility were built. According to Blair (2002), prior to his election, "crime was rising, there was escalating family breakdown, and social inequalities had widened." Identifiable neighborhoods, labeled "sink estates," were "marked by vandalism, violent crime and the loss of civility." The "mutuality of duty" and the "reciprocity of respect" had been lost. Social disintegration and diminished quality of life were evidence that the "moral fabric of community was unraveling." Civil society was being undermined by "abuse, vandalism, anti-social behavior."

In keeping with his Conservative predecessors, Blair attacked the criminal justice system as outmoded and overindulging offenders with punishments failing to reflect the seriousness of offenses. Only by remedying imbalances, addressing low-level crime and broadening the definitional scope of antisocial behavior, would "social cohesion" be restored to "fragmented communities." The message was simple: the state alone could not deliver safe communities, reduce crime, or protect its law-abiding citizens. Primary responsibility rested with parents and individual citizens. Rights, including rights of access to state support, intervention, and benefits, were presented as the flipside of civic responsibilities. Personal responsibility for challenging intimidating behavior, small-scale disorder, and criminal activity constituted one element of a network of "informal controls" contributing toward safer and more integrated communities. At the hub of this idealized notion of "community" was the relationship between families and interagency partnerships working toward common, agreed social objectives.

According to the Blair agenda, moral renewal, offering the corrective for crime and disruptive or disorderly behaviors, was two dimensional. First, affirming culpability and responsibility through the due process of criminal justice—from apprehension to punishment, incorporating the expectations of retribution and remorse. Second, reconstruction of and support for the values of positive families and strong communities. Following the brief period of consultation, in 1998 the Crime and Disorder Bill passed into legislation, establishing crime prevention as a responsibility within *all* public agencies. The objective was early intervention—targeting children's potentially criminal behavior while encouraging "appropriate" parenting. To this end the act introduced Antisocial Behavior Orders (ASBOs) and Parenting Orders, civil injunctions issued in magistrates' courts.

Despite Home Office guidelines reassuring that ASBOs would be used against children only in exceptional circumstances, they became employed disproportionately against under 18s. Children were named and shamed, their photographs published on the front pages of local newspapers. They were threatened with ASBOs by local government "antisocial behavior officers" employed in "antisocial behavior units" and by the police. Families lived in fear of being reported by neighbors, of being evicted should their children breach their ASBOs. Many children received prison sentences having never been convicted of a crime other than breach of their ASBOs (see Scraton, 2004). Subsequent legislation introduced "dispersal zones" outlawing the meeting together of two or more people on the street and night curfews on children.

Such disturbing developments were not lost on Alvaro Gil-Robles (2005, p. 4), European Human Rights Commissioner. He likened ASBOs to "personalized penal codes, where non-criminal behavior becomes criminal for individuals who have incurred the wrath of the community." ASBOs had been "touted as a miracle cure for urban nuisance" placing the police, local authorities, and others under considerable pressure. Gil-Robles recommended "respite from . . . ASBO-mania" with civil orders limited to "appropriate and serious cases." Troubled that children between ten and fourteen could be considered "criminally culpable," Gil-Robles concluded that ASBOs brought children to the "portal of the criminal justice system." Widespread publicity of cases involving children, central to Home Office guidelines, was "entirely disproportionate" in "aggressively informing members of the community who have no knowledge of the offending behavior" and "no need to know." Naming and shaming constituted a violation of the European Convention on Human Rights with the potential of transforming the "pesky into pariahs."

Despite a series of legal challenges, their continuing refinement and expansion of powers continued unabated, seriously breaching the United Nations Convention on the Rights of the Child, undermining the "best interests" principle, the presumption of innocence, due process, the right to a fair trial, and access to legal representation (Scraton, 2007). The Labour Government rhetoric, reminiscent of the Giuliani-Bratton zero tolerance agenda (Scraton, 2004), remains one of "reclaiming the streets" from lawless youth alongside disciplining "dysfunctional" families. It neglects the context of conflict in communities divided and dislocated by deeper, structural inequalities evident in poverty, racism, sectarianism, misogyny, and homophobia. In adopting an individual-social pathology model delivered with the force of virulent, punitive rhetoric, there is no consideration disruptive behavior is ignited by political-economic marginalization and criminalization. Most significantly, children and young people are well aware that for all the rhetoric of inclusion and stake-holding, they are peripheral, rarely consulted, and regularly vilified.

The veneer of risk, protection, and prevention coats a deepening, almost evangelical, commitment to discipline, regulation, and punishment. As the grip tightens on the behavior of children and young people minimal attention has been paid to social, political, and economic context. The reality is an authoritarian ideology mobilized locally and nationally to criminalize through the back door of civil injunctions. In-depth, case-based research already indicates that the problems faced by children and families are exacerbated by the stigma, rumor, and reprisals fed by the public process of naming and shaming. And the transactional perspective on rights and implementation is part of the Blair legacy. At the 2005 Labour Party Conference his heir apparent, Gordon Brown, reminisced that his "moral compass" was set by his parents; for "every opportunity there was an obligation" and for "every right there was a responsibility" (Conference Address, 26 September 2005).

IMPRISONED WOMEN

In 2003, after twenty-one years, I left Edge Hill to work in the Institute of Criminology and Criminal Justice at Queen's University, Belfast. In the North of Ireland the mid-1990s ceasefires, followed by the 1998 Good Friday Agreement, laid the ground for a lasting peace, a devolved assembly in government, and this included the release on license of politically-motivated prisoners. While considerable attention was given to these developments, particularly regarding the resettlement of prisoners, concern remained regarding the treatment, accommodation, and regimes for the "ordinary" prisoners incarcerated in what had been established as a high security system. The prisons inspectorate published a damning report of prison conditions for women and I was commissioned by the Northern Ireland Human Rights Commission to conduct in-depth research into the high security Mourne House Women's Unit within Maghaberry Prison.

Working alongside commission investigations worker Linda Moore, we gained unprecedented access to the jail and its prisoners. Following the inspectorate's severe criticisms we anticipated improvements in regime and evidence of strategy, policy, and staffing reform. Instead we found depleted programs reflecting an all-pervasive climate of indifference and complacency. No corporate strategy, no gender-specific policies, no discrete management structure and no gender-oriented training had emerged. Workshops were permanently closed, women rarely escorted to classes. They were locked alone in cells for a minimum seventeen hours a day, often unable to phone their children. Compulsorily strip-searched, there was no support on reception and no induction program. Sentence management and resettlement programs recommended by the Inspectorate had not materialized. In stagnation, Mourne House operated a high security regime. Men comprised 80 percent of discipline staff rising to 100 percent on night guard duty (see Scraton and Moore, 2005, 2007).

We met a grandmother mopping the corridor of the punishment block in which she was held. Epileptic and diabetic, she carried a colostomy bag and suffered open, weeping varicose veins. She was in solitary confinement for abusing guards. Prisoners stated she was taunted by guards who refused her tea unless she complied with their demands. A woman prisoner commented:

> She ate with her fingers. They'd taunt and laugh at her by blowing smoke through the door . . . She tried to hang herself and three of us saw her getting out of the ambulance. They walked her across the tarmac in February with a suicide blanket on. They all had riot gear on. She was crying. They were bringing her back from hospital and she was put back in the punishment block. We just kept our heads down. Just did our time.

This was how self-harming and ill women were "managed." We found deeply disturbed young prisoners held with adult women. In a strip cell within the punishment block we interviewed a child, her flesh torn and cut from her ankles to her hips, hands to her shoulders. She was dressed in a canvas gown, no underwear, lying on a concrete plinth, without a mattress or pillow. Reflecting on this experience I later wrote:

> As we walked from the cell, her words on tape, the emotional mix of sadness, anger and incredulity was overwhelming. Her circumstances typified the "duty of care" provided to women and girls imprisoned within an advanced democratic state constantly proclaiming values of "moral renewal" at home and abroad . . . if such "manifest injustice" prevailed in 2004, what had been done in the past? If this could be done to children, what was the fate of women prisoners? How had a process involving doctors, nurses, probation officers, clergy, prison visitors as well as prison officers and their managers become so institutionalised, so accepted, so routine, yet hidden from the world outside? Academics had researched recently in the prisons, why were they unconcerned? (Scraton, 2007, p. 4)

The most common response from prison guards was that girls and young women were manipulative, attention-seeking, and used self-harming behavior as a strategy. Young women were well aware that guards did not take seriously their "suicidal thoughts":

> They tell you to stop playing at hanging yourself. If you're suicidal they threaten you with the punishment block. 23 hour lock-up on the punishment block. . . . They don't even look in on you. I'm surprised this whole jail hasn't killed themselves.

Two years earlier Annie Kelly had died in a strip cell in the punishment block. In and out of Mourne House since she was fifteen, she had a history of disturbed and destructive behavior including self-harm and strangling herself until she lost consciousness. Immediately prior to her death she told the board of visitors she had "no ambition but to die." The board reported that a "different approach concerning Annie should be made with some urgency." She was held in a "ligature-free" strip cell modified for her use. Yet, undetected and unobserved, she was able to tear "non-destructible" fabric into ligatures and find, or make, a hole in the Perspex covering of the window and the diamond mesh inside it, of sufficient size to thread the ligature and take her weight.

During our research another prisoner, Roseanne Irvine, took her own life (see Scraton, 2006, 2007). Identified as vulnerable, the guard who found her was aware of a "strong possibility that she was liable to attempt suicide but it had been impossible to observe her continually . . . although we were aware of the situation, we were helpless to prevent it." Roseanne received no counseling, had little meaningful contact with discipline staff and was locked in her cell, unobserved, for extended periods. On the night she died she told guards she had taken "five blues" but she was locked without seeing medical staff.

Seemingly inevitable, her death was shocking. A professional worker stated that "everyone realised that Roseanne had great needs but it [the provision] fell short because no-one put their hand up for overall responsibility." Given Roseanne's personal history of self-harm and attempted suicide, the lack of an effective care plan for such a vulnerable young woman raised profound concerns about the circumstances of her death. She had arrived in prison in a deeply distressed state and was convinced she would lose access to her daughter. Another prisoner recalled:

> She was always talking about her wee daughter. She loved her so much she talked about [her] every day. She hadn't seen her daughter for three weeks and she . . . didn't think she would see her again because of what her social worker told the prison officer to tell her. She told Roseanne that [her daughter] was happy and it would not be right to bring her up to the prison to see her. That really hurt Roseanne. You could see it in her face when she was telling me. It was Roseanne's child and she had every right to see her.

Roseanne had suffered in the punishment block. She had been deeply distressed and tore out her hair. Although considered at risk, she was returned

to her normal landing where she had access to several ligatures in a cell with
multiple ligature points. A woman prisoner stated that on the evening of her
death:

> Roseanne told me not long before we got locked up that the staff did not check
> on the women every hour and she said to me that one of these nights they will
> find someone hanging and they will be dead. That very night Roseanne was
> found dead.

The impact on the other women prisoners was immediate:

> The next day I just sat and cried. I then had panic attacks. They didn't get the
> nurse over. I pushed the [emergency] button and they came to the door. I asked
> to see the nurse and they just said "No." They said, "You're not allowed to push
> the button. It's for emergencies only." I said I was having a panic attack. They
> said, "Take deep breaths." It was early evening. I sat up on the bed with a pillow
> and cried and cried.

Roseanne's closest friend on the landing was devastated and was transferred to the male prison hospital where we interviewed her several days later.
Throughout the interview she had difficulty in focusing and apologized constantly for her emotional and physical "state." Continually crying, she said:

> The way that girl was treated the system let her down. There should be a hos-
> pital for women. It was disgusting, dirty in here . . . I always told her not to do
> anything to herself. I tried to see her that night but we only got 20 minutes out
> [of the cells]. I started to write things down myself. I wrote there should be
> more support for women with mental health problems.

She talked about her own mental health problems: You get no support, the
staff ignore you." She had received two visits from a psychiatric nurse "then it
was stopped." There was "no support for women with depression" and in the
prison hospital "you're locked up twenty-three hours a day":

> If you're sitting there [in the cell] for hours there's stuff that goes through your
> mind. If I don't get out today I'll plan something. They think there's nothing
> I can do but I can. They think they know everything but they don't. I've got a
> plan, I know what I'll do. My first cousin hung himself.

She had resisted transfer to the male prison hospital: "it's filthy." Held in strip conditions, the bed was bolted to the floor and the metal toilet was open to guards' observation. It was described by a senior orderly as a "basic suite" which the staff tried "to keep as clean and tidy as possible given the circumstances." The impact of Roseanne's death and her transfer to the male prison hospital was devastating:

> I have four kids and four grandkids and I miss them all so much. I keep thinking to myself I will never see mine again. I love them all so much too. But to me time is running out for me. I can't take much more. Every day is a nightmare.

Eventually Linda Moore and I gave evidence and were cross-examined at the inquests into the deaths of Annie Kelly and Roseanne Irvine. While the juries returned verdicts of "suicide" their narratives reflected the disturbing circumstances in which they died, as noted in our research. The jury found the "main contributor" to Annie's death was "lack of communication and training at all levels," criticizing her "very long periods of isolation," the lack of appropriate "female facilities." The narrative called for the "provision of a therapeutic community." Roseanne had taken her own life while the "balance of her mind was disturbed." The jury noted the significance of the events leading up to her death including her long history of mental health difficulties, concluding: "The prison system failed Roseanne." There had been systemic "defects" including "severe lack of communication and inadequate recording" and a lack of health care and resources for women prisoners. The jury concluded that prison was "not a suitable environment for someone with a personality/mental health disorder," recommending "more ongoing training on suicide awareness for prison staff."

The Mourne House research demonstrated that regimes and programs were not gender specific in design or delivery yet the regulation, control, and punishment of girls and women were consistently gender specific. Fear, degradation, and dehumanization endured by women prisoners were institutionally gendered, most appropriately represented and analyzed through their location on a continuum of violence and violation. This ranged from lack of access to telephones or baths, through lock-ups, to strip-searches, personal abuse, and punishment. The sharp end of the continuum, where the body is the site of self-harm and strip searches, is related directly to the sexual comments, innuendo, and insults embedded in the prison's daily routine. The women's testimonies provide bleak reminders of the destructive force of imprisonment. While not reduced to total passivity, nor completely incapacitated, women's voices were effectively silenced, their self-esteem consistently undermined, and their physical and mental health deeply traumatized . . . and two women died.

THE RELUCTANT PROSELYTIZER

In February 2006 I presented a plenary to the annual conference of the Australia and New Zealand Society of Criminology. The theme was "Violence, Incarceration and the 'War on Terror.'" I opened the talk with a favorite quote:

> Humanity is male and man defines woman not in herself but as relative to him; she is not regarded as an autonomous being . . . she is defined and differentiated with reference to man and not he with reference to her; she is the incidental, the inessential as opposed to the essential. He is the Subject, he is the Absolute—she is the Other. (Simone de Beauvoir, 1972 (1949), p. 16)

There is considerable irony for me in celebrating the significance of Simone de Beauvoir's *The Second Sex* over half a century after its publication. Studying sociology, social theory, and social philosophy in the early 1970s, the only casual reference to her was as the "wife of Jean-Paul Sartre." De Beauvoir did not restrict her analysis of "Other," now a common but rarely attributed notion, to patriarchies. Central to conceiving and establishing their power and status as the essential, the absolute, the "One," she argued, powerful groups materially, politically, and ideologically create, define, and regulate "Others." These are strangers on "our" familiar streets, outsiders in "our" communities, aliens in "our" sovereign territories. As individuals their actions are immediately suspicious and together they are suspect communities. The currency of Otherness is fear, and the transaction is invariably hostile. Acknowledging structural inequalities of the time, de Beauvoir recorded the oppression of black people in the United States, aboriginals in the colonies, proletarians in capitalist economies, and women and girls throughout patriarchies. Reflecting Hegel she noted that "in consciousness itself there is present a fundamental hostility towards every other consciousness; the subject can be posed only in being opposed . . . the essential as opposed to the other, the inessential, the object" (de Beauvoir, 1972).

In my talk I made a connection between Simone de Beauvoir's analysis and Frantz Fanon's *The Wretched of the Earth* in which he exposes the relationship between structural relations and social action. The brutality of colonial subjugation through military occupation and police rule was secured and rationalized through the dehumanization of native populations:

> As if to show the totalitarian character of colonial exploitation the settler paints the native as a sort of quintessence of evil. Native society is not simply described as a society lacking in values, but also the negation of values . . . the enemy of values . . . the absolute evil . . . corrosive . . . destroying . . . disfiguring . . . (Fanon, 1967, pp. 31–32)

"Natives" are depicted and policed as "savages," "barbarians," "un-civilized," "pagans," without morality or religion. They are quintessential "others" in their homelands, "disfiguring all that has to do with beauty or morality" (Famon, 1967). As colonial powers seized land and natural resources, terrorized communities, and destroyed cultures, they built empires whose lasting legacy is today apparent in the global dynamics of "race" and racism. The colonial inheritance is profound. It is reflected in the rhetoric of patriotism, belonging, and purity, in the surveillance of suspect communities within and the "hordes" massing at the borders without. Populist interpretations of the "clash of civilizations" are predicated on the "civilized" (us) and the "uncivilized" (other).

Barbara Hudson (2003, pp. 35–36) identifies the undercurrents that flow beneath the surface discourses of dangerousness and risk management. Severe preemptive measures are introduced to eliminate potential danger through identifying, monitoring, and regulating those "classified as dangerous." Consequently, "dangerous offender legislation, internment and other forms of protection against suspected enemies" are enacted "often on a murky border between criminal law and national security regulations where they lack transparency and accountability and barely respect the liberal ideals of due process protections, and separation of governing powers." Such tangible outcomes are derived in authoritarian populism directed toward outsiders.

173

In my talk I demonstrated how U.S. President George Bush and U.K. Prime Minister Tony Blair had been deceitful in proclaiming Iraq's potential for mobilizing "weapons of mass destruction" and listed the consequences of Afghanistan and Iraq. These included: rewriting the preconditions of a "just war"; indiscriminate killing of civilians, particularly the use of cluster bombs; the atrocities of the Northern Alliance and allied special forces in Afghanistan; the denial of the Geneva Conventions culminating in Guantanamo Bay and rendition; detention without trial in the United Kingdom and Canada under new antiterror laws; attacks on academic freedom. A central issue was the use of torture and brutality administered by U.K. and U.S. interrogators and soldiers.

Using our primary research with women prisoners in the North of Ireland, demonstrating their endurance of brutality and neglect, my concern was to consider the institutionalization of violence as fundamental to incarceration. While recognizing the contextual differences between the local "war on crime" and the global "war on terror" the carceral consistencies were striking: the abuse of institutional, discretionary powers with confidence and impunity; the initiation of official inquiries as mechanisms of neutralization, incorporation, and legitimacy; the management, manipulation, and manufacture of information; inadequate and partial investigations; the nondisclosure of privileged evidence; the marginalization, condemnation, and silencing of victims and campaigners (see Scraton and McCulloch, 2009).

I quoted Edward Said's (2000, p. 51) poignant critique of U. S. punitive policies as manifestations of "a [burning] puritanical zeal decreeing the sternest possible attitude towards anyone deemed to be an unregenerate sinner." Zealots that "clearly guided U. S. policy towards the native American Indians, who were first demonized, then portrayed as wasteful savages, then exterminated, their tiny remnant confined to reservations and concentration camps." It is an "elemental anger" that "fuels a judgmental attitude" and while it has "no place in international politics" it has become, for the United States and its allies, "a central tenet." Thus "punishment is conceived in apocalyptic terms" and the "sinners," the prisoners "are condemned terminally, with the utmost cruelty regardless of whether or not they suffer the cruelest agonies" (Said, 2000).

Critical analysis, I continued, requires the analysis of what Foucault (1980) referred to as regimes of truth within democratic states—the mechanisms and instances that secure self-serving accounts and accord them value. It also turns on the political management of status caught definitively in Howard Becker's (1967) conceptualization of "hierarchies of credibility." My proposition was, and remains, that in seeking out the view from below, in committing to investigative research and in bearing witness to the experiences and contexts of everyday life the critical researcher builds an alternative analysis. I ended my talk with a quote taken from Stan Cohen's *States of Denial*:

> Intellectuals who keep silent about what they know, who ignore crimes that matter by moral standards, are even more culpable when society is free and open. They can speak freely, but choose not to. (Cohen, 2000, p. 286)

Walking from the lecture hall I overheard a comment about the talk. It was dismissive, my presentation reduced to "proselytizing." Addressing the profound injustices of the "war on terror" and bearing witness to women's incarceration in Northern Ireland through critical analysis of the determining contexts of power and authority was portrayed, in one word, as an attempted conversion "from one religion, belief or opinion to another" (apologies to the Oxford Dictionary). It was a comment designed to consolidate an assumed binary between "objectivity" and "subjectivity." The former the proclaimed product of value-free, unfettered scientific method, the latter the regrettable outcome of value-laden, tarnished standpointism.

The following day I copresented the opening plenary of the International Conference on Penal Abolition. I stood alongside Terry Hicks, the father of Australian Guantanamo prisoner David Hicks. Terry is a modest and reserved working-class man thrust by circumstances before an international gaze. Like so many people I have been privileged to meet, his direct experience of institutionalized injustice was the catalyst for knowledge and activism. He recounted the violence of his son's capture, interrogation, transportation, and detention. He talked of the helplessness experienced by a family faced with the might of the U.S. administration supported without equivocation by its Australian ally. It was a remarkable, moving presentation. Two years later in London I shared a platform with Moazzam Begg who illustrated in graphic detail what he, David, and all others experienced before and during their Guantanamo detention. It confirmed, with the precision of personal endurance, the humiliation, torture, inhumanity, vulnerability, and powerlessness of incarceration *in extremis*. Both experiences bore testimony to the importance of critical analysis in exposing the capability of advanced democratic states to marginalize, exclude, and punish those that they perceive and proscribe as threatening.

If, as some "critical researchers" in criminology have proposed, a progressive analysis is predicated on the desire to challenge inequality, inhumanity, and exclusion within a political context that is authentically democratic, can inherent structural contradictions—political, economic, cultural, ideological—be ignored? Of course social life, locally, nationally, and globally, is diverse and complex. People are not totally determined by their structural location. There is not only difference within families and communities, however "close-knit," but also within individuals through their lifecycle. It is self-evident that social life is multidimensional, that individual and collective understanding is a process and that institutional change is often the consequence of personal struggle and social movements.

REAFFIRMING A CRITICAL AGENDA

This brief, schematic excursion from early days through a series of in-depth research studies that form part of three decades' work returns the discussion to the context of the events and the circumstances in which they occurred. Each could be analyzed solely within their social and institutional contexts. Yet the institutionalized racism underpinning the policing of 1980s Liverpool and the deaths in custody of black people requires location within the determining contexts of "race" and class. The negative imagery and punitive consequences surrounding the ascribed "crisis" in childhood and its attendant "breakdown in law and order" was rooted in the formal and informal, public and private, manifestations of power inherent in adult-child relations. The deaths of two women in custody are not only about the failures of a particular prison to meet its duty of care but illustrative of the gendered responses to women in prison and to women enduring mental ill-health within patriarchal societies. These studies in their extended form demonstrate the full dynamic force of marginalization, exclusion, and criminalization when directed against the "Other."

Critical analysis foregrounds power, its relations to authority, and its processes of legitimacy. It contextualizes the determination of and resistance to the containment of personal action and social interaction. Acknowledging the fine legacy of C. Wright Mills (1959), it turns individual cases and personal troubles into public issues. Mills condemned the servile, servicing relationship adopted within the academy in meeting the lucrative commissions of public bodies and private corporations. Sociology's "reforming push" had diminished as its attention shifted toward sponsorship by the corporation, the army and the state" (Mills, 1959, p. 129). It had become a utilitarian relationship, "which is to say that we become technicians accepting their problems and aims, or ideologists promoting their prestige and authority" (Mills, 1959, p. 193).

Mills established a radical agenda derived in the "sociological imagination," critically self-reflective of personal context while mapping and interpreting the intersections of biography and history." The "personal troubles of milieu" reflected the accumulation of interpersonal interactions of everyday life. They were not devoid of context: the "public issues of social structure" (Mills, 1959, pp. 7–8). The social world of language, place, family, and community—local environments of the individual—"required location within the larger structure of social and historical life" (Mills, 1959, p. 8). Central to the contextualization of everyday life within structural relations is the analysis of power, not only in its routine institutionalized forms and expressions but also within the political, economic, and ideological determinants of multinational capital, the legacies of slavery and colonization, and the subjugation of women within patriarchies. From this foundation and inspired by a range of social movements—civil rights, women's liberation, anti-apartheid, prisoners' rights—radical criminology emerged in the United States shadowed by critical criminology in Europe.

As "radical criminology" took shape Nanette Davis (1975, p. 205) proposed that the processes of "institutionalization, defining, labeling and categorizing" central to the work of social reaction theorists reflected "commonsense reality" underpinning the mechanics of societal regulation and their operation. The broader context was "an unequal society divided by class, ethnicity, sex, and political and economic differences" dominated by "politically powerful groups" which formulated and enforced rules and laws "detrimental to the interests and needs of powerless groups." Recounting the emergence and profound significance of radical scholarship at the University of California's Berkeley School of Criminology, Schwendinger, et al. (2002, p. 43) note the deep analysis and questioning of "America's class, race and gender inequality" and the development of a "critical mass that produced an Enlightenment-like explosion of rich theoretical ideas about the nature of crime and criminal justice." For Barry Krisberg (1975, p. 19), the sociological imagination represented a commitment to social change, "intimately related to the struggles of oppressed people for equality, self-determination and social justice, because these are the groups that are actively seeking liberation, intellectually and politically" (Krisberg 1975, p. 19).

The radicalism central to critical scholarship was concerned with locating interpersonal and institutional relations within overarching historical and contemporary material contexts in which the dynamics of "crime," "deviance" and "conflict" originated. Platt and Takagi (1981, p. 39) note the acceleration in the growth of the poor, the over representation of black and Hispanic men, women, and children in their number and the "astronomic growth" in "police and criminal justice budgets, subsidized in the main by the working class" and the deterioration in "desperately needed social services."

In the United Kingdom and Ireland the "radical" or "critical" shift in criminology emerged in the late 1960s as the National Deviancy Conference fast became an umbrella forum for radical social workers, prison abolitionists, campaigners, and critical criminologists inside and outside academic institutions. Stan Cohen (1981, pp. 240–41) notes that "[p]erhaps its greatest achievement" was its central role "in creating (in 1974) the European Group for the Study of Deviance and Social Control" that became "an influential force in bringing together like-minded sociologists and activists in Western Europe." Six years later, as a young lecturer at the Open University I was intrigued by the stacks of bound European Group working papers occupying every inch of floor space in Martin Loney's study. He enthused relentlessly about the group to anyone who would listen.

Finally, in 1984 having moved to Edge Hill, Kathryn Chadwick and I went to the European Group's conference in Cardiff. It was a volatile moment. There was an accusatory debate over "left idealism" dominated entirely by British academics. Those outside the debate—geographically and politically—looked on in astonishment. To us, and we were not alone, the sometimes acrimonious exchanges over "realism" seemed a sideshow. The conference was held at height of the 1984–85 coal-miners dispute and the Thatcher administration's all-out attack on the unions, having orchestrated the sinking of the *Belgrano* and the deaths of ten Republican hunger strikers

in the H Blocks of Long Kesh. The New Right's authoritarian grip was exemplified by the continuing increase in the powers of the police and security
services and the expansion of European prisons accompanied by a parallel
diminution in political accountability. At the Cardiff conference the most
moving moment came on the final evening. We were guests of the miners at
a welfare club high in the South Wales valleys. Following passionate speeches
from miners' leaders and Women Against Pit Closures and the full emotion
of a male voice choir, Beppe Mosconi and Bill Rolston sang songs of struggle
from Italy and Ireland. I have not missed a conference since.

Never before had I attended an academic conference alongside striking
workers and their families. Sessions were packed, the atmosphere electric and
much of the broader European analysis has since proved prophetic. The group's
founders were committed to connecting academic research and community-
based activism, resisting the pre-eminence of "conservative, positivist and
functionalist orientations within criminology" and their translation into state
policy and institutional practice. It was resistance to what Nils Christie (1994,
p. 58), himself a founding member, named "useful knowledge"—useful only
to state institutions and their managers. Utility, in this context, erodes the
capacity and opportunity for "critical thinking." The European Group, initially focusing on the structural relations of class, political economy, and state
power, expanded its reach to "overcome other national, linguistic, ethnic,
sexual and gender barriers in an effort to develop a critical, empancipatory
and innovative criminology, particularly in research and dissemination.

Whatever the frustrations regarding the group's somewhat erratic communication, precarious finances, and uncertainty over venues, the collabora-
tions, support, exchanges, and friendships have had a lasting significance for
the many participants, occasional or regular. In terms of research, publication, teaching, and campaigns the European Group has made a marked and
lasting contribution that reflects the journey, and debates en route, within
critical criminological analysis. The European Group also became the inspiration for the edited collection *Law, Order and the Authoritarian State: Readings
in Critical Criminology* (Scraton, 1987).

Seven years and seven conference papers on from Cardiff, Kathryn Chadwick
and I reflected on the founding period of the NDC and the European Group.
"New" or "Radical" criminology, we argued, was grounded in the "diverse
and unique world of everyday life, the claimed location of interactionists, yet it

adapted and contextualized new deviancy theory within the structural dynamics of power and social control" (Scraton and Chadwick, 1991, p. 165). It emphasized the structural processes of economic marginalization and criminalization within the context of class divisions and conflict inherent within advanced capitalism. While provoking the opprobrium of mainstream criminology, the defenders of which caricatured "new" criminology as naive, determinist, and reductionist, the critical challenge to academic orthodoxies "returned to prominence the significance of structural relations, the question of power and the processes which underpinned its legitimacy" (Scraton and Chadwick, 1991, p.165). The emphasis was derived in the "*contexts* of social action and reaction" and the often less visible structural arrangements–"the political, economic and ideological management of social worlds" (Chadwick, 1991, p. 165).

Critical analyses of criminal justice, however, demonstrate how differential policing, discriminatory prosecution, and inconsistent punishment reinforce structural inequalities within society. Marginalization and exclusion through class, "race," gender, sexuality, and childhood are not arbitrary forms of subjugation. They are consistent and material manifestations of a "social order" derived in the overarching power relations of advanced capitalism, neocolonialism, patriarchy, and age. Restorative justice and its conferences of mediation are played out within the same determining contexts as criminal justice. What do the concepts of rehabiliatation, reintegration, and restoration mean if social injustice and material inequalities persist? Whether walking from a criminal justice prison or from a restorative justice conference the child or young person is returned to the interpersonal and structural relations that brought them into conflict with the law.

In the aftermath of September 11 Edward Said castigated "prominent intellectuals and commentators" who employed "self-righteous sophistry . . . uncritical self-flattery . . . [and] specious argument" in rationalizing and tolerating the Bush program of military intervention. Clearly, as critical analysis has demonstrated repeatedly, academic inquiry does not proceed unfettered by sponsors and gatekeepers. It feeds off and into what John Berger refers to as prevailing "ways of seeing," reflecting and reinforcing centers of power. Academic knowledge is incorporated into what Michel Foucault (1980) identifies as the state's general politics of truth: the mechanisms and instances which secure self-serving true or false statements; the techniques and procedures accorded value in the acquisition of truth; the political management of status, thereby establishing what Howard Becker referred to as hierarchies of credibility. This is truth as manufactured and produced, through which acts are ascribed meaning and given the *imprimatur* of official recognition.

Power, particularly its use and formulation within medico-legal discourses, institutionalizes, professionalizes, and rewards truth acquisition protecting and reproducing the status quo. This includes, indeed relies on, self-defining "scientific discourses" within academic and state institutions alike. It is no less than a process of production of formally sanctioned knowledge. As Henry Giroux (2002) notes: "The impoverishment of many intellectuals, with their growing refusal to speak about addressing, if not ending, human suffering is now matched by the poverty of a social order that recognizes no alternative to itself."

ACKNOWLEDGMENTS
Many thanks to my coresearchers and comrades especially at the Centre for Studies in Crime and Social Justice (Edge Hill), INQUEST, Statewatch, the Institute of Race Relations, and the European Group for the Study of Deviance and Social Control who have shared the long and winding road. Thanks to Kathryn Chadwick and my friends and my family, particularly my partner Deena Haydon, and my sons, Paul and Sean, whose work and support have been so significant.

REFERENCES
Becker, H. S. (1963). *Outsiders: Studies in the Sociology of Deviance*. New York: Free Press.

Becker, H. S. (1967). Whose side are we on? *Social Problems*, 14, 239–247.

Blair, T. (2002, November 10). My vision for Britain, *The Observer*.

Clendinnen, I. (1998). *Reading the Holocaust*. Melbourne: Text Publishing.

Cohen, S. (2000). Some thoroughly modern monsters, *Index on Censorship*, 29, pp. 36–43.

Coleman, S., Jemphrey, A., Scraton, P., and Skidmore, P. (1990). *Hillsborough and After: The Liverpool Experience*. Liverpool: Liverpool City Council.

De Beauvoir, S. (1972). *The Second Sex*. Harmondsworth: Penguin.

Fanon, F. (1967). *The Wretched of the Earth*. Harmondsworth: Penguin.

Foucault, M. (1980). *Power/Knowledge: Selected Interviews and Other Writings 1972–1977* (ed. C. Gordon). Brighton: Harvester Wheatsheaf.

Gil-Robles, A. (2005). *Report by Mr. Alvaro Gil-Robles, Commissioner for Human Rights, on his Visit to the United Kingdom, 4th–12th November 2004.* Strasbourg: Office of the Commissioner for Human Rights.

Giroux, H. A. (2002). Global capitalism and the return of the Garrison state: Rethinking hope in the age of uncertainty, *ARENA Journal,* 19, 141–160.

Goldson, B. and Coles, D. (2005). *In the Care of the State? Child Deaths in Penal Custody in England and Wales.* London: INQUEST.

Haydon, D., and Scraton, P. (2000). Condemn a little more, understand a little less: The political context and rights implications of the domestic and European rulings in the Venables-Thompson case, *Journal of Law and Society,* 27, 416–448.

Hudson, B. (2003). *Justice in the Risk Society.* London: Sage.

Keane, F. (1996). *Letter to Daniel: Despatches from the Heart.* London: Penguin/BBC Books.

McLure, J. (1980). *Spike Island: Portrait of a Police Division.* London: Macmillan.

Moore, C. (2003). *One Voice: My Life in Song.* London: Hodder and Stoughton.

North, M. (2000). *Dunblane: Never Forget.* Edinburgh: Mainstream.

Oxford, K. (1981). *Evidence to the Scarman Inquiry.* Liverpool: Merseyside Police.

Poulantzas, N. (1978). *State, Power, Socialism.* London: Verso.

Said, E. (2000). Apocalypse no, *Index on Censorship,* 29, 49–53.

Said, E. (2002, March 2). Thoughts about America, *Al-Ahram Weekly.*

Sandler, M., and Coles, D. (2008). *Dying on the Inside: Examining Women's Deaths in Prison.* London: INQUEST.

Scraton, P. (1976). *Images of Deviance and the Politics of Assimilation.* Unpublished MA Thesis, University of Liverpool.

Scraton, P. (1981). Policing and Institutionalised Racism on Merseyside. In D. Cowell, T. Jones, and J. Young [eds.]. *Policing the Riots.* London: Junction Books, 21–38.

Scraton, P., ed. (1987). *Law, Order and the Authoritarian State: Readings in Critical Criminology,* Milton Keynes: Open University Press.

Scraton, P. (1997) Whose "Childhood? What "Crisis?" in P. Scraton (ed). *"Childhood" in "Crisis?".* London: UCL Press/ Routledge.

Scraton, P. (1999), Policing with contempt: The degrading of truth and denial of justice in the aftermath of the hillsborough disaster, *Journal of Law and Society,* 26, 273–297.

Scraton, P (2000) *Hillsborough: The Truth.* Edinburgh: Mainstream.

Scraton, P (2004). Streets of terror: Marginalisation, criminalisation and moral renewal, *Social Justice,* 31, 130–158.

Scraton, P (2005). Death on the Terraces: The Contexts and Injustices of the 1989 Hillsborough Disaster. In P. Darby, M. Johnes and G. Mellor [eds]. *Soccer and Disaster: International Perspectives,* pp. 59–76. Routledge: London.

Scraton, P (2007). *Power, Conflict and Criminalisation.* Routledge: London.

Scraton, P., and Chadwick, K. (1986). The Experiment that went Wrong: The Crisis of Deaths in Custody at the Glenochil Youth Complex. In B. Rolston and M. Tomlinson (eds.). *The Expansion of European Prison Systems.* Belfast: EGSDSC Working Papers, No. 7.

Scraton, P., and Chadwick, K. (1987a). *In the Arms of the Law: Coroners" Inquests and Deaths in Custody.* London: Pluto.

Scraton, P., and Chadwick, K. (1987b) Speaking Ill of the Dead; Institutionalised Responses to Deaths in Custody. In P. Scraton (ed.). *Law, Order and the Authoritarian State: Readings in Critical Criminology.* Milton Keynes: Open University Press.

Scraton, P., and Chadwick, K. (1991). Challenging the New Orthodoxies: The Theoretical and Political Priorities of Critical Criminology. In K. Stenson and D. Cowell (eds). *The Politics of Crime Control.* London: Sage.

Scraton, P., Jemphrey, A., and Coleman, S. (1995). *No Last Rights: The Denial of Justice and the Promotion of Myth in the Aftermath of the Hillsborough Disaster.* Liverpool: Liverpool City Council/Alden Press.

Scraton, P., and Moore, L. (2005). *The Hurt Inside: The Imprisonment of Women and Girls in Northern Ireland.* Belfast: Northern Ireland Human Rights Commission.

Scraton, P., and Moore, L. (2007). *The Prison Within: The Imprisonment of Women in Hydebank Wood 2004–2006*. Belfast: Northern Ireland Human Rights Commission.

Scraton, P., Sim, J., and Skidmore, P. (1991). *Prisons Under Protest*. Milton Keynes: Open University Press.

10

Confessions of a Drive-By Intellectual

RAY MICHALOWSKI

I am an intellectual. More accurately I am a species of drive-by intellectual who, rather than pursuing a career-long focus on a single topic in criminology, has given serial attention to multiple social issues. Over the course of my career I have written about vehicular homicide, criminological theory, the political economy of crime and punishment, law and justice in socialist Cuba, corporate, political, and state-corporate crimes, motorcycle pilgrimage and the politics of memory, globalization and sex work, the criminality of war, and most recently, immigration and immigration control.

I suppose it sounds a bit elitist to characterize myself as an intellectual, even of the drive-by persuasion. But that is not at all how I mean it. For me, the term "intellectual" is shorthand for a work life devoted to creating ideas about crime and justice, and communicating these ideas to academic, student, and public audiences. In short, my work life has been a life of the mind, a life built around ideas.

Because of my working-class Italian and Polish peasant roots, I continue to draw deep satisfaction from working with my hands—building furniture and boats, turning bowls at my lathe, and tinkering with my motorcycles. Consequently, for me, being an intellectual has no more inherent worth as a life way than many others. While my work differs from people who earn their paychecks by using their hands and bodies more strenuously than I do, I have no sense that this difference makes me any "better." Indeed, the people

I admire most are not academics. They are songwriters, artists, and ordinary working folk who, despite the challenges of their daily lives laugh honestly, easily, and often without self-conscious examination of how they appear to others—as is so often the case with intellectuals.

I am not saying I do not love what I do. To the contrary; I love reading, and thinking, trying to figure out how societies function (or not), how they decide that some harmful behaviors should be punished and other equally harmful acts (like war and gross exploitation) should be rewarded, how they construct and pursue ideas and images of justice. Reading, thinking, teaching, and writing about these things have been my life's work, and it has been good work.

The question here is how did a would-be jock from a factory town in upstate New York become a Regents Professor of Criminology at Northern Arizona University? That's what I hope to explain to you—and to myself—in the following pages.

A NEW YORK STATE OF MIND

The scene: October 24, 1962, a dusty high school football practice field in Schenectady, New York. A squadron of F-86 Saber jet fighters screams low overhead. As they disappear over the horizon, their sound vibrating the autumn breeze, one of the players yells over—

"Hey Ray, ya' know the position to take in case of a nuclear attack?"

"No," I say.

"You sit in a chair, put your hands behind your head, put your head between your knees . . . and kiss your ass goodbye."

It was just a bit of adolescent male gallows humor during the Cuban Missile Crisis, but that dangerous moment in U.S. geopolitical history ignited a small spark of curiosity in me—someone who had never thought about much more than whether my football team would win, how fast I could make my car go, when my band would get its next gig, and how far my girlfriend would go during the Saturday night make-out session (this was, after all, before the birth control and the sexual revolution of the late 1960s). Why, I wondered, was I going to be blown to bits over some tiny Caribbean island where affluent folks—the "plutocrats" my dad called them—had once gone to gamble, and where now a charismatic, bearded revolutionary wanted to create a different kind of society? Somehow I sensed the conflict was about more than evil "commies" threatening the "free world" as the politicians, priests, and pundits in our small mill town were telling us. Just what that "more" might be, I had no idea.

Many years on, when I was a graduate student and then a university professor, I came to know people who had grown up in leftist households where critiquing the dominant economic and political order had been commonplace. Unlike them, however, even though the Cuban Missile Crisis left me with a vague sense that there was more to the story than I was being told, I had no cultural or intellectual tools to help me see behind the dominant geopolitical ideology of the time. So, I went back to my usual less-than-intellectual pursuits, including smashing bodies on the football field in the hopes of getting an athletic scholarship that would pay my way through college. And I did. By my senior year I had football scholarships to Boston College and the Merchant Marine Academy at Kings Point.

Then something odd happened. I woke up one morning in the fall of my senior year with the realization that I didn't want to be a jock. Why? I have never been sure. After all, I was good at smashing bodies. Maybe it was the time I had spent teaching young children how to play the guitar, or weekend evenings spent making dance music with various bands, or hours spent listening to jazz with my musician friends. Or maybe it was a sense that the world was more complex than my working-class jock culture was willing to admit, a world that I somehow sensed would remain beyond my grasp if college was primarily about smashing bodies and the locker-room smells of sweaty uniforms, antiseptic, and communal showers. Whatever the reason, I rejected the scholarships (much to the annoyance of my high school principal), and enrolled in Fordham University in the Bronx, even though this would mean I would have to figure out how to pay my own way.

Being a college student in New York City in the late 1960s was an intellectually and socially exhilarating experience. At Fordham, we were taught by a formidable phalanx of Jesuit scholars and secular academics who were passionate about the world of ideas. They struggled to give us the tools of philosophical reasoning, rational discourse, and intellectual engagement. More than that, the Jesuits compelled us to social action. In my case, it was

Father Grady, the hall rector in my freshman dormitory who pressured me into working with a youth group at St. Charles Parish in Harlem.

Every Friday evening of my freshman year, there I was, a naive white boy from upstate New York, meeting with and supposedly "helping" African American ghetto youth understand what life was all about. Needless to say, those young men and women, many who were nearly my age, taught me far more about life's realities than I could ever teach them. It was there, in the church and on the streets of Harlem after our regular meetings that I first began to understand how deeply racism permeates American society; how deeply it had permeated me. It was consciousness shattering. Once I made friends with people for whom America's race question was not social theory, but lived reality, I felt as if I had tasted of the fruit of forbidden knowledge. I could not simply forget what I saw and learned on the streets of Harlem. I could no longer go back to being that naive white guy from upstate New York once I understood that whatever the liabilities I might suffer from having grown up working-class rather than affluent, I enjoyed something my new African American friends did not—the twisted privilege of having a white face.

My Harlem experience was heightened by a broader climate of political turmoil and social change: the civil rights movement, ban-the-bomb marches, the rise of Students for a Democratic Society, the folk music scene in Greenwich Village, the beginnings of the anti-Vietnam War peace movement. Some Fordham students opened a coffee shop—the Compleat Works of Charles Dickens—across the street from the college. Here we gathered to drink coffee or Orzato, perhaps indulge in illicit smoke, but mostly to argue politics, philosophy, and religion late into the night. Here I found a world that could help me explain the Cuban Missile Crisis and much more in ways that went beyond the knee-jerk patriotism of my youth.

As I said it was a heady environment. By the end of my second year, I had shed the mindless "my-country-right-or-wrong" ideals of my working-class upbringing, and had begun reading Marx and Gandhi in philosophy classes, Weber and Durkheim in sociology, and Bierstadt and Roper in history. My personal cosmic shell cracked as I entered a new, more complex world by crawling through the portal of ideas. It was at that point I became an intellectual, that is, somebody who saw ideas as the most exciting thing on the block—better than a winning season, a fast car, or a cheap feel.

My own particular foothold in the world of ideas, however, was less within any particular academic discipline (although I was majoring in English and sociology) than it was in the world of journalism. About the time I was losing the blinders of my upbringing, I also discovered photojournalism and Fordham's student newspaper, *The Ram*. Soon I was roaming the city, camera in hand, looking for slice-of-life photos in ghetto neighborhoods, covering antiwar demonstrations, and eventually writing newspaper copy and editorials. By the time I was appointed managing editor of the *Ram* in my junior year, I decided I was headed for a life in print journalism.

As a would-be journalist, I held myself somewhat aloof from full-blown participation in the political ferment underway in my university, the city, and the nation. While I sympathized with the social justice movements of the times, with SDS and the antiwar movement, and was a hanger-on to the sex, drugs, and rock-and-roll culture of the age, I also felt that if I became a fully engaged participant in any of these scenes, I would compromise what I then believed to be the "objective" eye of the journalist. Once, while photographing an antiwar sit-in, a protestor I knew looked up at me from her position on the floor and asked,

> "Are you ever going to commit yourself to anything, Ray, or are you just going to take pictures of the Revolution when it comes?"

I didn't answer, but I remember a voice in my head saying, "Yes, that's just what I am going to do—take pictures. I am going to document events and write about them. That's what journalists do."

What I didn't realize was that my journalistic standpoint was a step toward the personal marginality necessary for "sociological imagination" (Mills, 1959). I remember reading Peter Berger's (1963) observation in *Invitation to Sociology* that a sociologist is someone who wants to know what is going on behind every door and window shade, and thinking, "That's just like being a journalist. That's just like me!" While I continued to be peripherally involved with a wide range of movement activities, I stayed true to what I thought were the ethics of "unbiased" journalism, and eventually garnered a graduate scholarship to the Columbia School of Journalism.

Reality, in the form of the Vietnam War, however, altered my plans. Few students were heading to graduate school in 1968 unless they were 4-F (ineligible for the draft) or had a high draft lottery number (which I didn't). As someone who opposed the Vietnam War, and who, despite my journalistic ethics, was being gradually drawn into the War Resisters League, I found myself in a quandary. I had been raised to be a patriot, to "do my duty." My father, my uncles, and the fathers of my friends had served in World War II. I knew that these, the most important men in my life, expected me to do the same if I was drafted. I considered enlisting in the Air Force as a photographer. I considered going to Officer Candidate School (OCS) to avoid becoming a "grunt." But I also knew the war was wrong. And then friends on leave from the military started coming back with the same story: "This war is fucked, man. Whatever you do, don't go." I considered resisting the draft and going to jail. But I feared the shame. It was surprising to learn that I had enough courage to go to war, but not enough to go to jail.

The eventual resolution to my moral dilemma was neither dramatic nor heroic. After about four months of draft eligibility during which I figured I would go if called, I started teaching English in a Catholic girls' high school in New Rochelle, New York. In addition to a paycheck, the job also came with a draft deferment due to a teacher shortage in the greater New York City area. The following year I became a father, and was again deferred as the "sole support" of a family. The Vietnam War, however, did not exit from my life at that moment. In fact its role was only beginning, and would eventually lead to one of the most personally compelling research projects of my career—so far.

ON BEING A GRADUATE STUDENT

Before I graduated from Fordham with my BA in sociology, I had applied to a variety of journalism and sociology graduate programs, including Fordham as a backup. Since I was unable to attend any graduate program full-time, I began the 1968 fall semester as a full-time teacher of high-school English and a part-time graduate student in the sociology M. A. program at Fordham. Along the way to my master's degree, I encountered two very different educators who would each make a significant impact on my early intellectual development.

The first was Dr. John Martin, a professor and one of Fordham's two prominent criminologists at that time. I signed up for his graduate seminar in criminology, not because I was particularly interested in the subject, but because it fit my rather constraining work schedule. Nevertheless, I soon found myself fascinated by the course and the man. I had always wondered why some of my high school friends who were no more delinquent than I had been (and that was more than a little) had ended up with limited life options and lower aspirations after they had been caught and prosecuted as juvenile delinquents, while I, who by sheer dumb luck was never caught, had gone on to college and a professional teaching job.

John Martin introduced me to labeling theory, which offered an intellectual framework for understanding something I had experienced and observed, but never understood. But he did more than that; he made me aware that law is not the blind expression of universally held "values and mores," but rather the result of conflict. He did this less by assigning us readings in conflict criminology, or taking particularly radical positions himself, but by his narratives about how the justice system forged adult criminals out of minor juvenile offenders.

Along with John Martin's criminology, I began taking courses in social psychology with Dr. Charles Elliot who deepened my understanding of labeling theory by exposing me to the larger thought system of symbolic interaction, from George Herbert Mead's (1934) foundational work, *Mind, Self and Society,* to what were then relatively new and groundbreaking writings by Howard Becker (1963), Peter Berger and Thomas Luckman (1966), Herbert Blumer (1969), and Erving Goffman (1959). It was here, in the sociology of symbolic interactionism, that I thought I had found a wider framework to understand social life. With that bit of expectation in my kit bag, and a year as a psychiatric social worker at Rockland State Mental Hospital (I had been fired from the teaching job for helping students dramatize antiwar poetry), I headed off to pursue a PhD at Ohio State University where John Martin told me I would "like what was going on."

I've always wondered what Dr. Martin was thinking when he said I would like what was going on at Ohio State. I certainly was pleased to receive a tuition-plus-salary position as a teaching assistant there. I had discovered I enjoyed the role of educator during my year as a high school English teacher, so I was glad to be back in the classroom leading "discussion groups" in introductory sociology. However, having moved from the intellectual richness of Fordham and the political ferment of New York City, I found both the bland structural-functionalist sociology that dominated the OSU department and the white-bread city of Columbus, Ohio unexciting. I took a lot of courses from a lot of very smart and committed scholars at Ohio State. The problem was that while I was learning a good bit of sociology, relatively little of it helped me understand the social conflicts taking place beyond the classroom door. I remember vividly a moment in a course rather poorly titled "Race Relations"—as if the racial dynamics in America were rooted in the inability of people to "just get along." The professor had just dismissed the concept of institutional racism, saying that only individuals, not institutions, could be guilty of racism. At that point, one of my classmates, a black "sister" with full dreadlocks, stood up and said, "You don't think there's institutional racism. I'll show you institutional racism." With this claim hanging in the air, she turned her backside to the professor and pointed to her buttocks. "You see this ass," she said. "It's impossible for me to find a pair of pants to fit my butt because they're all made for skinny-assed white girls. That's institutional racism!" I wanted to cheer (but I didn't). Finally someone—in this case, a student, not a professor—was connecting the sociological dots for me.

I learned. I earned decent grades. I progressed to the dissertation phase of my doctoral education. But I was not intellectually inspired. I was fortunate, however, in working with Dr. Simon Dinitz, the department's leading criminologist of the time. Like most of his professional peers, Si was an orthodox criminologist. By this I mean that he understood criminology as a discipline dedicated to identifying the personal or interpersonal *defects* that produced the "kind of people" who would break the law. Having once been a delinquent myself, I suspected this question was at least too narrow, if not downright wrong, although I wasn't sure yet what might constitute an alternative criminology.

Si may have been an orthodox criminologist, but in addition to being one of the smartest and most creative orthodox criminologists I knew, he was by far the kindest professor I had met. Si was always concerned about his students as people, not just as budding intellects. He never humiliated students in class, no matter how boneheaded their answers or statements might have been. He had a quiet ego that enabled him to actively attend to what other people were saying, rather than focusing on what he would say next. In short, he became, and remains, my role model for what an educator should be.

About the time I started working with Si, an academic whirlwind blew into the department in the form of Dr. Paul Friday. Paul was a recent PhD from Wisconsin University, and brought with him a more politically engaged form of sociology than was common at Ohio State University. While Paul helped me recognize there were other ways of doing sociology, his most important intellectual contribution to my development took less than thirty seconds. One day he leaned inside the door of my graduate student cubicle, tossed a grey-covered hardback book on my desk, and said: "I think you might like this." It was the first edition of *Law, Order and Power*, by William Chambliss and Robert Seidman (1971). I started reading it that day, and by the time I had finished two days later, I knew I had found the way out of the intellectual dead zone in which I had been wandering.

Here were writers who actually talked about *society*, about how social arrangements, not personal defects, determined the content of law *and* the content of jails. Here were analysts who considered political economy an important sociological topic.

Imagine this: To that point in my career as a sociology graduate student not one single professor ever required or even suggested that I read anything by Karl Marx or any of the subsequent Marxian thinkers who contributed so much to modernist social thought. It was as if, for the sociologists who had been teaching me, the entire realm of Marxian sociological inquiry simply did not exist. What Marxism I knew I had acquired in philosophy and theology courses at Fordham, but nowhere had it been connected to the problematics of sociology. As I read *Law, Order and Power*, I began to understand how ideological hegemony works: Not through the constant imposition of messages that support the dominant order, but through the silencing of messages that might challenge it.

By the time I encountered Chambliss and Seidman, I had already begun the preliminaries for dissertation research on vehicular homicide. This itself was a bit of rebellion. I had been working as a research assistant on a federally funded study of "shock probation" in Ohio, the first state to explore the strategy of using "quick dip" sentencing as a rehabilitation tool. The assumption was that my dissertation research would be based on data from this project. It was easy and efficient: The data were already there. All that remained was to wrap it in some theory, add a literature review, run a few SPSS programs, and bingo, I would have a PhD! At first, that sounded pretty good. In addition to being a graduate student I was also a father with a wife whose work constituted over one-half of our small household income, so getting done and getting a "real" job was a high priority. Despite these pressures, in the end, I balked at doing a "quick-and-dirty" dissertation. I felt that I wanted to undertake a project that was my own, not an extension of someone else's larger research agenda. So I conceived of a dissertation examining offenses charged under Ohio's relatively new vehicular homicide law.

While my dissertation research produced some interesting findings about wrongful death by vehicle and the meanings of violence, the most valuable outcome was my discovery that, for the most part, American criminologists in the early 1970s did not view vehicular death as a particularly meaningful topic for criminological inquiry, no matter how wrong or how criminalized these deaths might be. This reality was clarified for me in a letter of rejection from a prominent criminology journal in which the editor stated "While the research is well done, traffic accidents lack sufficient importance to warrant publication in this journal." After the initial moment of disappointment and annoyance, I was fascinated by the logic of this rejection. Why, I wondered, are arrests for gambling, or public intoxication, or minor theft more important for criminologists, public policy makers, and the public in general than wrongful deaths by vehicle? This question was particularly compelling because, at that time, nearly twice as many people were being killed on the road as were being murdered, and about half of these deaths resulted from some traffic violation, many of them egregious violations such as drunkenness and speeding.[1] This was the root of the question that would become the central theme of my sociological and criminological career: What determines the selection of some harm for criminalization, and others for reluctant tolerance, acceptance, or even public approval?

SOUTHERN (DIS)COMFORT

When I completed my doctoral studies, my primary question was not intellectual, it was practical: Where could I find a job? The year I entered the academic job market, 1973, was a miserable one. Colleges were cutting back rather than adding new faculty positions. I interviewed for several attractive jobs. Unfortunately, in each case the departments were unable to hire due to budget and position cuts.

In late April of my final year at Ohio State I had one more interview, this one at a small college I had never heard of—the University of North Carolina at Charlotte. This time I was offered a job. I was grateful and relieved. I was also depressed and horrified. To end up deep in the Deep South, at a school with no academic prestige, in a department with no graduate program, no well-known sociologists, but with a heavy teaching load, felt like professional and intellectual death. My personal circumstances, however, did not allow me to wait out a year or two and search again in a better recruitment season, as did some of my graduate student friends. With working-class gratification that I had some kind of job, and a scholar's sadness of being exiled to "nowhere," I packed up and hauled my wife and son to North Carolina. My plan was to stay a while, and then move to a better position. And that's what I did—except "a while" turned out to be eighteen years, and my next job was even more remote than Charlotte—but I'm getting ahead of myself.

Not long before I left Charlotte in 1991, I saw a card which had a flower growing through a crack in a sidewalk on the front. The message on the inside read: "Grow where you are planted." It made me smile. Through a lot of good fortune and a bit of work, my eighteen years in Charlotte turned out to be years of intellectual and personal growth, due largely to the friends and intellectual companions I met both there and through my participation in various professional organizations. These people and their contributions are far too numerous to name. There are a few, however, who are essential to this narrative.

First and foremost is Jill Dubisch, a brilliant social theorist, ethnographer, and anthropologist who had joined the faculty at UNC Charlotte the year before me. Jill expanded, and as my life partner, continues to expand, my intellectual horizons more than I ever thought possible. In 1985, I published a book, *Order, Law and Crime*, that some critical criminologists found notable for its use of anthropological imagination to examine the deep roots of how societies construct their categories of wrongful and acceptable social injuries. Without the benefit of Jill's anthropological vision (and gracious access to her personal library) the anthropological insights of *Order, Law and Crime* would never have emerged.

About the same time I was settling into Charlotte and beginning to absorb a degree of anthropological vision from Jill, my intellectual trajectory was impacted by several other forces. One was my exposure to "radical criminology," a Marxist-oriented approach to problems of crime and justice that had reached critical mass at the School of Criminology at U Cal Berkeley. At the 1974 meeting of the American Society of Criminology I attended a session on radical criminology and first heard many of its core thinkers—Tony Platt, Paul Takagi, Richard Quinney, and Herman and Julia Schwendinger.

After this meeting, I began to refashion my intellectual project along more explicitly radical and Marxist lines, a decision that would have far-reaching impacts on the balance of my career. When I first started moving in this direction, Si had warned me to "stay in the mainstream" of criminology. If I didn't, he cautioned, I would never garner the "big grants" that were essential to moving out of Charlotte to what he termed a "good university." Si was a politically savvy criminologist, and he was right. After I moved away from mainstream criminology, the chances for research funding were almost nil. Not so much because of specific discrimination based on my political-economic and Marxian theoretical orientation, but rather because there was no funding for the questions that would interest someone with that orientation—such as, "why are major harms caused by political and economic elites so rarely punished while minor harms caused by poor young men of color are the focus of the justice system?"

Despite Si's warnings, the radical scholars from Berkeley I met in 1974, and many others who were influenced by them, became my intellectual community for the next ten years, a time during which I explored and deepened my own version of a Marxian understanding of law, crime, and justice, and began, myself, to write for the community of radical criminologists, particularly in the journal *Crime and Social Justice* (now *Social Justice*). As my development of a political-economic understanding of crime and justice expanded, it began to demand more extensive treatment than I could give it in articles, and led eventually to the publication of the aforementioned *Order, Law and Crime*.

The 1974 ASC meeting was foundational for my intellectual development in another curious way. As a fully employed recent graduate from Ohio State University with socialist sentiments, I offered my room in the meeting hotel as a crash pad to Stephen Pfhol, a graduate student friend who remained at Ohio State, and any other underemployed OSU graduate students he might care to bring. One of the people Steve brought along was Ron Kramer, now a distinguished sociologist and peace activist at Western Michigan University. As a result of that first meeting Ron and I first became professional acquaintances, then co-authors, and ultimately close friends. Over the intervening years we wrote and spoke about political and corporate social injustices in more pages and on more occasions than I can ever remember, crafted the widely-used concept of state-corporate-crime, and most recently developed a criminological critique of the U.S. war in Iraq (Kramer and Michalowski,

2005, 2006). Also, as an echo of that first meeting in Chicago, Ron has been my hotel roommate at the American Society of Criminology for over twenty-five years—except now he pays for his share of the room.

My years in Charlotte offered other deep, intellectual influences, among them the historian James Livingston and the Michaels. Jim Livingston came to Charlotte in 1985, and although he stayed for only a few years, his intellect and his capacity for expression deepened my understanding of historical forces and historiography in ways that have remained critical for my thinking.

The Michaels, Mike Pearson, Mike Sheely, and Mike Fennel, respectively a sociologist, a lawyer, and a carpenter, each contributed to my thought in distinct ways. Michael Pearson was the most widely read sociologist I have *ever* known, with a personal library to match. Over fifteen years as colleagues we shared ideas and books, political activism, hours of sociological and political talk, and a deep friendship. Mike P. worked with me on an analysis of the political economy of punishment, but other than that he wrote little. He was, however, proof that the strength of a scholar's intellect cannot be judged by the length of his publication record. Mike P. may have published very little sociology, but he understood a great deal of sociology, and was better at communicating it to students than anyone I have ever known. Sadly, he died much too young.

Mike Sheely was an intellectual of a different stripe. He was a labor lawyer who engaged me as a data analyst and expert witness in employment discrimination class action suits. His legal acumen and my statistics won a number of race, sex, and age discrimination cases against major corporations such as Eastern Airlines, Duke Power, First Union National Bank, and Thurston Motor Lines. To him I will always be grateful for the opportunity to use my sociological training to put real dollars in the pockets of working people who had been the victims of labor injustice, as well as to force changes in the employment practices of the corporations we took down. We became good friends. As a pair of displaced New Englanders we understood each other on many levels, and Mike S. never failed to increase my understanding of how law works at the practical level of the courtroom. Sadly, he too died much too young.

The third Mike, Mike Fennel was a scrappy Chicago Irishman who made his living as an independent home repairman and remodeler, but who also loved to think and argue about society. He devoured history and social science writings at a rate that would shame most graduate students, always holding his own in debate with academics, including Livingston and myself. More than that, he brought an unsentimental vision of daily life to our discussions. For him, the gritty reality of the working-class struggle to earn one's daily bread was experiential, not academic. His perceptive understanding of economic, political, and social life in Charlotte led to semi-regular appearances on the op-ed pages of the *Charlotte Observer* where the tag line at the bottom identified him as a "Charlotte carpenter and writer," a most fitting description for someone who seamlessly linked manual and mental labor. Fortunately, he is still around and raising hell.

In the mid-1980s, I had the opportunity to shift my academic lens to Cuba. Finally, thanks to the easing of travel restrictions under President Jimmy Carter, I was able to experience, firsthand, the island that had started my intellectual journey so many years before. In addition to a number of briefer trips, I was able to live in Havana during the spring semester of 1989 while undertaking an ethnography of a *bufete colectivo*—a law collective. During my years of connection to Cuba, many Cubans, from lawyers, to scholars, to ordinary citizens, gave me the gift of their time and energy to help me better understand the realities of life in a socialist society in terms that were colored neither by the rosy tint of Marxian orthodoxy nor the jaundiced negativity of U.S. anti-communism.

In my last two years in Charlotte, a new colleague, Dr. Susan Carlson joined the faculty. Her capacity to link complex critical theory to complex statistical analyses expanded my horizons in another direction. I had, by that time, come to an intellectual impasse, feeling as if the dynamics of contemporary political-economic life involved something more intricate than the structural Marxist framework within which I had been working. Susan introduced me to the theory of social structures of accumulation which helped better explain the changes in justice system practices that I had been observing and studying. It remains the theoretical framework that I use whenever I am attempting to understand broad changes in patterns of crime and penal practices.

GO WEST NOT-SO-YOUNG MAN
In 1993 Jill and I grabbed, what for many academic couples, was the brass ring. We were offered positions as professors in the same university in a part

of the country we wanted to try living. The state was Arizona, the city was Flagstaff, and the school was the Northern Arizona University. The problem was that accepting this offer required that I do two things I had promised myself I would never do; leave a department of sociology for a department of criminal justice, and become an administrator. But that was the deal—to make it work I had to agree to serve as chair of a newly formed department of criminal justice. I was reluctant. I also knew, however, that I did not want to spend my entire career at UNCC. I had never been fully at home in the South, though I had good friends there and loved its coastal regions. I also felt that I wanted to experience more than one university in the course of my career. So, faced with becoming the chair of a criminal justice department or possibly staying in Charlotte for the balance of my career (I had already reached my mid-40s), I chose Arizona, hoping that the dean's promise that I would "thrive" if I came to NAU would hold true. Fortunately, it did.

I experienced a few difficult early years as an administrator as I tried to forge a department committed to social justice, not just criminal justice. However, I was blessed with a fine set of young colleagues, in particular Alex Alvarez, Larry Gould, Marianne Nielsen, Neil Websdale, and Nancy Wonders, who shared my vision, and were willing to work energetically to make it a reality. Through their efforts, the Department of Criminology and Criminal Justice at Northern Arizona University has, over the years, earned recognition both nationally and internationally as a center for critical criminological inquiry.

My time in Arizona and NAU brought other intellectual and personal rewards. Shortly before reaching Flagstaff, Ron Kramer and I had begun examining wrongdoing at the intersection of business and government—what we termed "state-corporate" crime. During my time in Flagstaff, this idea matured, was taken up by a number of young scholars, and eventually led to a collection of studies of criminality at the highest reaches of power and politics (Michalowski and Kramer, 2007).

In another vein, the many beautiful roads that crisscross Arizona and the greater far West led Jill and I back to motorcycling—an echo of our early years in Charlotte when we would strap a cheap cardboard suitcase to my little 400cc Honda and ride off to Myrtle Beach, South Carolina for the weekend. After a few years of recreational riding around the West, we became involved with an annual motorcycle pilgrimage that rides from Los Angeles to the Vietnam

Veterans Memorial in Washington, D.C. When we first joined the Run, we saw it as a way to address some personal sorrows we carried as a result of the Vietnam War. After several years of riding with the Run, however, we began to turn our ethnographic eyes to understanding how pilgrimage, ritual, and the political (re)construction of memory intersected in ways that made the Run a powerful experience for its participants, and a remarkable example of American culture at work. The result was our 2001 volume, *Run For the Wall: Remembering Vietnam on a Motorcycle Pilgrimage*, a book that for both of us was not only an intellectual project, but also a labor of love written in memory of all those who have suffered at the hands of careless politicians who destroy or damage legions of warriors and citizens to pursue dreams of international dominance. Today, when I listen to the stories of Iraq war veterans, I hear such stunningly clear echoes of America's Vietnam experience that I am deeply saddened and angered by the failure of our national leadership to care about the consequences of their criminal military adventures.

Today my intellectual central project focuses on two intersecting areas, the linkages among globalization, immigration, and the sociopolitical construction of national sovereignty (Wonders and Michalowski, 2002; Michalowski, 2008), and the criminology of war and empire (Michalowski, 2003, 2009). While these are at a far remove from my early interests in vehicular homicide, they are really continuations of the question provoked by my dissertation work thirty-five years ago—how do powerful elites decide what harms and what harm-causing individuals to criminalize, and what harms and what harm-causing individuals to tolerate, or even to celebrate? Today, I look for answers less at the national, and more at the transnational and global level. In this endeavor I have learned much from my Flagstaff colleague, co-author, and friend, Nancy Wonders, and my colleague, friend, and sailing partner Piers Beirne. The intelligence and energy Nancy brings to understanding intersection of identity, borders, and techniques of state boundary-maintenance have done much to deepen my own understanding of these questions. I count on Piers for his always sharp-eyed and unforgiving critique of any muddle-headed thinking.

If I have any regrets it is that I have not been able to teach doctoral students. This is, of course, no surprise. Most of the radical and/or critical criminologists of my generation were excluded from "Research 1" institutions, in some cases by outright repression as in the case of the closing of the School of

Criminology at Berkeley, and in others by the inability of radical researchers to obtain major research funding—a key criterion for positions at flagship universities.

While I am somewhat sorry that I do not teach doctoral students, I also recognize that this is a condition of my own choosing. After all, I could have followed Si's advice to "stay in the mainstream." It is just that the mainstream did not then, and does not now, ask particularly interesting questions about crime and justice —at least in my view. If there is joy in being an intellectual, it is in asking and trying to answer the questions that are meaningful to you, not to federal granting agencies. If the two happen to coincide then one will enjoy mainstream benefits. If not, then the choice is either to sell out one's own questions, or manage without mainstream rewards. I chose the latter path. Having done this, however, I take comfort in knowing I am in good company. Many of the founding radical criminologists I admire, and who did much more to shape the field than I, such as William Chambliss, Tony Piatt, Julia and Herman Schwendinger, and Richard Quinney, ended up in non-doctoral programs as well. Yet, all of them continued to write and influence critical criminology with strong and clear voices.

The gates to doctoral granting programs widened somewhat for the generation of critical scholars entering the professorate in the 1980s. By then both feminism and postmodernism had breached the upper echelons of higher education, and radical critiques of the dominant order became more tolerated as the vehement anti-communist McCarthyism that still lingered over the Academy in the 1960s and early 1970s began to wane. I do find it interesting, however, that the one set of radical critiques that still remains largely unacceptable in the highest reaches of the Academy is those focused on social class. Federal and state governments now fund research shaped by the feminist critique of patriarchy in areas such as the study and prevention of domestic violence. There are no similar initiatives, however, informed by a socialist understanding of social class. That is the one critique capitalist society cannot allow to obtain a high platform.

CONCLUSION

Many years ago, I heard a story from an anthropologist friend who had worked in a Pacific Island community. It is a culture where people bring gifts—"grave goods"—to burial ceremonies to help the deceased along the way to their next life. She wanted to understand how far these obligations extended, so she asked one of her subjects whether he would be obliged to bring grave goods to someone who had done nothing more than sell him some palm trees. The man replied, "Of course." When she asked why he would bring grave goods to someone with whom he had had nothing more than a fleeting business transaction, his reply was "Because he grew me."

I have always liked that sentiment, the simple (or maybe not so simple) recognition that so many of the people we meet along our life path help grow us into the persons we become. So the answer to the question of how did I, a would-be jock from upstate New York become a sociologist of law, crime, and justice, is that I have been fortunate to meet people who grew me in the ways that I needed at the times that I needed.

NOTE

1. This was in the years 1973–1975, before the emergence of Mothers Against Drunk Driving made vehicular deaths a matter of widespread public anger and mobilization. It is also interesting to note that the rise of the movement against drunk driving occurred, not at a time when road deaths were rising, but when they were declining due to increased vehicle safety and road improvements.

REFERENCES

Becker, H. (1963). *Outsiders*. New York: Free Press.

Berger, P. (1963). *Invitation to Sociology*. New York: Anchor Books.

Berger, P., and Luckman, T. (1966). *The Social Construction of Reality: A Treatise in the Sociology of Knowledge*. Garden City, NY: Doubleday.

Blumer, H. (1969). *Symbolic Interactionism: Perspective and Method*. Chicago: University of Chicago Press.

Chambliss, W., and Seidman, R. (1971). *Law, Order and Power*. Reading, MA.: Addison-Wesley.

Goffman, E. (1959). The Presentation of Self in Everyday Life. Doubleday: Garden City, NY.

Mead, G. H. (1934). *Mind, Self, and Society*, C.W. Morris (ed.). Chicago: University of Chicago Press.

Michalowski, R. (1985). *Order, Law and Crime.* New York: Random House.

Michalowski, R. (2008). Border militarization and migrant suffering: A case of transnational social injury. *Social Justice,* 31 No. 5 (Spring).

Michalowski, R. (2009). Power and crime in the global age: Theorizing intersections of state, economy, and politics. *Crime, Law and Social Change* (Forthcoming, 2009). Michalowski, R., and Dubisch, J. (2001). *Run for the Wall: Remembering Vietnam on a Motorcycle Pilgrimage.* New Brunswick: Rutgers University Press.

Michalowski, R., and Kramer, R. (2007). *State-Corporate Crime: Wrongdoing at the Intersection of Business and Politics.* New Brunswick: Rutgers University Press.

Mills, C. W. (1959). *The Sociological Imagination.* London: Oxford University Press.

11

Hither and Thither No More: Reflections of a Retiring, But Not Shy, Professor[1]

GARY T. MARX

After putting on Beethoven's *Pastorale Symphony No. 6*, 1 scanned the horizon, the wind gauge, and the knot log. At that moment I realized I was living my life about as well as I could. The sun was preparing a colorful departure to the other side of the world, and the breeze was holding steady. I offered my friend another glass of wine and steered west.

—*Jimmy Buffet*, Tales From Margaritaville

In a never finished novel about a novelist who could no longer write, Dashiell Hammett advises, "if you are tired, you ought to rest, I think, and not try to fool yourself and your customers with colored bubbles" (Wolfe, 1980).

I am not really tired, just a little weary. Besides the illusion offered by colored bubbles ain't all bad and the hustler has a kind of perverse appeal. I fortunately don't have Hammett's health or drinking problems. But I do have nothing more to say about the academic career issues treated in this and other recent books. Thanks to the serendipity that defines so much of life, I wrote far more on the subject than I ever planned to in spite of an inclination to reticence in personal matters.[2] Table 1 summarizes my advice to beginning scholars.

I will instead write about a topic that has been scarcely touched in the burgeoning academic self-reflection literature—retirement and being out of the academic organization.

There are many reasons for reflecting back on one's life. The pleasures of good memories and nostalgia; revisiting people and places that were formative in one's development; musing about roads not taken and imagining what might have happened if they had been; answering the question who am I now and how does that connect with who I was at the beginning of a career; finding the knowledge (or perhaps just new beliefs and interpretations) that can emerge from straining a career through five decades of experience; and channeling one's lingering narcissistic needs into a socially acceptable form under the rationale of leaving a record for family, friends, and fellow travelers.[3] Furthermore, if it is correct as Eli Wiesel observes in *Night* that we are our memories then involvement with them is fundamental to our sense of self.

Such reflections are like reversing the vista of a telescope by looking in the wrong end—taking in the width of a life and narrowing it to one's present. We can't with much certitude turn to an unknown future. But the cornucopia of a lifetime's memories, however blurry, faded, and selective are there to be worked with.

Getting one's cognitive and emotional bearings on the terrain as a human and as a cultural and biological descendant is enhanced by knowing ancestor's stories. How I wish I had the life stories and moral precepts of my hundreds (the number doubles with each generation) of grandparents, great-grandparents, and their siblings going back to the first ancestor born in 1642 whose name I know. Among them were rabbis (one who traced his ancestry to the Maharal of Prague [a humble guy who claimed he was a direct descendant of King David]), merchants, leather workers, horse traders, revolutionaries, jewelers, peddlers, ragmen, maids, sweat shop seamstresses, a circus worker, a hooker, farmers, soldiers, hoteliers, developers, gamblers, restauranteurs, and manufacturers —even an imbiber of rat poison and the nineteenth century owner of an abode overwrought with Renaissance paintings (the Villa Hertziana) next to the Spanish Steps in Rome.

What written record would be left by relatives who sailed to Surinam from Amsterdam in the early 1800s; the imprisoned leaders of the failed 1848 revolution in Bonn; a plantation owner whose South Carolina home was reportedly burned down the day after a Sabbath dinner was shared with General Sherman; a great grandfather who left the U.S. in 1906 for Palestine to be buried on the Mount of Olives in order to be on hand for the messiah; a great uncle said to have been with Lenin in Switzerland and with him on the sealed train back to Russia and a great grandfather, the Mayor of Borisov who died in the civil war following the revolution; or a rags to riches to almost rags grandfather who lost ownership of a square block in downtown Los Angeles and his large estate in Topanga Canyon in the depression. A golf lover and hater of Roosevelt, he was a founder of Hillcrest Country Club because people of his persuasion could not join the established clubs. Since 1938 his ashes have been part of the turf there. As well, I wish I knew even more about the seller of California Mohave desert land to suckers in the early 1930s (he was smart enough not to buy any himself) and the owner for a short time of a pre-Bugsy Siegel gambling casino in Las Vegas (the Kit Kat Club) and later a restaurant on the Sunset strip.[4]

SILENT GRASS-GROWING MOODS

I'm goin' up the country, baby don't you wanna go? . . . Got to get away.—
Canned Heat

In 1851 Herman Melville wrote to Nathaniel Hawthorne, "I am so pulled hither and thither by circumstances. The calm, the coolness, the silent grass-growing mood in which a [person] ought always to compose,—that, I fear, can seldom be mine." (Melville, 1972) At the height of an active career as a college professor I knew the feeling.

But that is the case no longer. In 1996 I became an emeritus professor, retiring but not shy, while still at the top of my game and earlier than most colleagues. Like a diver avoiding the bends I did not exit quickly. I spent the next two years decompressing (but not deflating) via fellowships in California and Washington, D.C. Since then I have been pastured on an island in the Pacific Northwest and warmed in the Sonoran desert with a kind of sabbatical for life.[5]

In these remarks I will compare the situation of the retired academic to others and suggest some reasons why retirement may be easier for the former; note the increased importance of retirement as a third major stage of life; and reflect on career success and failure and visits to places that were formative in my growing up.

Common complaints for the newly retired include loss of an important identity, boredom in the face of so much unstructured time, unease over the absence of a distinction between workdays and weekends, and loneliness. I have been fortunate not to experience these in any serious fashion. Being an academic offers some natural preparation for retirement.

There are of course honorific titles such as "professor emeritus" which portage a bit of esteem for the informed, relative to those who can only say, "I worked on the assembly line at Ford." But beyond what you can say about yourself is the issue of how you see yourself relative to your work career. I feel fortunate that my identity as a social studies scholar is strong and I don't need a literal or locational badge or tag to remind me who I am. In most settings it doesn't matter whether others are aware of my former activities. My identity involves commitment to the discipline rather than the profession, a given organization, or place per se.[6]

As a result of light and flexible academic schedules with abundant leaves and holidays, the limits of time and place tethers were modest—be on campus several days a week for a few hours to meet a class or two and be available for meetings. Early in their career successful academics come to terms with the enormous amount of discretionary time they are offered.

Nor have I experienced the loneliness or lack of direction many retirees report. Living close to our offspring and having made some new friends (although far fewer than as a youth) helps. But so too does the kind of work done. When experienced as a calling or a compulsion, mental work is portable and migratory. It is always with you (although there is a down side there as well). Scholars and artists live to a significant degree in a symbolic world of imagined interactions that can be called up at any point, apart from the constraints of physical location and time period. One doesn't have to be at work to work. You still have a job, you just don't get paid for it. Changes in geography and unspringing the clock don't affect this. Moving slowly out of the regular job and occasionally dipping back into it has also smoothed the transition. But there are other issues.

On my last major move from Colorado to Washington State in 1996 I shipped ninety boxes of assorted unsorted books, journals, correspondence, and documents, and two trunks that had been shipped to Colorado from Boston in 1992 in a prior move and not opened since then. After unpacking a few high priority boxes, most remained unpacked. With continuing deadlines or the seductions of new leisure, I just did not want to spend the time unpacking and sorting them. Most of the boxes continue to gather dust (and no doubt worse in our barn), whether from the weather, insects, or rodents.[7] The more time goes on, the harder it becomes to face them.

The boxes generate ambivalence and a solution to that is of course avoidance. I feel affection and curiosity toward their contents, but also feel pushed away by them. They bring a certain lingering sadness and melancholy involving disillusionment about the profession (if not the discipline), a bemused view of what all the sound and fury was about, less than full enthusiasm about the continual weakening of the borders between the university and the society—especially the commercialization of university research and efforts to run universities along business models, to judge faculty by the size of their grants, and a share-the-spoils politicization in the distribution of university resources that seems more appropriate to big city politics than to the repository of the highest ideals of Western civilization. The boxes contain bittersweet reminders of defeats as well as victories—some weakened, if residual, bad feelings about the former and sadness that the latter are no longer a significant part of my life. A career stored in boxes also leads one to ask, why, if I am now likely a better scholar as a result of so much accumulated knowledge and experience, am I not still formally part of the institution that most values scholarly work, let alone at its apex? Yet there is also much to be said for moving on.

My twice almost colleague at the University of California at San Diego Joe Gusfield (1990) put it well:

> The thought of being outside the swirl of institutional life is appealing to me. The idea of a life without a schedule of places to be at set times, without guilt of responsibilities not fulfilled or deadlines not met, and without the need to manufacture opinions seems an attractive Utopia.

Robert Merton (1985) captures a tension experienced by the highly motivated (driven?) overcommitted scholar when he notes that for Schopenhauer, "the chief sin against the Holy Ghost of the intellectual life is to put down one's own work in order to take up another's." Of course helping others can improve one's work as well, not to mention being politically useful, or a reasonable expectation for a member of a community. Being away from such demands on a daily basis however is salutary, even as some loss is felt. The demanding swirl of academic life which serves to socially locate and validate the professor goes, but the time to reflect on what the activity means and the choice of how much of it to continue is gained.[8]

It's the little things you notice—waiting in line at the post office, paying for office supplies and computer help and doing your own copying. Then there are the occasional meetings with new colleagues who seem to evidence a vague familiarity with your work (or perhaps they are just being polite). This is reminiscent of the person who said to the retired actress, "didn't you used to be Joan Crawford?"

The recognition that comes with longevity can be bittersweet. I was surprised and pleased to see myself referred to as "the doyen" of the kind of research I now do. But I must admit to ambivalence in another account in being referred to as, "the grand old man of surveillance studies." I can accept the first adjective, but the second is a blow to the solar plexus of a guy who, although he can no longer palm a basketball, still does over 150 push ups and likes to run and bike long distances, having fun and trying to avoid being, and being seen, as too old. Yet moving on in life requires coming to terms with how others see us and getting out of the way of those who run faster or at least more freshly.[9] Having been in the academic biz for five decades it is ok and maybe even accurate to be called old and to slow down without apology or self-deprecation. With time can even come surprising good news—some of the old worries about consuming too much chocolate, liquor, and coffee turn out to be misplaced.

Beyond any literal slowing down (which might be balanced by greater experience and wisdom), there is the increased difficulty of effectively communicating with (and understanding) students who are forever young and always undergoing a unique cohort experience.[10] The currents of life carry (or sometimes catapult) the teacher ever further downstream away from the slang, dress style, media culture, and sentiments of the students. One risks being seen either as a pathetic, emulative poseur or as hopelessly out of it, even a bit quaint and comical in one's datedness. Not sharing as much of a common culture makes communication more difficult. Most students for example are only familiar with films and current events that appeared when they reached adolescence.

We must acknowledge American society's fetish of youthfulness but not accept it. As Popeye might have said, "we y'am what we y'am." We can not be what they are, nor what we were. The deliciousness of having been on the right side of the 1960s generation gap with one's students I experienced as a young teacher remains memorable, but not relivable.

Another lesson is realizing how much sociability among colleagues is intermingled with instrumentality and when the latter goes, the former can decline precipitously. When you have no official position and no specific reasons to interact and can't directly help or harm others professionally (and even worse have moved geographically away) you are out of sight and given lower priority. I am struck by the number of times letters or e-mails sent to colleagues (e.g., a note congratulating them on an award or promotion, a request for information, a paper I sent, a suggestion to get together, an offer to give a talk, a query about a part-time job) have gone unanswered or belatedly responded to, relative to when I had a regular position. This is not out of malevolence, but simply reflects prioritization among busy, instrumentally oriented people. Being out of the game erodes the veneer of civility that often envelops work relationships, even holding apart the information overwhelm that the Internet has brought.

Not to worry. The limelight can blind and burn as well as warm. Mark Twain got it right when he wrote, "obscurity and a competence—that is the life that is best worth living."[11] (Twain) It is even better if one can add "and the time to be left alone and do fulfilling work, in serene and beautiful environs surrounded by those you love with sensuous delights, challenges and recreation never far away."

When I look out at Puget Sound and see great blue herons and bald eagles against a backdrop of the Seattle skyline and the Cascades and hear the seals and coyotes it is easy to forget the larger world and to agree with a neighbor who wrote:

> I find more and more that I don't like to leave Bainbridge Island very often.
> It worries me, now that I think about it, but no destination seems to me
> worth leaving home to get to.
> Andrew Ward (1991)

> As Mose Allison sings:
> I'm a certified senior citizen
> Its true it could happen to you. . .
> raise hell in Arizona.

Being nourished by the warm sands of the Ringtail Trail at the Arizona Sonoran Preserve, while seeing the sunset through the Cholla cactus, smelling the creosote after a desert rain and sidestepping an ancient tortoise, it is easy to reverse Yeats and have an abiding sense of the good life which can sustain one through temporary periods of tragedy.

Early in my career I recall historian Oscar Handlin who was about to retire proudly recounting that he did not read a daily newspaper. I was shocked and it even seemed a major dereliction of civic responsibility.

But as the man in the movie said, "things change." At the same age, I now understand Handlin's reasons. There are times I agree with Paul Simon's, "I get all the news I need on the weather report." Or Bruce Springsteen singing, "I've seen enough, I don't want to see anymore." The faithful reading of a local newspaper and the several national dailies requires too much precious time and offers little of enduring importance and much that is conducive to depression, anger, and cynicism.

Reading habits change —I now don't miss an issue of the AARP Bulletin. I also often read the financial and obituary sections of the newspaper. The latter had previously seemed irrelevant and slightly tainted. Everyone I knew was young and healthy. Yet imperceptively people only a little older than you who were always there are gone. When you don't have a regular income slight perturbations in the market take on exaggerated importance. The business section ceases to be the stuff of soulless materialists.

My declining income, travel, mail, e-mail, fax, and phone communications suggest a move from "Who's Who" to "Who's He?"[12] But who cares? With this change there has come time and the need for new kinds of reflection and even leisure.

By self-definition, I am not retired and have never taken up golf (which is different from putting it down). Research and writing continue to be deeply engaging. Yet I am organizationally homeless, even as I feel well-niched in some broader dispersed community of social studies scholars. Can you gracefully move from status defined by respectful placement in a prestigious organization to status defined (for most of those you encounter, especially if you move away) by general attributes such as gender and age? Who are you stripped of the resources, symbols, and borders that organizations offer? There is a strong link between identity and organizational affiliation and our culture doesn't provide ready identity pegs when that link is broken.

I am uncertain how to respond to the ever-present demand for occupation on questionnaires and the eternal, "what do you do?" question. I still publish and occasionally lecture, yet I can't honestly say I am a college professor. While I have been writing professionally for forty years, it doesn't feel quite right to think of myself as a writer. Given the largesse of research support and occasional work, I have not dipped much into my retirement funds. I certainly don't feel retired, yet I do not have a regular employer. By the standards of the Bureau of Labor Statistics I might even be unemployed, since I have unsuccessfully applied for jobs. But it doesn't seem right to say that I am unemployed.

The amplitude of requests from students, colleagues, editors, administrators, journalists, and others, and the constant meetings and classes to prepare for (or to feel bad about not having prepared for) moves from a flood to an ever smaller trickle the longer one is out. In facing far fewer external demands there is time for inner dialogue and the slow replaying of a life. As Frank Sinatra sang, "nice work if you can get it"—most of the time.

STAGES

I always thought there were two basic life stages: growing up and being a grown up. The growing-up stage is essentially preparation for life—learning the culture and all that entails. This is the standard material of introductory social science textbooks involving socialization and rites of passage—going to school, experiencing and experimenting, getting certified, and selecting a career.

Then graduation arrives and you are out in the world. There are an astounding array of choices regarding what to do, where to live, how to live, who to live with, and what kind of a person to become. For the privileged this seems a time of almost infinite possibility. It is relatively open-ended with untold degrees of freedom.

The stage of active involvement is just doing it—getting married, raising children, working, and perhaps moving up. The degrees of freedom are less now. This is your life as an old television program proclaimed.

Yet with the good fortune of affluence and health, the above is only two-thirds or three-quarters of the story. There is a third stage which is harder to characterize because it is relatively new as a result of people living longer with greater affluence. This stage is more contradictory and less linear than the earlier two stages—involving both new freedoms and new restrictions. Many people will spend as much or more time in retirement as they did in their career.

Four components of this third stage are: enhanced consumption and leisure, risk-taking, departure preparation, and nostaligia/interpretation/sense-making. I will emphasize the last after brief mention of the others.

Consumption: For the privileged (but not wildly rich) middle classes, it can be a time for consumption and expenditures on a scale previously unimagined (or if imagined, seemingly unrealizable). Growing up in the 1940s and 1950s with parents as the walking wounded from the Depression, you didn't have to be Protestant to love deferred gratification. Being successful and being moral meant deferring or minimizing immediate gratification for the long run.

In addition you likely had very little wealth and were too busy saving to meet your needs for a home or a car and then for better ones, for children's needs, and of course for that rainy day or emergency that could always arrive. But those demands are largely behind you. You got through it. You are free. What is more, given the growth of the economy, wealth transfers from parents, smart or lucky investing, tax-deferred savings for retirement, and health insurance, you are comfortable and don't have those worries.

You also have the time to enjoy indulging yourself in activities unrelated to work. You were too busy before to do enough of that. A sense of impending (or at least closer) doom can also generate a sense of abandon. There is greater awareness of the ticking clock.

The illness and death of mentors and even former students is a jarring awakening. There might not be time to finish a book, undertake a long planned project, or take that trip to Alaska.[13] This recalls the hedonistic and indulgent arguments of the later 1950s and early 1960s when we thought the world would soon face nuclear destruction summarized in the song "enjoy yourself, enjoy yourself, it's later than you think." That was a time of both heightened anxiety and hedonism.

This ethos is also reflected in the last meal of the condemned person and tales of sexual escapades the night before an individual joins a monastery or convent. Grab it while you still can. Don't wait for next year in Jerusalem. This is the last chance cafe. As the folk song says about the last train, "If you miss this one there'll never be another one." The desire to do this can be intensified by a dirty little secret —what if I die before I get to enjoy enough of this hard-earned money and the leisure it offers, or do some things I have always wanted to do?

Risk-taking: It can also be a time for greater risk-taking, if guided by greater wisdom and experience. You have the financial means to maximize safe risk-taking (if that is not a contradiction). On the other hand, you also have less to prove and less physical ability. In a sense you have less to lose. A professional innovation at which you might not be successful —mixing fiction with your social science won't hurt your career. Your children are safely into adulthood. One friend in commenting on the mountains he now climbs in Asia said he would never think of having done that until after his children were on their own. My modest mountain biking and kayaking forays have the same quality.

Adieu bidding: As Tom Rush sings "I am going on a journey and I pray all things go well."[14] This is a time for consolidation, contraction, account settling (although discretion is required here since some of the appealing ways of settling nonfinancial accounts are wrong even if delicious to contemplate), and leave taking.

It is the reverse of the initial stage of preparation for life. It is a time for passing on the baton and preparation for departure, a time to think about the unthinkable and divide up the spoils. A time to get lean rather than fatten up. A time to divest not invest. Who gets what? How to insure that one's children are helped without being corrupted? What causes and charities to help? And in what proportions? And how does one do this while keeping enough to live well in the interim and avoid becoming morbid, sentimental, and weepy?

Wills need to be drawn up, attics cleaned out, correspondence and libraries culled. Such house-cleaning and preparing for the big move is not only fair to descendants, but also extends your control. After all it is or was your life.

Interpretation: For the reflective classes it is above all likely to be a time for interpreting, indulging in nostalgia, summing up, and pretty final sense making. Strands of curiosity and a hunger to know whipsaw through consciousness as a reward and penalty for being blessed and cursed with a good memory, powers of introspection, and the scholar's passion for wondering and analyzing. This quest for understanding works best when its deeply personal and idiosyncratic roots can be connected with its broader social, cultural, and historical contexts.

You have the advantage of hindsight. The future (or the vast majority of it) has arrived. You know in great detail what the story is thus far and the general direction it will probably take. In many ways that is a relief. There is little struggle and angst over the concerns that took up so much energy in the earlier stages and in worrying about the future. You also have a much greater stock of information to work with in making sense out of your life and life in general. The folk knowledge about age and wisdom reflects this. This is your best shot at understanding. As you get nearer to the top of the mountain, the view gets better. It is more sweeping and you can see further. You may even see what kind of a story it is. In this case it is not one of redemption, nor is it a Horatio Alger tale. I started in the middle not at the bottom in a resource rich time and place with expanding opportunity.

Our friend Morrie Schwartz (Albom, 2002) in explaining why he was very public about his dying from Gehrig's disease said, "I want someone to hear my story." The literal person goes, but memories and lessons live on in those whose lives we have touched.

This sense-making is for one's self and others. Most importantly, this involves one's immediate family and their descendants, but I also feel a desire to pass on my sense of things to colleagues and students. This may be hubris and a silly quest for some level of immortality. Schwartz observes that written records, tapes, photographs, and videos "are a desperate attempt to steal something from death's suitcase." Perhaps. But they are also something we can offer later generations.

MEMORIES ARE MADE OF THIS
While it may well be that, "nostalgia's just another word for nothing left to lose," I find it very pleasurable. There are musings in which I am only partly in control. They sometimes just wash over and mentally carry me away (although other memories noted below with respect to mentors, career events, and places, I approach more analytically). They often involve my formative years: Ayn Rand and her sophomoric characters in *The Fountainhead* and *Atlas Shrugged*, Sinatra's swingingly having it his way, Hemingway, Chandler, Hammet, Bogart, Brando, Newman, Dean, Traven, Kipling, Sartre, Camus, Kerouac, the lyrics of Cole Porter and the Gershwins, the singing of Chet Baker, June Christie, Chris Connor, Anita O'Day, Johnny Cash, Buddy Holly, The Beach Boys, and Mose Allison, Southern California in the 30s, 40s, and

50s, the hazy, lazy days of summer, the beach and desert, palm trees and stucco homes with red tile roofs, on a clear day you can see Catalina, convertibles and girls, girls, girls. In the background Sandburg, Mencken, Twain, Whitman, Thoreau, Emerson, Conrad, Kafka, Orwell, Huxley, and Europe. And closer to home Groucho Marx, Jack Webb, James Dean, Natalie Wood, Lenny Bruce, Mort Sahl, Shelley Berman, Martin Luther King, Malcolm X, Bobby Kennedy, and Erving Goffman.

These form pieces of a hazy, softly nostalgic puzzle. They provide the psychic backdrop against which to order a life and define a sense of self and an idealized and preferred personal style (its degree of realization is of course another matter).

Some common strands:

—the concrete as against the grand abstraction, authenticity/honesty, a distaste for hypocrisy, appreciation of the intellect, rationality, empiricism, irony, paradox, thresholds, and curvilinear truths and wisdom, surprise, humor, individualism, and a naive belief in an almost presocial self able to endure the slings and spears of destiny and the pressures of the crowd, courage, perseverance, and struggle against the odds, performance, cool, hot, precision, passion, testing but respecting legitimate limits and asking "says who and why?" fascination with the outsider, awe, enthusiasm, nature reverence, challenges, tentativeness but with awareness of the need to believe and act, the struggle for justice, and being a person of integrity.

HEY SPORT

One type of well-formed memory which is often present involves sports. Why does a man approaching seventy years of age who is not now an avid sports fan, so often think of his own athletic moments, some going back to the sixth grade? [15] Jumping up amidst a crowd in the end zone to catch a touchdown pass; down by one point, stealing the ball, running down the court and scoring the winning basket just before the buzzer goes off in a high school game on a championship team; and that cinema-perfect Hollywood May day more than fifty years ago, when I broke the school record in the shot put (50'3"), but it didn't count because I stepped over the line.

Why do I still yearn for it to have been otherwise? In retrospect why do I feel deprived and imagine what I might have done if I had the real coaches, weight and diet training, video analyses, and all the other techniques that now enhance performance? What possible difference could it make since I won the meet?

It would not have made the world a better place, satisfied my youthful sexual longings, nor made me tougher on the schoolyard. Perhaps it is liking or needing to think of myself and imagining being known by others as the kind of guy who broke school records. But what are records? My best effort that counted was 48'10" and the record was 49'6." Who today knows or cares who held, or even what the class B shot put record for John Marshall High School was in 1956? But there it is replaying in my mind as an unbroken broken record.

Those close, but no cigar musings, and fantasies of greater sports achievement are mostly restricted only to my high school years. I almost never think about being only a finalist for the C. Wright Mills award in 1968, failed job applications, or rejected articles. I am not sure why.

More analytic are thoughts involving less clear memories. Take a note from a student written in 1978:

> *Professor Marx how can I thank you for giving us so much? More than any other professor, you challenged me to think more analytically, to be more objective, and to work harder. But on top of that, you have always been personally warm and receptive, willing to talk, anxious to listen. During my four years at this school I have found very few professors who meet this standard, but that just makes you all the more special. As I sat in your last lecture for Soc. 10. I tried to comprehend not having someone like you to be here encouraging and helping us to think, to question, to learn. I felt very scared and realized the ultimate goal of the best professor is to teach his or her students to do all of those things for themselves. And, I felt better, confident that once I'm "out in the world" all by myself, your lessons will be with me, confident that now I am prepared to think for myself, to question, to wonder. And for that, I thank you.*
>
> —Vicki

Wow. I'd like to have a teacher like that! But who is Vicki? I have no recollection of her, nor of most of the other students on the class lists I have kept for forty years. Does it matter? Does Vicki still remember me and that course? It is quite likely she does not. Does that matter? If you are over thirty, how many of your professors can you recall, how many names from your high

school yearbook are familiar? How many faces do you recognize from summer camp and Sunday school pictures? With each year the number declines.

Looking back raises deep issues about reality, at least as it appears to us
within our individual consciousness. I am not going to lose too much sleep
over my failure of memory. I am glad I kept the customers satisfied. At the
end of a career there is so much more to remember than when starting out.
In addition, with age comes the slowing down of memory. Besides, in our
surveillance society, with a little archaeological digging, it is often possible to
recover the facts should one be so inclined.

The failure of memory in such matters is not of great import and offers
ample fuel for novelists, philosophers, and psychologists. But it does give one
pause and is a reminder of the ethereal and ephemeral nature of human experience. It is an eerie feeling to have some evidence from a material record or a
current conversation and yet to have no memory of the matter at hand.

FORGETTING THE BAD NEWS (AT LEAST MOST OF IT AND HOW IT FELT)

Yet selective memory can be a friend as well. I recall the content and emotion
of great career moments, however with moments of great anger and defeat I
recall the content, but can't capture the emotion.

I have certainly had my share of failures in dealing with the established
professional field of criminology. As many of the articles in this volume suggest, institutional location, resources for research and the acceptance of one's
work can be related to one's view of criminology as primarily concerned with
understanding and improving responses to traditional crime, as against asking critical questions about this. If critical voices were dominant, one would
hardly see special sections devoted to critical criminology.

Has my critical, or I think more accurately, independent perspective (ideally owing allegiance to a higher calling of truth pursuit rather than to the
conventional labels) hurt me? Certainly in some settings. I am not a fellow
of the American Society of Criminology, although I have been nominated
several times.[16] My project on undercover police was rejected by the National
Institute of Justice, as were several other applications. Several conservative
traditional criminologists were prominent on NIJ and other projects for
which I was rejected. With all the attention to surveillance and security issues since 9/11 (in 2003 there were 3,512 companies with homeland security
contracts; by 2006 the number was 33,890—$130 billion in contracts and

still counting), I have never received a call from any government or private agency about the issues. The number of places to apply for funds to ask critical questions about homeland security efforts is minuscule relative to sources to develop it, and even with funds, gaining deep access is most unlikely. My surveillance research is much better known and appreciated in European policy circles than in the U.S. There are no doubt more job openings for quantitative than qualitative researchers and more opportunities for applied (in which the agenda is set by the organization) than for basic research.

On the other side, for some industrial strength critical criminologists my approach was too tentative and balanced—asking for logical development and empirical assessment of sacred holy trinity ideas taken to be self-evident.

But my lack of greater success within the field of criminology also reflects choices I made. As with the character played by Peter Fonda in *Easy Rider*, I favored, "doing your own thing in your own time." I moved away from large quantitative research projects, favored basic research, and did not want a career as a research manager, nor as a consultant, nor did I want to be in environments so clearly tied to a particular institution. I wanted to follow my muse, not the five-year plan to keep a department on, or propel it onto, the A-tier. Adopting what Kenneth Burke called, "a perspective on perspectives" and being a good listener who tries to hear all sides a la the empathetic methodology called for by symbolic interaction can also come at a cost of an uncomfortable tilt toward relativism. Greater specialization as an easily definable type of criminologist would likely have brought greater career rewards and influence, if not necessarily greater wisdom or authenticity.

Yet the richness of this society, the multiplicity of legitimate interest groups, academic freedom, norms about listening to all sides and examining the evidence offers space (if hardly equal for all groups) to express alternative views.

In other settings an independent voice may have helped. The mainstream news media have been very welcoming of op-ed articles and requests for interviews. A "liberal" foundation readily provided support for the undercover book. I have received support a number of times from NSF and I have served on several panels involving surveillance and privacy questions for the National Research Council and had a number of chances to testify before Congress. I helped secure a seat at the table (even if not at its head), for privacy and surveillance issues and helped define research agendas and the national cultural conversation re these issues.

In these cases my critical approach helped, but beyond content, form mattered as well. George Bernard Shaw said something like, "in the right key one
can sing any song." Wrapping critical questions in the language of scholarly
inquiry will get one further than wrapping them in the rhetoric of the political manifesto.

If I had done equivalent work in the areas of education or health (even not
being a grade school teacher or medical doctor) rather than in criminal justice, I would have no doubt had appreciably more contact with and influence
upon practitioners in those worlds than in the more closed world of criminal
justice.[17] But I would probably not have had equivalent contact with civil liberties and public interest groups.

In general, my experience suggests that the quality of the research product
and the prestige of one's school and sponsors are much more significant in resource and attention allocation and influence, than the politics of the applicant
(although that is not to suggest that the door is equally wide for all applicants).
Of course I have seen critical, as well as establishment scholars treated unfairly
(for the former particularly during the anti-Vietnam War period), but the
larger issue generally touches more subtle sociology of knowledge questions
involving what doesn't get studied (rather than scientific failings of what does).
For example where is a budget equivalent to NIJ's to study crimes of authority
and white-collar and environmental violations (including the ability to shape
the law such that highly unethical behavior is not defined as criminal)?

Beyond criminology, with respect to career slights I can still readily recall
some interactions that were hurtful. I served on the committee that established one of the first Afro-American studies departments, an event partly in
response to Martin Luther King's killing. There were time pressures and I was
charged with writing the introduction to our report. I stayed up all night doing it and was pleased with the rough first draft. At our meeting the chair of
the committee said in his most officious Cambridge tone, "Mr. Marx where
did you go to high school?"noting its grammatical failings not its contents.

When my book *Protest and Prejudice* appeared, a senior colleague advised
me to give inscribed copies to the tenured professors. One colleague thanked
me and came over to me the next day, having already finished the book. While
not exactly counting the kudos, I was pleased that he had read it so quickly
but was immediately deflated when he bluntly said, "well it doesn't exactly
burn your eyes out."

A senior political scientist wrote an atrocious article which I thought was a political tract masquerading as scholarship. A journal editor asked me to comment in print on it and asked him to respond. He refused stating that it wasn't appropriate for an assistant professor to review a distinguished professor.

At a reception at Harvard a high official of the university on learning that I was in the social relations department tried to be friendly. He said, "Ah, George Homans—you can tell he is an Adams by his forehead" while dribbling his drink on my tie. I got his drift and nodded, but as an outsider at the time I had no clear idea of what the Adamses looked like, something that was not true of those whose office contained Adamses oil paintings viewed daily.

In May 1964 as a young instructor in the social science integrated course at Berkeley, after collecting the final exams for my course, I left for Europe. Why put off traveling even for a day, when I could grade the exams en route and phone in the grades? That jejune move might have violated university policy, but it made Professor Lewis Feuer under whose auspices I was teaching apoplectic. He called my parent's home and hurled invectives at my mother telling her my career was finished because of the cardinal sin I had committed. When I learned of this I felt like flying 6000 miles back to Berkeley to confront him about his cardinal sin of misplacing his indignation and on my mother no less. If I had returned my career might well have been harmed, if not ended.[18]

My concepts, ideas, and data have sometimes been used without attribution, in a few cases by people who are still household names.[19] I felt cheated at the time, but now I am merely bemused and maybe even flattered. Perhaps the thief was unaware of it, having lifted the ideas from an earlier thief in a long chain of misappropriation. We all swim in the same cultural sea and beyond forgetting, it is easy not to know where the water was previously. If others independently come up with common terms such as the surveillance society, maximum security society, surveillance creep, ironies of social control, covert facilitation, and issueless riots, that might suggest that they usefully correspond to something. In writing about social issues the important thing is the idea not the author.[20] But in the competitive, individualistic environment of the academy that is hard to remember, at least until you get out. On the other hand, on at least one occasion I was accused in a book review of taking ideas from a scholar I had never even read (it would have been more judicious for the reviewer to simply say related ideas are expressed by . . .).

I can recall three times when invited articles were rejected. I was angry, although in only one of the cases had I actually written a new article. I now see that in each case the editor was not a sociologist and I can smile at the rejection on the basis of different disciplinary approaches. In the case of journal rejections, it was always easier to just find another one. With hundreds of journals in sociology and on criminology-related topics, one never runs out of hope.

The more established one becomes, the more writing is done in response to pretty sure thing invitations, rather than to taking one's chances in journals that sometimes seem to survive only because you are forced to subscribe to them as a condition of membership in a professional association. Those with big reputations also sometimes wrongly slide by with so-so articles, although there may be some interest for historical reasons in having a hero's current work or even a perverse motive on the part of an editor to expose feet of clay.

There were jobs I thought I would get but did not, although I was on the short list. Those were humbling experiences, but also productive of cynicism since I knew the politics of the department (or the university administration) didn't go my way even though I thought I had a stronger record than the persons who were hired. Yet there is much room for differences of opinion about the relative merits of a candidate and about what a department most needs. An older candidate may have a much better record, but also reflect more traditional concerns and perhaps soon bail out of productive work relative to a promising young scholar working in an emerging area. Also if nonmeritocratic factors work against you, at other times they no doubt work in your favor.

I have learned to take some satisfaction in making short lists and waiting lists, even when one is not chosen. At least you were in the ball park. You can also sometimes learn what they were looking for, or where you went wrong and that can help in re-applying.[21] In such a competitive world where chance factors play a major role, one can't expect more. Human existence is dominated by vast contingent forces that we gamely try to channel and control. That we sometimes succeed should no more lull us into thinking we can continually pull it off than should failure lead us to stop trying.

If the goal is not redefined and still matters, you need to go with the odds and keep at it, knowing that at some point things may go your way. The future has a wonderful open-ended quality. Also with a career strewn with victories, it is easier to face rejection and move beyond an infantile sense of entitlement and grandiosity.

With respect to teaching (and most else) I came to see the impossibility of trying to please everyone. One student who checked "not intellectually stimulating" on the course evaluation wrote "it was just one big brainstorm—with what about this and what about that? I felt like we were going in circles." Another student who checked "very intellectually stimulating" wrote "the class made me ask 'why' and see that the answer to that often depends." Yet another complained about too many essay questions and another didn't want any multiple choice questions.

This variety of expectations and evaluations also applies to research. Everyway of seeing is also a way of not seeing. Consider the responses to an article I submitted, "This is the best article I have ever reviewed for this journal—an absolutely outstanding contribution" versus "This tiresome review of things everyone knows does not merit publication here." The response to a grant request: "An extraordinarily important project. . . absolutely indispensable. I urge strongly and without reservation that this request for support be approved" versus "This study offers little that would improve the infrastructure of science. Do not fund it."

Negative evaluations—whether from students or colleagues became less stinging over the years. Some judicious mixture of being true to one's self and yet trying to be at least somewhat responsive to audiences that are usually heterogeneous is required. Truth in advertising requires making clear to students at the start what one's teaching style is and what is expected of them permits self-selection. In the case of editors, I generally chose to send my missives to those who value qualitative, conceptual, interdisciplinary, issue-raising work.

Perhaps repression is functional. But more likely increased sophistication and maturity made it possible to understand and sometimes to even agree with the rejection. In place of an infantile, egoistic, insatiable need and sense of entitlement, I became philosophical and grateful for the use of the hall and the chance to try. No one can win them all. Perhaps there is a dilution effect in which failures are drowned out by successes. It seems petty and greedy to wish for more when you are already full. In some cases I agreed that there was a poor fit between my approach and the need of an institution or an editor, or that I had not developed my argument or data in a clear enough fashion, or that I had not adequately changed an already published article, or I could see that the winner was more qualified.

Deeper emotions are involved in reflecting on what the competition means. I have written about that elsewhere (table 2) and will try not to repeat.

THE GOOD NEWS STILL FEELS GOOD

While the above memories are very clear, the anger and pain I felt are long gone. In contrast, with respect to good news, I can recall both the content and the intense positive emotion I felt.

As a first semester graduate student I was worried about whether or not I would flunk out—especially after our orientation meeting in which the unsupportive faculty advisor said, "look to your left, look to your right, next year at this time half of you won't be here." Having drifted into graduate school with moderate preparation and socialization I was scared. That was no doubt functional and drove me to study harder than some of my over-confident and intimidating fellow students from Ivy League schools who wore ties and carried briefcases. I wore Bermuda shorts and was carried in a Corvette.

Our task for the required methods course was to write a research proposal for the secondary analysis of survey data from the Academic Mind study by Lazarsfeld and Thielens. The comment on my paper:

> This is a very good effort. I will be most interested to see what you come up with next semester.[22]

Shout it from the hilltops! I felt a great sense of relief and excitement. I had a reprieve! At least I would be there another semester before they discovered that I was just pretending.

Then there was the gracious letter I received from Professor Morris Jano-witz of the University of Chicago about my thesis on Father Coughlin. Janow-itz offered some critical suggestions, but was appreciative of the thesis. One line I read over and over, "I look forward to reading your future work." Wow, I hadn't thought that far ahead and had no confidence that there would, or could be future work. Here a leader of the field just assumed there would be more. Such small steps built my confidence and changed my self-image. Becoming a professor became a desirable and realistic goal. Previously I had been simply exploring and having fun learning.

But my best memory was that beautiful Berkeley day in November 1966 when the mail brought a formal job offer from Harvard and the mock up pages of my forthcoming book. That day will live in famy (doesn't seem to be any such word but there should be given infamy). I sat outside on a bench by the Campanile with its two bridge view and very slowly opened both letters feeling exultation beyond words.

In April 1970 I vividly recall standing in a phone booth in Grand Central Station calling to get directions to the building where I was to give a paper and being told by the department chair I had been awarded a coveted fellowship. Another senior colleague had told me not even to apply because the odds were so small. The sweetness was enhanced by the tenured job offer that followed my visit. But I could not envision raising a family on an associate professor's salary and living in Manhattan. Instead I used the offer to negotiate a higher salary and longer contract in Cambridge.

After a recent presentation, a colleague I didn't remember came over and said, "good to see you again. I've never forgotten that great talk you gave at the American Political Science Association meetings in Washington, D.C. in 1968 when we first met." That must have been a helluva talk. I wish I could remember something about it.

In an evaluation a student wrote, "I have never had a class with this much intellectual stimulation—this professor rocks." Something must be going on because a few months later a graduate student at a conference left me speechless (not easy to do) when she said, "meeting you for me is like meeting a rock star"[23]—yeah and how do you like my limo? Then there was the colleague whose class I visited and at semester's end jokingly said he was angry because I made him look bad. I was bewildered until he explained that in response to the course evaluation question, "what was the best part of the course?" several students said Professor Marx's lecture.

Then there are the times when one feels good about one's work not because of praise but because it touches other's lives or effects public policy. Here I put being asked to write introductions to colleague's books and receiving dedications such as, "I hold him in the highest regard as a mentor, scholar, and human being. He provided encouragement, scholarly guidance, and I much appreciated his words of wisdom on living the good life."

Kind words from students and seeing them (and their students) succeed has been very rewarding. Among the most satisfying aspects of teaching has been working with thirteen students on co-authored papers (in most of these cases this was only once and was the student's first published paper). Sponsoring and supporting international students, including several from China was particularly meaningful.

Work on the Kerner Commission, the Senate Select Committee on Undercover Activities and on privacy and equity issues in new information technologies for various national committees has been very satisfying. The results of my first book *Protest and Prejudice* helped in civil rights fund-raising and brought data to the topic of black–white and the connected black–Jewish relations.

Salman Rushdie (1995) has observed that "our lives teach us who we are." In bits and pieces over time one gets a sense of how others see us and sometimes that felt good and sometimes bad. That may particularly happen during crisis periods.[24] Thus in the midst of a departmental struggle at Colorado, in an environment closer to an alpine surreal circus than the highest expression of Western civilization, my leadership style was severely maligned. Learning of this, a former colleague expressed great surprise and said in a note, "you are among the most soft-spoken people I know, soft spoken but with an undercurrent of unrelenting strength." Others wrote and thanked me for standing for principle when so few of the timid bureaucrats and faculty members would. Being told by one of my role models—the late Lew Coser "you are one of us" meant more than almost anything.

The discovery that one not only has lots to say, but has a distinctive voice to say it with was also satisfying.[25] Forms of expression, whether artistic or academic come, to varying degrees with the distinctive signature of their authors.[26] This realization was something I simply backed into. But it was gratifying to hear colleagues says things such as, "its vintage Gary Marx" or "your voice comes through beautifully, even in an e-mail" or to be described as "a crafty literate pro" who knows "how to milk a metaphor." Being aware of the craftsmanship and style that define one's work footprint, can (for better and worse) mean raising the bar of self-expectations.

Elements of my style include identifying and disaggregating new morally and socially important topics, approaching these comprehensively and synoptically in essay form with a bit of wit, and even humor, and believing that data are where you find them, whether in sophisticated experiments and with numbers or in cartoons and literature. We need to access commonly held assumptions, yet only reject them when empirical and logical evidence demands it. I like to follow the questions, not the method or theory. Making distinctions among elements usually treated in an undifferentiated fashion is central to my approach.

Georg Simmel (1994) observes "We are at any moment those who separate the connected or connect the separate." We need to disaggregate and then to aggregate (or in the motto of the paleontological society, Frango ut patefaciam—"I break in order to reveal."

I was drawn to topics that involved taken for granted views and seeming contradictions. Given the interdependencies of social environments and the multiple levels and kinds of data for considering causes and consequences, I have moved from youthful frustration in the face of duality, irony, and paradox to patronly appreciation (or at least tolerance for these) and to (at least initially) suspicion of certainty and simplicity when contentious social issues are involved.

In the last scenes of the film *Chinatown*, Jack Nicholson is interrogating Faye Dunaway about her relationship with a young woman. Dunaway alternatively and repeatedly states, "she is my daughter" and under Nicholson's more coercive questioning, "she is my sister." Finally she says, "she is my sister and my daughter," indicating an atypical relationship with her father.

So it is with our research, we are posed (and in the best of cases also poised) between a rich variety of tensions and the answer sometimes is "yes and no" and "both." Thus societies need both liberty and order; group life is impossible without normative boundaries, yet rule-breaking can be creative and a factor in positive social change; environmental surveillance and boundary maintenance is central to any life form yet when inappropriate it can also destroy life; our sense of self is defined by our ability to control personal information, yet sharing is central for intimacy and in a democratic society, openness and encouraging accountability through visibility are fundamental. These concerns have helped frame a lifetime research agenda.

Confidence may come by accident. I once drove a hundred miles to give a talk and as I approached the podium realized I had forgotten my prepared remarks. I winged it and gave one of the best talks ever. After one has been in the biz for awhile, it is almost a sign of weakness to rely on the security of the written lecture, although the mores of the disciplines vary here. The written talk fails to honor what can be the bubbling creativity of the mind and the colliding and overflowing of ideas when one is cranked and into the topic and the synapses are firing. I now prefer to talk from an outline.

In an overflowing cauldron of work experiences, among the more memorable was having a student from India introduce himself and say, "Just call me Sid." His full name was Siddartha, a name hallowed by 1960s seekers of the way. The occasional unsigned love notes were interesting, as was the careless student who wrote a fine paper on riots that seemed familiar. It should have, as it was taken verbatim from my article in the *Encyclopedia Britannica*.

Then there was the curious case of the student who failed the midterm and the final and yet wrote a note saying, "Professor Marx, I just wanted to let you know that I really enjoyed your class even though I may not have shown it through my work, [sic] Through the class I have become so much more interested in law and I now know that this is the direction I want to head in. . . . I wanted to thank you for a great class and for helping me find what I really am interested in." God save the law. What might have been written if the student had received an A grade? Then there was the student who gave me a poor grade in the course evaluation because, "he uses far too many big words that get you lost in what he is actually trying to say." Calling Brutus on the fault line.

Newspaper stories such as one that referred to "Karl Marx's stimulating lecture last night on surveillance" and being cited several times in book reviews—not for one's ideas but because of sharing a name ("the only Marx in the bibliography is Gary Marx") were amusing.

OFF AND ON THE ROAD AGAIN: CALIFORNIA DREAMIN'
CALIFORNIA HERE I COME RIGHT BACK WHERE I STARTED FROM

B. De Sylva and J. Meyer—A clear sky was almost the most important thing— D. H. Lawrence. The subsidized travel opportunities available to academics (whether for meetings, summer, or sabbatical teaching) have been highly beneficial. Travel counters the parochial and the routine, expands one's knowledge and networks and supplies audiences. I have had shorter term teaching gigs in more than twenty universities in Asia and Europe and given lectures in over 100 other schools. Now, not having a regular job means even greater freedom to take advantage of such travel.

This has permitted returning for short-term teaching to places where I was once rooted such as Berkeley and Los Angeles and seeing what they feel like decades later, as well as to Chicago to imagine what life was like for great grandparents in the nineteenth century and to regionally distinct places such as West Virginia, Kentucky, and Puerto Rico that make one aware of the limitations of bicoastality). I wouldn't agree entirely with Joan Didion who observes, "all that is constant about the California of my childhood is the rate at which it disappears." But returning was a shock. You can't go home in any real sense, but you can clearly visit with the eye of the outsider. Launching pads needn't (and perhaps shouldn't) be homes, even if they remain tourist attractions.

The visits share something with Woody Allen's character in *Sleeper* who awakes in a strange, but strangely familiar place. The Berkeley light and the bay view from the hills didn't change, even with an unduly dense campus with a hodgepodge of architectural styles. Yet on balance almost four decades later, it was in Maurice Sendak's children's story, now "someone else's nut tree."

Much of current Berkeley was run down, tired, dirty, and dreary —a caricature of its former self. Reflective not of the British philosopher for whom it was named, but rather Bererkly—a self-conscious ministrelization show. Consider the Pink Man who, in his unicycle and leotard, leads an annual parade celebrating Berkeley's self-affirmed craziness. In this political milieu liberals are called conservatives and few conservatives will cop to it.

Skates, skateboards, and scooters are no longer the exclusive vehicle of children —gangly adolescents seem to come at you from all sides as one crosses a street. The side streets off Telegraph Avenue were littered with needles not beer cans. The Rexall drug store on Telegraph is that in name only, having closed its pharmaceutical section for security reasons.

This was not your father's Berkeley. *The Daily Cal* reports on students' lack of knowledge of the university's health workers who dispense information and also condoms and lubricants. Ads are prominent for "Sperm Donors Wanted—We need men of all ethnicities" and "Women Be An Angel! Donate Eggs—All Nationalities Needed."

An advertisement for a religious meeting advocates the need to "transcend all forms of Jewish chauvinism and goyim-bashing and recognize that we are part of the Unity of All Being." The gathering is "perfect for families, welcoming to singles of all ages, to interfaith couples, and to gays, lesbians, and bisexuals."

In 1963 students were invited to "Join the Shop-In at Lucky's Market— Fight Discrimination in Employment." Today they (at least those of a certain non-hue) are invited to join a group that promises "UNtraining White Liberal

Racism" for only $10. "The UN training offers personal work in a supportive setting for white people to address our unconscious racial conditioning." This appeal is offered adjacent to an ad promoting "Massage Therapy for Pets."

There are new issues such as MCS (multiple chemical sensitivity). According to an article in the *Berkeley Daily Planet* MCS is a "legitimate disability under the Americans with Disabilities Act." The Berkeley city council adopted a resolution asking citizens not to wear scents at public meetings out of respect for those whose health is compromised by fragrances.

There are the changes in culinary culture. Food carts have largely displaced advocacy tables from the corner of Bancroft and Telegraph. The formerly more bohemian Northside of campus is now known as "the gourmet ghetto." Restaurants' signs promise, "no pesticides, hormones, anti-biotics or msg"— to which some might add "no taste." The faculty club serves soy milk. The Ratskeller, that rah rah sporty American paragon of steak and potatoes, favored in my day by alumni, football players, and sorority sisters features tofu and wraps in barbecue sauce in a punk environment. Diversity now comes in many forms, including the addition of a real delicatessen with "challah French toast." The *Berkeley Gazette* contains an ad for: Help Wanted: experienced baker with collective interests.

In the 1960s bumper stickers said, "make love not war" and "question authority."[27] Now one sees "Dykes on Bikes," "Question Reality," "I take my pet to a holistic vet" and "All those who wander are not lost."

Yet Berkeley remained inspirational and provocative. Not many other cities declare a Nuclear Free Zone or seek their own foreign policy. If there are political Edsels there are also kernels for a better world. With the passion and optimism of youth, it was a place pulsating with question-asking, experimentation, and innovation. It was nostalgically reminiscent of one prong of the good society which must forever involve questioning, imagining, and taking nothing for granted.[28] With worldly experience, maturity, and distance from Berkeley, the second prong of the good society involving appreciation of tradition, ritual and institutions, and awareness of the limits of human perfectibility, and the horrors of trying to achieve it at any cost, can cause one to forget the first prong.

The significance of utopian dreams lies not in their failure, but in the search they inspire. Many ideas that seemed wildly utopian in the nineteenth century became partial realities in the twentieth. The 1960s matter as well.

The times did not change to the degree that Bob Dylan claimed they were, but they did change. The moral high ground is also needed to remind the realpolitikniks that there must be limits to compromise.

All the professors I knew are now retired or dead. The few still around the campus seemed frozen in another era, rarely venturing from the cozy consensus of Berkeley, perfectly cast for the role of aging radicals. If I had stayed there and taken an assistant professor position (which I never gave serious consideration to), I no doubt would have ended up the same. Wombs are hard to leave. However given a more peripatetic and varied career with respect to geographical places, intellectual areas, methods of inquiry, and kinds of departments and audiences, I feel very privileged to have been able to see more "of the world and what it is" as the Bible advises and to have been at and left Berkeley when it was at its height.

While the current sociology faculty contains leading scholars, in general they don't seem as towering as those who were there in the 1960s, nor are they likely to be as important as foundational figures for the discipline. Herbert Blumer was brought to Berkeley in the 1950s and given resources to build the best department in the nation. There was little competition and he was able to recruit laterally, something rarely done today. Philip Selznick, Reinhard Bendix, Marty Lipset, Erving Goffman, Kingsley Davis, and Neil Smelser, along with younger leading colleagues, established Berkeley sociology as a mecca, drawing on the best of the Columbia, Chicago, and Harvard traditions in rapidly expanding fields that required founding figures.[29] They were in on the ground floor—their destiny was favored by their demography, as well by their brilliance. Given the explosion of knowledge and technique since then, the fragmentation of sociology and the social sciences in recent decades—and the rise to competitive prominence of many more universities, it is unlikely that we will see such a formidable and influential cohort again in one place. They were sociology's greatest generation.

Glory days well they'll pass you by—Bruce Springsteen

Another form of looking back is to consider who one was in high school as against who one is today.[30] I was initially enthusiastic about going to my fiftieth reunion. I drafted the requested 500 word life story and read with great interest about the lives of others. I was unfortunately unable to attend the event. A large majority of the class (or at least those who wrote) had stayed within the greater Los Angeles area (why would they want to leave?) and I remembered far fewer persons than I thought I would. I wasn't sure with Gertrude Stein how much there was there.[31] I would have enjoyed going, but there is also something to be said for keeping the visual memories I have frozen in 1956. For my entry I wrote:

> Spent the better part of the 1960s at Berkeley, doing Berkeley things, but mostly studying for a PhD in sociology. . . . Spent twenty-five years in Boston, doing Boston things, teaching and researching at Harvard and M.I.T. with sojourns to teach in France, Belgium, Austria, Spain and China and work with government and non-profit organizations on issues involving race relations, policing, civil liberties and technology. . . .Thomas Starr King Junior High School and Marshall left indelible positive impressions, in spite of adolescent unease and various hidden, and not so hidden curricula that favored some doubtful aspects of our society. I don't know how much was me, and how much was the school's failure to make learning exciting, but I learned very little about science, art, history or literature and what is perhaps worse, did not learn to appreciate these. What I did learn was how to get along with others and be noticed. The fuel of my high school experience was competition. This meant persevering and often winning—whether elections, writing and speech contests, basketball, track events. . . . Related to this was a desire to look "sharp" and to impress girls. Perhaps if excellent grades had come more easily, I might have added them to my exterior impression arsenal, but alas they did not. I did just enough work to qualify for college admittance. But as with the other endeavors, it was the prize not the process that mattered. I have since learned to reverse the emphasis. Note the words of poet Henry Newbolt, "to set the cause above renown, to love the game beyond the prize."

In reflecting on the image of that person I am no less competitive, but that is mostly because I can't help it. It's like a reflex and it is fun. I am curious to see how well I can do, whatever the activity. Yet it is no longer "look ma no hands" or a quest for the days of yesteryear Bruce Springsteen sings of. Rather it is part of an ethos linked to doing one's best and giving it your all. The emphasis is on competing with oneself rather than besting others. I no longer have the need to prove anything or for the acclaim/recognition success can bring in advertising to others. Giving up the avaricious and insatiable carrot always in front of the donkey ghost of status acclaim has been salutatory and among the best parts of being a lapsed, but recovering academic.

Qualified Angels. A related aspect is giving up an unenviable self-righteousness acquired during the 1960s Berkeley years that involved a never-doubted moral superiority and political correctness. In this view Los Angeles was seen to epitomize all (or at least most) of what was wrong with society.[32] It was easy to form an identity in opposition to this.

One of the enduring banalities of the middle-class mobile (whether geographical or cultural) learned from Hemingway and Wolfe is that you can't return.[33] But you can visit, filtering impressions through the strainer of age and experience. As both sustenance and opposition, my identity was resolutely shaped by growing up in Southern California.

My recent time in the Los Angeles area was certainly not Yogi Berra's deja vu all over again. It was more a dream-like experience in which recognizable fragments of a past were interwoven with architectural and cultural clichés from contemporary mass culture. The street names and grid pattern of east Hollywood between Franklin and Santa Monica were the same, but most of the buildings were new. Some of the previous structures were hidden behind face-lifts. The few recognizable buildings were in disrepair and some were boarded up. Yet the generic video, convenience, and fast food outlets were all too familiar. There were constant jarring reminders that this was not chez moi. Missing was the unreflective sense of familiarity, security, and predictability that flows from the automatic emotional pilot of a known environment.

How can you describe the feeling of going to your father's factory on Sunset Boulevard (where in making cardboard boxes you drove a staple into your thumb or listen to the Amboy Dukes in the privacy of a labyrinthine stock room) and seeing it as a parking lot for Circuit City? What is there to say about the Brown Derby restaurant on Los Feliz that is now Louisa's Trattoria? Where are the words to express the feeling of seeing the stately home on Mariposa Avenue your grandparents built in 1914 replaced by a crumbling apartment building with broken windows and for rent signs? How to express the indignity of seeing Mariposa become a dead end —literally slashed at a rakish angle by the Hollywood Freeway?

The palm trees, birds of paradise, and other exotic plants, decaying stucco buildings, dirty streets, street vendors offering everything from oranges to furniture to themselves, along with the scrubbed, buttoned up, tightly guarded quality of the structures inhabited by the more privileged (with armed guard signs, video-surveillance, controlled entries, and high walls and fences) seemed vaguely third world and mysterious—a place better suited to my adulthood encounters with Graham Greene than my adolescent encounters with Raymond Chandler.

To see that the Pacific Coast Highway (that ultimate California symbol of carefree youth, openness and infinity, with its western ocean and eastern golden hills views awaiting the driver of a convertible who has hurled down Sunset Boulevard to the sea to come to the end of the country) has become just another six-lane traffic-clogged highway with strip malls and pseudo-Mediterranean developments with streets named after the developer's daughters or wives, was a final reminder of the perils of returning.

Los Angeles is not a world I chose (or perhaps it rejected me). The slickly marketed Hollywood worlds of eternal youth, beauty, and acquisition are all too familiar. Yet the university was not quite Universal City and Cambridge, the Bay area and the Northwest are not Southern California. But like scars which are clinically functional, if aesthetically displeasing, childhood experiences don't really go away, even as we build upon them. I now view those early years in L. A. as a vaccination giving me a mild version of an illness in the service of later protections enhanced by twenty-five years in Boston. I feel very fortunate to have grown up in, and then to have escaped from Los Angeles. But I now feel more bemused than critical.

Whether it is seeing that the tentacles of the L.A. culture are everywhere or the mellowing that comes with age, I am less certain that Los Angeles is peopled with a disproportionate number of vain, materialistic, instrumental, superficial, shallow plastic people. And even if it is, why should I spend time judging them? Today I would not so automatically take Dustin Hoffman's side in the film *The Graduate*.[34]

Plastic clearly has a place in the economy and in self-presentations and interaction. One must choose one's battles and fight the important ones. Self-righteousness and fundamentalism of course must be challenged, even as one tries to avoid sinking into an indefensible moral relativism. Among the many good lessons from one brand of sociology is the need to take the point of view of the other and to realize the extent to which choices are socially determined (excusing to a degree individual responsibility). Perhaps that is what maturity in its best version is about —perspective and tolerance.

Part of that perspective sees the evolving nature of human experience and existence. Things change and nothing lasts. Life can be thought of as a series of temporally and often spatially bounded events. Some are of short duration such as thirst, a sporting event, a play, a meeting, a visit to the dentist, a job rejection. Others are longer such as a summer camp or a vacation, or longer still as with high school, a relationship, a job, or a career. Some are one way streets with no going back. Others are cyclical. But a shared feature is beginning and ending.

One can rally against this dynamism, but it seems far more productive to apply some cognitive jujitsu and go with the force. When a life event is good, appreciatively seize it and soar in the moment. If it is bad, there may be solace in knowing that it may pass. What is endures, at least in the short run, are temporal sequences of varying durations.

There can be optimism here for the social reformer otherwise prone to pessimism. The less than full realization of the inspiring ideals of the 1960s was a surprise to the youthful and inexperienced idealists of that era. Most abandoned activism for more personal concerns, believing that change was an impossible dream.

However, George M. Hauser, a leader of efforts to end colonialism in Africa, an organizer of the first freedom ride in the South in 1947, and a founder with Bayard Rustin of the Congress of Racial Equality, has never given up. In an interview he reports that his experience has taught him that over the stretch of history a small group of people can have a large impact. (*New York Times*, December 12, 2007). It is necessary to take the initial steps even if one does not know where they will lead. His theme comes from an old hymm, "Lead kindly light against the encircling gloom/lead thou me on. . . .I do not ask to see the distant scene/ One step is enough for me." Hauser says, "I believe one step is enough and you take it as long as you have faith you're doing the right thing to begin with."

A Grandparent Not A Conquistador Erich Goode in memorializing his distinguished father, sociologist Si Goode, notes a common, if rarely openly acknowledged sentiment among successful academics and a sociological explanation for the perennial unhappiness among many players.

Si wanted to be an intellectual conquistador . . . a sociologist in the grand scale of Max Weber and Emile Durkheim. He didn't appreciate the fact that in a fractured, fragmented field, and in an era, like ours, such titans do not and cannot exist. Si felt his work on social theory was insufficiently appreciated, believing that lesser scholars received greater acclaim. He told me about his bitter disappointment at the response to a book he had just published. He thought he was commanding the field, "Come on, everybody, let's take that hill!" Yet when he looked around, he realized no one was following him." (Goode, 2003)

Perhaps surprisingly success has been much more conducive to reflection and analysis than failure. I am not sure why. But now with time and perspective and removed from the daily validating impact of colleagues, I have become more doubtful of much of the social science and humanities academic writing status hustle enterprise. The more time goes by, the less I am a firm believer. Too much of it is self-promotional and mutual back scratching involving esoteric, arcane ramblings among isolated tribes—unread, unremembered—and unremarkable, and sometimes stronger on technique or ideology than scholarship. I feel I have pretty much left the profession but not the discipline. There are also issues about the payoff.

For example, I spent the better part of an uncompensated year working on a very long book review essay on recent empirical studies of surveillance (Marx, 2005). The assignment gave me the impetus to read material that I needed for the book I was working on. I feel very good about the article and know from a web page counter that it has been read many times. Yet almost no one has mentioned the article.[35] That enormous expenditure of effort went into a void. It has generated no interactional wave to ride, nor even any current to fight. Just a lot of ideas poured into a swallowing ocean of words.

Yet as Henry James wrote, "We work in the dark. We do what we can. We give what we have." And of course one can never know the impact of ideas and I would have done it even knowing the modesty of the direct response. But it does give one pause. Is this what I really want to continue to do with my shrinking commodity of time, once my current book is finished?

There is also the issue of being a commentarial spectator rather than directly involved in the action and making a difference in some immediate sense. One of our sons is a firefighter and a labor union leader. When I asked him recently how his shift went he said, "pretty exciting, we saved a man's life last night. He was on fire trapped in a burning car. We cut him out with the Jaws of Life and got him to the hospital just in time. If he had crashed a few miles further away he would have died. He lost both legs but he will live." Our other son is an environmental planner who is responsible for innovative programs linking soil quality and salmon and keeping organic material out of landfills.

I sit comfortably in park-like settings and write while listening to classical guitar music. I sometimes feel almost parasitic and a betrayer of Teddy Roosevelt's stirring words about being in the arena.[36] I know all the fine rationalizations about effecting climates of opinion and training students in the highest liberal arts critical tradition (whether those we teach or who read what we write). But it does seem more than a little removed and safe within the confines of the university —clever retorts, secret ballots for tenure, anonymous reviews, and with tenure, a job and salary whether one succeeds or fails. In the roads not taken genre, I miss the risks, action, and having a more direct influence on other's lives that an alternative career would offer. At times I identify more with a disfavored character D. H. Lawrence (1993) described as "a buck of the King Edward school, who thought life was life and the scribbling fellows were somewhere else,"[37] than with the sedate life of the professor.

Even granted all the good civilizational issues for the life of the mind, when you deal with social questions that concern you, impact matters. Most of us lack the energy, the means, and the will to take our ideas to market. In contrast, the widely heard (if not always agreed with) George Soros, who almost got a PhD with Karl Popper, is correct in observing, "I have a platform because I made a lot of money. If I were just an intellectual, an obscure university professor I wouldn't be saying these things and I wouldn't be heard" (Solomon, 2006). Take it from an obscure university professor, George, you got it right! Or rather you might be saying them, but no one beyond your subspecialization would hear them and, with ever new cohorts appearing, long remember them.

Being out of the game brings some redefining of what is most important in life and of what success means. There is less need for occupational self-promotion and the courting of public exposure once you have had time to see how rapidly books go out of print and unread journals are given or thrown away—there is always a fresh morning paper, another edition of the six o'clock news, and the arrival of the next issue of a journal. New scholarship replaces the old, only to be replaced itself. Reputations are not only perishable and short-lived, but they are not very transferable across fads and fashions, disciplines, cliques, and countries, nor translatable into other languages. You might be a hero on your block in our own time, but you tread on dangerous ground if you portage that reputation very far from home. Yet if you don't, you remain insular and parochial.

Climbing high up can bring hubris, but it also brings a view of the immensity of the fields wherein reputations may lie (with homage to Goffman, 1956) or better perhaps may rest. The criteria must be responding to your need to write and pleasure in the process, not the outcome. When the research does find audience approval, it must be viewed as a master chef might view producing a glorious meal—appreciated as it is consumed, but more or less destroyed in the process, as the audience moves on to the next meal, the leftovers soon spoil, and new chefs appear. If you can tolerate the slightly sentimental and sappy tone, words commonly attributed to Emerson come to be more fully believed:[38]

> To laugh often and much;
> To win the respect of intelligent people
> and the affection of children;
> To earn the appreciation of honest critics
> and endure the betrayal of false friends;
> To appreciate beauty, to find the best in others;
> To leave the world a bit better,
> whether by a healthy child,
> a garden patch,
> or a redeemed social condition;
> To know that even one life has breathed easier
> because you have lived.

That is to have succeeded. Amidst the enduring pulls between the individual and the community, the national and the international, the earth and the world, ideals and practices, the present and the future, as W. C. Fields said, "A man's got to believe in something." His solution, "I believe I'll have a drink" will work for some. But for others, salvation may lie in the acceptance of polarities and a deft wending of one's way through their contradictions. But certainly not at a cost of having fun or denying one's self a drink.[39]

I continue with my academic projects, even though after forty-eight years there ought to be time off for good behavior. Yet, I am not quite at the same place as a recently retired colleague, who said, "I looked back on my career, declared victory, and now am moving on." There is still writing that I want to do and some fellowship opportunities to pursue. But I am moving closer toward the leisure that might enable me not to feel like such a failure at woodworking and guitar playing.

I am very appreciative of the greater time now for family, recreation, consumption, and citizenship activities. I am thankful for the indulgence of imagination and the faded memory-maps of biography and place with the quest for a life lived with truth, integrity, love, civility, beauty, humor, fun, and challenge.

A colleague near retirement asked me for advice. Bad move. As C. W. Mills said, "in the end a man must go to bat alone."[40] Yet as with temptation, I can resist anything but responding to such questions. To summarize some of this article—be in the moment. Don't put off things you have wanted to do. "Let it be" as the Beatles sang—both your expectations for, and your anger at others; be appreciative of all that has been, and continues to be, good in your life and in life; stay active within your physical limits; stay engaged a la Sartre with whatever moves you and doesn't hurt others; keep the faith and the passion; come to terms with the transitory nature of recognition and success and see their accidental and environmental correlates; try and merge means and ends; appreciate dualities, polarities, and ironies and the fascinating elements of the individual and the social in which individuals die, but the culture that nourished them and that they contributed to lives on and finally, stay curious and be filled with wonderment and laugher. Remember wherever you go, there you are.

NOTES

1. I am grateful to Glenn Muschert and Jeff Ross for critical comments. A longer version of this article is available at http://web.mit.edu/gtmarx/www/hitherthither.html

2. For example Marx 1990, 1997, 2000. These are at garymarx.net.
    I had the good fortune to spend almost my entire academic career in Berkeley and Cambridge at institutions a recent *Times of London Higher Education Supplement* ranked as the three best universities in the world.

Looking back it seems strange and even disingenuous that I could be so taken with a few modest career downturns and moved enough to write the first of these kinds of article in 1990 about perceived failure. Of course I was writing about how it *felt*, something frequently only tenuously tied to how it *is* by some objective standard. A part of this was dramatic effect in essay writing and the appeal to others of stories about success and the fall from grace. Yet it also reflects a frame of reference conditioned by social location and, as we used to say, relative deprivation. In such high octane environments one looks up to those more accomplished (in 1970 for me in Cambridge this meant frequent contact with living scholars such as Parsons, Homans, Riesman, and Lipset, and those who had only recently died such as Allport and Sorokin). Stouffer, et al.'s classic work in *The American Soldier* that found soldiers in units with the highest rates of promotion were the most dissatisfied speaks to the subjective quality of evaluations.

3. Such writing as a form of impression management also offers the chance to rewrite history—covering up or correcting one's mistakes—something Ben Franklin was accused of doing.

4. The latter was my father Donald. The desert land is now downtown Palm Springs. The restaurant was the Coronet Club. As a midwestern migrant to California in the 1920s seeking fame in the film industry (with the added benefit of being able to pick oranges off of trees in winter), my father was not alone. He did find work in the film industry—as a laborer, following by a few years in the footsteps of John Wayne who began the same way. Wayne went on to bigger things. My father stayed at Warner Brothers moving sets around, although he did sing at least once on the radio. The glamour and opportunity Hollywood offered, however chimerical, elusive, illusive, and tainted dies hard. Perhaps with the image of Humphrey Bogart in Casa blanca in his mind, my father, wearing his own white linen sport coat (which I was draped in for my Senior Prom), wanted to be "maitred' to the stars." The restaurant did well for a few years, carried by a popular singer who refused to expand her repertoire of five songs. My father told her to add songs or be fired. Kay Starr ("Come On a My House") then went on to a record contract with Capitol. My father went on to bankruptcy. I would love to understand why I can recall (or so strongly believe I can recall) short memorable lines of conversation. In this case a car ride on the way to a civil hearing (my parents were suing their French chef whose double billing they claimed led to the bankruptcy—a charge he denied). At the age of eight, I asked (to my parents' surprise and consternation), "who is right?" My mother in the most serious tone

this gentle woman could muster said, "who do you think is right?" The opposing attorney was named Lincoln. To my father's credit and pride, he felt a strong responsibility to pay his debts. He was eventually able to do so, in spite of being legally excused from them.

5. With respect to the latter, and being a part-time, privileged, *resident alien* in Scottsdale of course offers problems as well—the biggest finding a place to park in the megamalls, followed closely by trying to remember where one has parked.

6. The profession refers to sociology or criminology incorporated—the organizations that promote the "professional" political and other interests of those who join them, including offering credit cards and life insurance. Their democratic structure gives all groups the chance to compete over the meager resources the profession controls and a hunting license to seek out the impure. The discipline is a less tangible ethos or spirit of unfettered social inquiry carried out within the traditions of scholarship and sometimes against those of the discipline. The discipline owes allegiance to a more transcendent and higher set of individualistic, Enlightenment (or at least as our belief system holds, more enduring and universal) ideals, than to those of whatever political winds happen to be dominant at the time, although in the best of circumstances these overlap.

7. In the case of the latter, one might say thought for food.

8. Here we see competing needs for independence and community. It is important to keep moving in a state of almost perpetual homelessness. There are paradoxes to be confronted in saying "yes" to both freedom and connection, while seeing the dangers of too much or too little of either and avoiding both anomie and root strangulation. Paul Bowles' (1949) image of the traveler (as against the tourist) who is on the move (whether physically a la travel and exercise or mentally a la changes in topic and perspective) offers one response. In this case the individual may be "somewhat homeless perhaps, but not heartless, staying fresh by keeping on the move. Life can be enriched by occupying multiple and changing physical and cultural worlds,—like mercury or a boxer constantly in motion and never able to be pinned down. The "on the road" ethos is a metaphor for much more than physical travel. New environments require and extend attention. That check draws against the inflationary introspective account, with its risk of solipsistic and self-elegiac bankruptcy that may hit those over fifty particularly hard. Looking outward means not looking inward (although to never look inward is to commit the sin of the unexamined life)" (Marx, 2000).

9. The extent *to* which, taken together, they also run *further* is a challenging issue involving one's view of the possibility of progress in social inquiry and whether it is seen as a cumulative undertaking a la the natural sciences or as something else.

10. To take one example a student in a recent class said in describing the scene at a nightclub, "you can get whippets there." That seemed curious and I asked why would such a place be selling dogs? There was immediate laughter and the student explained the jargon for nitrous oxide, something previously encountered only at a dentist's office or unknowingly in cans of whipped cream. In my brief early career as a box boy I was very familiar with whipped cream cans. In the 1950s they came without safety seals and offered a quick sugar fix to those stocking refrigerated market cabinets from behind.

11. Descartes' motto, "he lives well who is well hidden" also applies, although it conflicts with ideas of accountability and solidarity through openness.

12. In an age of academics as third rate, wannabe celebrities, instant media pundits who receive phone calls and e-mails from the media that say, "Professor I'm working on a deadline can you get back to me within the hour?" it is very easy to see the wisdom of my grandfather's saying, "fools' names and fools' faces are always seen in public places."

13. This can also push toward work rather than leisure and can lead to a sharpening of priorities and more selectivity in what is worked on and what invitations are accepted. I now try to only work on material that will inform the surveillance book I have been finishing for ten years.

At the same time as noted elsewhere, there is a countervoice which says "hey, let it be;" it doesn't matter that much, do what feels comfortable, you have done enough. There is the joke about the old man who goes to see a urologist, complaining about the difficulty of urination. To the doctor's question, "how old are you?" The man responds, "eighty" and the doctor says, "forget about it! You have pissed enough."

14. The journey as experience and metaphor has been central since a boy scout trip across the United States in 1950 to the National Jamboree at Valley Forge and the 1960s on the road ethos from 1960 travels in Mexico onward (Marx, 2000).

15. Of course school yard athletes are not alone in having such feelings. Consider fellow UCLA graduate Bill Walton, among the best and most honored college basketball players of the 20th century, re his 1974 season, "I look back at my college

244 GARY T. MARX

career as one of frustration, disappointment and ultimate embarrassment. For us to give 4 games away out of our last 10 was just totally unacceptable, and I will never be able to erase the stigma, the stain from my soul *about what could have been*" (italics added). Ok Bill, but how *about all that was!* I think we need a theory about reference groups here. *New York Times,* March 26, 2007. B5.

16. I find such invidious designations silly and inappropriate in a professional society of equals.

17. The goals of liberal arts academic research, whether within disciplinary or interdisciplinary environments, contrast with the more pragmatic concerns of those within (or seeking to join) criminal justice organizations (Leo, 1996; Deflem, 2002).

18. My control, or at least common sense in doing nothing at the time, contrasts with the volatile Feuer who was notoriously lacking in impulse control, a philosopher who earlier in his career actually got in a fist fight over a philosophical disagreement.

19. Awareness of the shelf life of reputations is another insight that comes with time.

20. A highlight here was meeting with Hubert Humphrey and hearing him use my ideas on the national media a few days later. Seeing my unacknowledged ideas and phrases used on editorial pages also seemed appropriate.

21. On the virtue of persistence in the face of the odds in beginning a career see Ross, 2005 and Shaw, 2000.

22. This was in contrast to a comment in the files from another professor that same semester, "this is a very marginal student. I would be surprised if he receives a master's degree. He certainly will not receive a PhD." Fortunately I did not see that until I was on the Berkeley faculty and dipped into my file one Sunday evening. I did receive a B- in the class, but I partly blame the instructor. Re the term paper he said read Durkheim and tell us what you think he is saying. I did just that with no argument or central question for analysis. I simply followed orders and did not have the slightest idea of what an original term paper looked like. Was that my fault or the teacher's for failing to communicate? Maybe both, but it introduced a certain caution in seeing evaluations of students absent a second opinion or only one indicator. I feel the same way about the marked difference between my achievement levels on time pressured vs. untimed tests.

23. I wasn't sure what she meant here since there actually was a singer named Marc Pearman who sang as Gary Marx with a group called the Sisters of Mercy.

24. Seeing what I was against helped me become clearer about what I was for. I have expressed this in thirty-seven moral mandates that would characterize my ideal department.

25. In the beginning I didn't know that I would meet with success and thought that a goodly proportion of other graduate students were better educated and trained, and more mature, smarter, and insightful than I, if a bit square. Gradually I came to see that I could effectively compete and beyond the tangible symbols of that, I was able to quickly verbally untangle some unseen aspects of complex social issues through distanciation and reflexive thinking. But sometimes the insights were not grasped by others of a different turn of mind, intended humor went unheard or a serious remark was taken to be humorous. Clever interventions may be seen as chattering class arrogance or simply be too clever for the audience. There can be a tension here. It is not only what you say, but how you say it. The issue also applies to teaching—do you aim at the middle, the poorest students who might profit the most or the best students who may not even need you? Among the greatest of pedagogical performing arts is finding the line that permits subtlety without going over an audience's head and being able to register thermostatic adjustments while maintaining some degree of authenticity.

26. Among the most influential, distinctive and memorable is that of Erving Goffman, an enduring role model.

27. But things had started to change even by 1965 relative to the peaceful, integrated, drop-in efforts of the earlier period, in which coats and ties and dresses were worn on picket lines and nonviolence was both principled and strategic. I recall my shock and sense of loss in coming to campus in the fall of 1965 and seeing a student demonstration (?) that involved smoking dried banana peels on the steps of Sproul Hall while the Beatles' sang, "We all live in a yellow submarine." That was one end of the disillusionment continuum anchored on the other end by the turn toward violent rhetoric and violence on the part of protestors and authorities.

28. This is well put in lines from Brecht's (1965) play *The Exception and the Rule* whose yellowed and brittle pages I still have from the student newspaper:

> find it estranging even if not very strange [and]
> We particularly ask you

When a thing continually occurs—
Not on that account to find it natural. . . .

29. I have written on Goffman and Lipset as mentors in Marx, 1984 and 2007 and on Smelser with Alexander, Marx, and Williams, 2003.

30. Or better how one remembers that. Note Proust's observation that he offered a theory of the past not a record. Such recollections have more the quality of impressionist painting than of photography (which itself of course is simply a selective representation shaped by the media of presentation).

31. Re her dated comment on Oakland, "there is no there there."

32. Of course while growing up there I had no conception of how bad it would appear from the vista of Berkeley in the 1960s. In the 1950s imbued with the myths of the Promised Land found at last, we felt superior to those snow and tradition bound in the Midwest and east. We not only had the ocean, we had Hollywood and all it represented.

Beyond the Hitching Post theater that only showed western films and endless drives up and down Hollywood Blvd. in the hope that the next group of girls we slowed down for would be available (they never were), I had a few vicarious Hollywood moments. My grandfather played golf with Groucho Marx, although they were not related. I tried out for the Al Jolson story and while I didn't get the part, I did get some small change for coming to the casting call. Tony Curtis and Janet Leigh came to our Purim carnival in the parking lot of Temple Israel of Hollywood. Our rabbi Max Nussbaum married Eddie Fisher and Elizabeth Taylor and Sammy Davis Jr. and Mae Britt. I have a copy of *The Wizard of Oz* signed by "the wife of the author" and the father of a Sunday school teacher was the voice of the cowardly lion in the film version. Parts of *Rebel Without a Cause* were filmed on my street and at the nearby Griffith Park Observatory. Piper Laurie once rented my grandmother's house above Sunset Boulevard and John Raitt (of the musical *Oklahoma*) almost bought our Los Feliz house. I had a brief social encounter with Kathy Kohner (AKA Gidget) and once almost took out the daughter of a famous film composer. My friend Noel Blanc succeeded his father Mel as the voice of Daffy Duck, Bugs Bunny, and of course Porky Pig. A brother of a good friend is now a very famous film star with a different name. Not even close to getting a cigar, but certainly growing up in Hollywood in the 1950s was a formidable experience, frequently relived now by seeing films on American Movie Classics.

33. The former writes, "and for Christ's sake don't ever go back—not under any circumstances" . . . "we can't ever go back to old things or try to get the 'old kick' out of something . . . the old things are nowhere except in our minds now" (Mellow, 1992, p. 168).

34. Here I read from his facial expression when a family friend in offering advice to the recent college graduate, says, "Plastics, Benjamin, Plastics."

35. The centripetal forces are far weaker today then when I entered the field and there seems to be less optimism and passion. The contrast with the late 1960s is striking. In one case I received more than 100 requests for a paper delivered at a conference and the discussion of social issues at sociology and political science meetings was far more intense and energized.

36. "It is not the critic who counts; not the man who points out how the strong man stumbles, or where the doer of deeds could have done them better. The credit belongs to the man who is actually in the arena, whose face is marred by dust and sweat and blood; who strives valiantly; who errs, who comes short again and again, because there is no effort without error and shortcoming; but who does actually strive to do the deeds; who knows great enthusiasms, the great devotions; who spends himself in a worthy cause; who at the best knows in the end the triumph of high achievement, and who at the worst, if he fails, at least fails while daring greatly, so that his place shall never be with those cold and timid souls who neither know victory nor defeat. Shame on the man of cultivated taste who permits refinement to develop into fastidiousness that unfits him for doing the rough work of a workaday world. Among the free peoples who govern themselves there is but a small field of usefulness open for the men of cloistered life who shrink from contact with their fellows. . . . There is little use for the being whose tepid soul knows nothing of great and generous emotion, of the high pride, the stern belief, the lofty enthusiasm, of the men who quell the storm and ride the thunder." www.theodoreroosevelt.org/life/quotes.htm.

Ok Teddy, riding the thunder is a rush and we all need edge work, but words give us the means to make sense of things and a division of labor may be appropriate across types of persons, as well as within a career. Society would not necessarily be better with more talk and less action, but it certainly would be better with more talk before action and with more empirical, logical, and moral analysis of the beliefs that undergird action.

37. This also reflects an ambivalence that is both generic given America anti-intellectualism and the specifics of my situation. Note the G. B. Shaw expression, "those who can do, those who can't, teach."

In an earlier article I wrote of being . . . "the intensely driven, hardworking, competitive, ambitious person" (like those I encountered early in my career) and the laid-back bohemian surfer of my California days; the intellectual interested in ideas for their own sake and one of the progeny of Karl Marx and C. Wright Mills who wanted to see ideas linked to change (perhaps a committed spectator, as Raymond Aron termed it); the quantitative and systematic sociologist and the journalist seeking to describe in language that people could understand what Robert Park called the big story; the scholar and the handyman; the athletic, river-running, beer-drinking, former fraternity man who could admit to still having some Neanderthal-like macho attitudes and feelings and the righteous carrier of a new gender morality. . . . Instead of worrying about what I "really" was and what I valued most, I saw that I was probably more marginal than most people. I came to value being something of an invisible person and social chameleon, able to fit into, and move in and out of, different worlds. This particularly helps when one's method requires taking the point of view of the other and the tentativeness of science.

38. Kipling's poem "If," which served as a powerful adolescent guide was among my first cognitive exposures to distanciation and marginality.

39. One study on having a happy retirement is encouraging here. A central factor is, "learning how to play again"—defined as gratifying activities that offer no economic gain, don't hurt others and needn't involve praise or recognition. Fun and games are defined as being ends in themselves (Valiant and Mukamal, 2001).

40. The full quote in the book with his letters, "My father asks, do we need anything. Does man ever really need anything but what is in him? The things I need no one else can give me: such things as warm sun and lazy afternoons and leisure to think things through. There is a certain type of man who spends his life finding and refinding what is within him, and I suppose I am of that type. No, there is nothing I need that can be given to me by others. In the end a man must go to bat alone." A bit heavy on individual determinism from a sociologist, but provocative.

Some Moral Imperatives for Aspiring Social Scientists

Develop the habits of critical thought, evaluation, and observation.

Write with clarity, logic, and vigor.

Write everywhere, all the time, on everything.

Have a fresh argument.

Write books, don't read them.

Take short cuts.

Learn how to be an effective public speaker.

Don't be scriptocentric.

Disaggregate and aggregate.

Be wary of sociologists bearing overbroad generalizations.

Be wary of "Jack Webb-Badge 714 'Just the facts ma'am'" sociologists.

Avoid the dangers that can arise from rigidly taking sides in doctrinal debates over theory and method.

Diversify—don't stay a specialist in one area too long.

Be problem and interdisciplinary as well as discipline focused.

Be wary of sociologists denying the desirability and possibility of scientific approaches to understanding society.

Treasure and develop the unique position of sociology as both a scientific and humanistic undertaking and should you choose not to straddle the fence, be tolerant of those sitting elsewhere.

Know what the questions are.

Be bold. Take risks!

Cultivate marginality.

Have short and long range plans and goals.

Life and sociology are about unfinished business and process.

Create real and virtual communities.

Actively look for mentors and role models, as well as antirole models.

Seek out those who are more knowledgeable, clever, and/or successful than you are.

Learn to "meet with Triumph and Disaster and treat those two imposters just the same."

Don't be selfish! Give of your time and your thoughts to others.

(continued)

(continued)

Be proud to be an academic.

Tell it like it is. Speak truth to power and others.

Believe in the sociology of knowledge and use it responsibly for insights.

Learn to deftly walk back and forth between the point of view of the actor and the observer.

Know the difference between a scholar and a fundamentalist.

Avoid the exclusionary notion that you must belong to a group in order to study it and that individuals have some special obligation to study groups they belong to.

Don't join the thought-police or spend undue amounts of time looking for any possible evidence of racism, sexism, classism, homophobia, or ageism on the part of your peers.

Be aware when you are operating as a scientist and trying to be value-free and when you are a more explicit political actor.

Have fun! Enjoy what you do!

Have a sense of humor!

Keep the faith! . . . Know that both principles and ideas matter and that the individual can make a difference. Believe that knowledge is better than ignorance—that knowledge is possible, and that empirical and scientific knowledge about human and social conditions can result in the improvement of those conditions.

Seven Characteristics of Success

1. It does not last.
2. You can never be successful enough (at least in your own eyes).
3. The more success you have, the harder it becomes to reach the next level of achievement.
4. There is a diminishing-returns effect. For those with youthful success everything afterwards may savor of anticlimax.
5. Success may have costly and unintended side effects (apart from the price initially paid to achieve it).
6. The correlation between ability, or merit, and success is far from perfect.
7. There is no reason to expect that what you do next will be better, by your own standards, than what you have done in the past or will necessarily bring equivalent or greater recognition and reward.

REFERENCES

Albom, M. (2002). *Tuesdays With Morrie.* New York: Broadway.

Alexander, J., Marx, G., Williams, C. (2003). *Self, Social Structure and Beliefs: Essays in Honor of Neil Smelser.* Berkeley: University of California Press.

Allison, M. "Certified Senior Citizen." Capital Records, 1994.

Bowles, P. (1949). *The Sheltering Sky.* New York: Vintage Books.

Brecht, B. (1965). *The Jewish Wife and Other Short Stories.* New York: Grove Press.

Buffet, J. (2002). Tales from Margaritaville. Boston: Mariner.

Canned Heat. "Goin' Up the Country." Liberty Records, 1968.

Deflem, M. (2002). Teaching Criminal Justice in Liberal Arts Education: A Sociologist's Confessions, *ACLS Today*, 22, 3–5.

Goffman, E. (1956). *The Presentation of Self in Everyday Life.* New York: Doubleday.

Goode, E. (2003). Remembering Si Goode, *Footnotes.* American Sociological Association, July/August.

Gusfeld, J. (1990). My Life and Soft Times. In B. Berger, (ed.), *Authors of Their Own Lives.* Berkeley: University of California Press.

Lawrence, D.H. (1993). *Lady Chatterley's Lover.* New York: Cambridge University Press.

Leo, R. (1996). Police scholarship for the future: Resisting the pull of the policy audience. *Law & Society Review*, 30, 865–880.

Marx, G. T. (1984). Role models and role distance: A remembrance of Erving Goffman. *Theory and Society*, 13, 649–662.

Marx, G. T. (1990). Reflections on Academic Success and Failure. In B. Berger (ed.), *Authors of Their Own Lives.* Berkeley: University of California Press.

Marx, G. T. (1997). Of methods and manners for aspiring sociologists: Thirty seven moral imperatives. *The American Sociologist*, 28.

Marx, G. T. (2000). Famished ardor: Some reflections on sociology and travel and on a trip to China. *The American Sociologist*, 31.

Marx, G. T. (2007). Travels with Marty: Seymour Martin Lipset as a mentor. *The American Sociologist*, 38.

Melville, H. (1972). *Moby Dick.* New York: Penguin.

Mellow, J. R. (1992). *Hemingway: A Life Without Consequences.* New York: Scribner.

Merton. R. K. (1985). George Sarton: Episodic recollections by an unruly apprentice. *ISIS,* 76, 470–486.

Ross, J. I. (2005). On the road again: Surviving the structural and procedural dynamics of interviewing for assistant professor jobs. *Professional Studies Review.* 2, 13–30.

Shaw, V. (2000). Toward professional civility: An analysis of rejection letters from sociology departments. *The American Sociologist,* 31, 32–4.

Springsteen, B. "Glory Days." Sony Records, 1984.

Simmel, G. (1994). Bridge and door. *Theory, Culture and Society,* 11, 5–10

Stouffer, S., et al. (1949). *The American Soldier.* Princeton: Princeton University Press.

Twain, M. *Notebooks and Journals,* Vol. 1. Berkeley: University of California, 1975.

Valiant, G., and Mukamal, K. (2001). Successful aging. *American Journal of Psychiatry,* 158, 839–847.

Ward, A. (1991). *Out Here: A Newcomer's Notes from the Great Northwest.* New York: Viking.

Wolfe, P. (1980). *The Art of Dashiell Hammett.* Bowling Green: Bowling Green University Popular Press.

About the Contributors

EDITOR

Chris Powell is professor and chair of the criminology department at the University of Southern Maine. He has lectured on criminology and social theory at a number of British Universities, most recently at Bangor. Besides the sociology of criminology, he has written on humor and social control, restorative justice and various other "control" related themes—in a "butterfly" kind of way.

CONTRIBUTORS

Luis A. Fernandez is an assistant professor in the Department of Criminology and Criminal Justice at Northern Arizona University. He holds an MA in political science and a PhD in Justice Studies from Arizona State University. Dr. Fernandez has worked for several research institutions, including the National Council on Crime and Delinquency and the Morrison Institute for Public Policy. He is the author of *Policing Dissent: Social Control and the Anti-Globalization Movement.*

Gary T. Marx is professor emeritus at M.I.T. He has also taught at the University of California at Berkeley (from where he received his PhD), Harvard University, the University of Colorado, and for shorter periods at twenty other schools. He has written a bunch of stuff including *Protest and Prejudice,*

Undercover: Police Surveillance in America, and *Windows into the Soul: Surveillance and Society in an Age of High Technology*.

Raymond Michalowski is a sociologist and Arizona Regents Professor in the Department of Criminology at Northern Arizona University. His works include *Order, Law, and Crime, Crime Power and Identity, Run for the Wall: Remembering Vietnam on a Motorcycle Pilgrimage*, and *State-Corporate Crime: Wrongdoing at the Intersection of Business and Government*. He is currently studying the social construction of unauthorized immigration, third-wave nativism, and moral panic in the US.–Mexico borderlands.

Alan Mobley is assistant professor of public affairs and criminal justice at San Diego State University, where he leads experiential, community-based courses in restorative and community justice. He first became interested in criminal justice issues in 1984, when he was arrested on narcotics charges. While in federal prison, Alan Mobley earned bachelor's and master's degrees in economics and sociology, respectively, and studied eastern philosophy and yoga. Upon release from prison in 1994, he entered the doctoral program in criminology, law and society at the University of California, Irvine. Dr. Mobley's teaching, learning, and action-oriented research aim to enliven the spirits of participation, collaboration, and integration. Among his current projects are All Of Us Or None, a national organizing initiative for the rights of the currently and formerly incarcerated, One Thousand Days, a holistic reentry partnership in California, and Just Business, an effort to bring meaningful, equitable, and sustainable work to high reentry communities, beginning in Detroit.

Sharon Pickering is associate professor in criminology at Monash University, Australia. Her recent works include *Counter-Terrorism Policing: Community, Cohesion and Security* (with Jude McCulloch and David Wright-Neville), *Borders, Mobility and Technologies of Control* (with Leanne Weber), *Refugees and State Crime*, and *Critical Chatter: Women and Human Rights in South East Asia* (with Caroline Lambert and Christine Alder). She coconvenes the Prato roundtable on transnational crime and is coeditor (with McCulloch) of the special edition of *Social Justice Beyond Transnational Crime*.

Hillary Potter is assistant professor of sociology at the University of Colorado at Boulder, where she also received her PhD in 2004. Her current research and teaching interests are feminist and black feminist criminology, racialized perceptions of crime, the intersections of race, gender, class, and crime, and race and intimate partner violence. Dr. Potter's published works include *Racing the Storm: Racial Implications and Lessons Learned from Hurricane Katrina* and *Battle Cries: Black Women and Intimate Partner Abuse.*

Phil Scraton is professor of criminology in the Institute of Criminology and Criminal Justice, Queen's University, Belfast, United Kingdom. Widely published in the area of critical analysis and its application, his most recent books include: *Childhood in Crisis, Hillsborough: The Truth, Beyond September 11, Power, Conflict and Criminalisation,* and *The Violence of Incarceration.*

Ruth Waterhouse was born in the North West of England and received a state education. She did an undergraduate degree in sociology followed by postgraduate degrees in criminology and later in counseling. She has taught sociology, criminology, women's studies, and counseling at University level for over thirty years. She has worked in a voluntary capacity for a rape crisis center. She lives in North Wales, United Kingdom.

Nancy Wonders is professor and chair of the Department of Criminology and Criminal Justice at Northern Arizona University. Her research and teaching focuses on the relationships between social inequality, difference, and justice, with an emphasis on underrepresented and vulnerable populations both in the United States and internationally. She has published numerous high profile journal articles and book chapters and has been recognized for innovation in teaching about difference and underrepresented groups. She is a former chair of the ASC's division on Women and Crime and recipient of the Western Society of Criminology's award for significant improvement to the quality of justice.

Roger Yates completed his doctoral thesis on human-nonhuman relations in 2005 following more than a decade working in the animal protection movement. He has taught undergraduate courses on social movements and protest, critical theory, and the sociology of humor at the University of Wales, Bangor, United Kingdom. He is currently employed at University College, Dublin, teaching undergraduate social theory, qualitative methodology, and a variety of "lifelong learning" evening courses for mature students. He is currently examining the relationship between theorists as producers of ideas and social movement activists as producers of action.

CPSIA information can be obtained at www.ICGtesting.com
Printed in the USA
244793LV00007B/92/P

9 780739 120330